HINTERLAND

ALSO BY CHRIS MULLIN

Diaries
A View from the Foothills
Decline & Fall
A Walk-On Part

Novels
A Very British Coup
The Last Man Out of Saigon
The Year of the Fire Monkey

Non-fiction
Error of Judgement: the truth about the Birmingham bombings

HINTERLAND

A Memoir

Chris Mullin

PROFILE BOOKS

First published in Great Britain in 2016 by
PROFILE BOOKS LTD
3 Holford Yard
Bevin Way
London WC1X 9HD
www.profilebooks.com

1 3 5 7 9 10 8 6 4 2

Text design by Sue Lamble
Typeset in Stone Serif by MacGuru Ltd

Printed and bound in Great Britain by Clays, St Ives plc

The moral right of the author has been asserted.

A CIP catalogue record for this book is available from the British Library.

ISBN 978 1 78125 605 3
eISBN 978 1 78283 232 4

FSC
www.fsc.org
MIX
Paper from
responsible sources
FSC® C018072

To my friends in high and low places,
with thanks for the pleasure of their company.

CONTENTS

Preface

Every so often I am approached by a young person seeking advice about how to embark on a political career. My advice has always been the same: Go away and do something else first and then you will be more use if and when you are elected to Parliament. On reflection this may be wrong. The careers of many of today's brightest and most successful politicians have followed an entirely different trajectory: university (usually Oxford), a job in the office of an MP or as a policy wonk in a think tank, leading perhaps to work in the private office of a minister or a member of the Shadow Cabinet, before being shoehorned into a safe seat (often with the help of powerful allies acquired en route). This trend was especially apparent during the New Labour era.

Rightly or wrongly, Tony Blair had a low opinion of the parliamentary Labour party and was determined to lever into Parliament bright young people in his own image and likeness with a view to making them ministers at the earliest opportunity. As a result, a sort of first- and second-class carriage developed in the House of Commons tea room. Once elected, the former special advisers were a race apart from those of us who had laboured in the salt mines of Opposition for decades. To be sure, they were usually highly intelligent and personable, but many of them had never knocked on a door on behalf of anyone but themselves at election time. Most had never asked a question even mildly sceptical of the official point of view. Nor had they done much else in life, apart from politics. They did not linger long on the back benches. Usually they were wafted into government within months of election and the brightest of them were soon in the

Cabinet. By their early forties some had burned out and moved on. This cult of youth was not confined to the Labour Party. Remarkably, by the 2010 general election all three main party leaders had been elected to that post within five years of entering Parliament.

I must not exaggerate. Not all Blair's protégés were young. And not all of them lacked hinterland. Alan Johnson, a most capable politician who would have made an excellent Labour leader, had hinterland in spades. Likewise, no one could argue that Charlie Falconer was not up to the job. Nor is the cult of youth an entirely new phenomenon – Harold Wilson was in the Cabinet by the age of thirty-one. There is, however, such a thing as political nous, which cannot be learned from textbooks or policy papers and tends to be acquired gradually as a result of experience. One can't, for example, help wondering whether, had he spent more time at ground level, Liam Byrne would have left that notorious note for his successor at the Treasury, to the consternation of both Byrne himself and his party.* Anyway, for the time being at least, the astonishing rise of Jeremy Corbyn has (if only temporarily) brought the cult of youth in politics to a shuddering halt.

Perhaps there is no right answer. Maybe what is required for a healthy democracy is a mix of politicians of all ages and professions, male and female. Our political system requires not only MPs who are capable of governing, but also individuals capable of holding the executive to account for the power they wield. On balance, however, it remains my view that hinterland is a useful attribute for any budding politician, whichever path they follow. For better or worse, I was a politician with hinterland. By the time I was elected, aged thirty-nine, I had lived and campaigned for many years in one of the toughest parts of inner London. I had been active in politics for the best part of twenty years. As a journalist I had travelled widely, reporting from, among other places, the wars in Vietnam, Laos and Cambodia. I had seen the sun rise over the Himalayas and go down over the Gobi desert. I was the author of three novels (one of which is still in

---

*On leaving office in 2010, Byrne wrote, 'Dear Chief Secretary, I am afraid there is no money. Kind regards, Liam – and good luck.' It was meant as a joke, of course, but the Tories exploited it mercilessly.

print thirty-five years after publication) and I had travelled down some very dark alleyways in search of the perpetrators of the Birmingham bombings. This is the story of my life.

Chris Mullin

Acknowledgements

My thanks to the following: Judy Burg, former university archivist at the Hull History Centre, where my papers are stored; also to her successor Simon Wilson and his most helpful colleague, Claire Weatherall; my friend Jean Corston, a colleague on the Home Affairs Select Committee and who later chaired the parliamentary Labour party; my late uncles Brian, Peter and Terence Foley for their account of family history; Alastair Logan, for running his expert eye over my account of the Guildford Four case; Kevin Marquis, my agent during four general elections; Colin Moore and his late wife Jean (née Martin), for help with my recollections of my much loved childhood neighbours Georgina and Charlie Martin; Leslie and Teresa Mullin, my late parents, for an account of their lives; Carol Roberton, Neil Sinclair and Doug Smith, for their help with background on Sunderland; Marina Warner, for her recollection of the John Anstey regime at the *Telegraph* magazine; my good friend the distinguished journalist Martin Woollacott, for looking over my account of our two weeks in Cambodia in that fraught summer of 1973; Sheila Williams and Ruth Winstone, for reviewing the manuscript and making many helpful suggestions; Andrew Franklin and his team at Profile Books, in particular my editor Cecily Gayford, for much useful help and advice; my agent Caroline Dawnay and her assistant Sophie Scard for their efforts on my behalf. Last but not least, my wife, Ngoc, for her account of growing up in war-torn Vietnam and for the life we have shared together.

CHAPTER ONE

Poor Sunderland

'What has gone wrong in Sunderland?' asked Neil Kinnock reacting to the news of my selection as a candidate for the Labour stronghold of Sunderland South. The leader of my party was on a visit to the north-east of England. Finding himself in the Dragonara Hotel in Middlesbrough, and believing himself to be in safe company, he began to make his mouth go, as he was occasionally inclined to do.

'First,' he said, 'Sunderland has an MP who is a boil on the arse of the Labour Party.' A reference to my estimable former colleague, Bob Clay. 'Now,' he added, 'they have gone and selected a certifiable lunatic.'

This had not always been his view. Neil and I had once been good friends. I first got to know him and his lovely wife, Glenys, in 1973 when they were living in Dysart Avenue, Kingston upon Thames, and I was the local Labour candidate, standing against a young merchant banker called Norman Lamont. Neil had been elected to Parliament three years earlier for an impregnably safe Labour seat in the Welsh valleys. He was the life and soul of any party. A fund of hilarious anecdotes, a passionate orator with a fine singing voice and a leading light in the Labour left, following the disappointments of the Wilson years. I was duly impressed. More than that, I felt utterly outclassed. On my first visit to Dysart Avenue the other guests were Norman Willis, assistant general secretary of the TUC, and his wife. The evening was a riot. From Neil and Norman, a continuous flow of wit and wisdom to which I had little or nothing to contribute. What's more, I made the mistake of taking with me a young woman who was into Tibetan mysticism and I could see their eyes roll whenever she opened her mouth.

From the moment I set eyes on him, I knew it was inevitable that Neil Kinnock would one day lead the Labour Party and I told anyone who cared to listen. As time passed, one or two reservations crept in. Neil was sometimes long-winded, a common affliction for politicians from the valleys. He was ambitious – nothing wrong with that, the Labour left urgently needed charismatic leadership – and had a quick temper which occasionally got him into trouble. I was with him in a restaurant in Blackpool when he claimed to have spotted a fellow diner sporting a National Front tiepin. 'I'm not eating my dinner with a fascist,' he loudly declared, and it was all that Glenys and I could do to restrain him from launching an all-out assault on the hapless fellow diner whose NF tiepin might, for all I know, have been displaying his initials rather than his political affiliation. For months afterwards Glenys was apologising to me, but no matter, I took it lightly. He was a star. Even now the glow still lingers. Occasionally there is a fleeting encounter. A tap on the shoulder followed by the inevitable, 'How you doing, boyo?' I still feel a twinge of nostalgia for the Kinnock of old.

The Americans had spotted him, too. Every American embassy has political officers whose job it is to attach themselves to upwardly mobile politicians in the main parties. There was nothing particularly sinister about it. They were usually sympathetic people of broadly similar politics. Republicans for the Tories. Democrats for Labour. Over the years I, too, received the occasional visit, and sometimes an offer of lunch, from the political officer whose job it was to monitor the Labour Party and report back to Washington. But in the case of the Kinnocks they became close personal friends. Each New Year's Eve there was a party, the venue for which used to alternate between the homes of Neil and several of his close friends. One memorable gathering was held at the US political attaché's residence in Connaught Square. In my mind's eye I can still see the marvellous spectacle of Norman Willis, later to become general secretary of the TUC, on a table leading a chorus of 'I am the man, the very fat man, wot waters the workers' beer'. Some years later, outside the Winter Gardens in Blackpool, I was approached by an American who said how much he had enjoyed reading my novel, *A Very British Coup*, 'particularly the scene in the house at Connaught Square'. He added, 'Mr Mullin, I live in that house.'

As the 1970s drew to a close, the civil war that rent the Labour Party intensified. The disappointments of the Wilson years increasingly gave rise to demands that the party leadership be made more accountable to members. The Callaghan government's controversial surrender to the IMF and the savage cuts in public spending which followed served only to fuel the flames. Uprisings among the foot soldiers were nothing new in Labour Party history, but this one was better organised. Neil Kinnock was an early member of the Campaign for Labour Party Democracy and, as a result, was quickly swept on to the Labour Party National Executive Committee, where he provided a sympathetic ear for the advocates of reform and voted accordingly. In the late 1970s he had been offered a job in the Callaghan government which he turned down, preferring instead to build his base among the grass roots. His friend and hero, Michael Foot, a veteran of earlier uprisings in the 1950s and 60s, took the opposite track and accepted a job in the Cabinet.

By the late 1970s the left in Parliament were pretty much clapped out. Exhausted, ineffective, content to remain powerless and in many cases resentful that the focus for dissent in the party had moved beyond Parliament to a new generation of younger members for whom newly elected MPs like Neil Kinnock and Dennis Skinner became the standard bearers. This was reflected in *Tribune*, the weekly journal of the Labour left, which had once provided a platform for such luminaries as Nye Bevan, Michael Foot and George Orwell. By the late 1970s *Tribune* was in steep decline. Edited for more than twenty years by Dick Clements, an affable, verbose Stakhanovite, it had lost its way and was shedding readers rapidly. It was Neil who in 1978 suggested that I give up my job as a sub-editor in the newsroom of the BBC World Service, and go to work for *Tribune* in the hope of injecting some new life into it. To begin with all was well. 'Glenys has started reading *Tribune* again,' he remarked a little while after I joined. Four years later, when Dick Clements finally stood down, it was a different story: Neil and others moved heaven and earth to stop me taking over the editorship. As he left the board meeting at which I was appointed, he was overheard to remark, '*Tribune* will be dead in six months.' Thirty years later it was still going, but it was – to quote the Duke of Wellington – a damn close-run thing.

The decision of Tony Benn to challenge Denis Healey for the deputy leadership of the Labour Party was the event that caused the parting of the ways. By January 1981, despite the bitter resistance of the party Establishment, the long struggle to democratise the Labour Party was triumphant on all fronts. Future leaders would no longer be chosen solely by MPs, but by an electoral college representing all three wings of the party – MPs, members and unions. Also, Labour MPs who had the good fortune to be elected for safe seats could no longer assume they would be there for life. Instead, once during every Parliament, they would be obliged to compete for renomination.

No sooner had these reforms been agreed than several senior members of the Labour Establishment – the so-called Gang of Four – announced that they were leaving to set up their own Social Democratic Party. A little later Tony Benn launched his challenge to Healey, and since the choice would now be made by the new electoral college and not, as before, by Labour MPs alone, the result was not predictable. It was a struggle for the soul of the party. On the one side were the party Establishment, the trade union barons, wielders of the big block votes at Labour Party conferences, and a majority of MPs, some deeply resentful of Benn for the part he had played in bringing about the reforms that threatened the comfortable world many of them had so long inhabited. Unlike in the 2015 leadership election, when much of Jeremy Corbyn's political base comprised those who had given up on the Labour Party, Benn's core support lay with rank-and-file members, the poor bloody infantry whose support the party leadership had for so long taken for granted and who were determined that there would be no repeat of earlier disappointments. He also had considerable support among active trade unionists. This came as an unpleasant surprise to those union leaders who had long behaved as if the block votes they wielded were their personal property. Caught between these two opposing camps was a large block of MPs, the so-called soft-left, who just wished it would all go away. They had no love for Healey, a former Chancellor, whose harsh pay policy many blamed for triggering the so-called 'Winter of Discontent' which lost

Labour the 1979 election, but they were not keen on Benn either. By now Michael Foot was leader of the Labour Party and they had voted for him in the hope of a quiet life. As it turned out, however, life in the Labour Party under Foot's leadership was anything but quiet.

Benn's decision to stand unleashed near hysteria. At first the Labour Establishment were confident that he would be defeated, but as the months passed and a number of trade union leaders were delivered to their conferences bound hand and foot by resolutions demanding they cast their union's votes in support of Benn, nerves began to fray. Michael Foot at first appealed to Benn to stand down and, when that failed, he launched an all-out assault. One after another Benn's erstwhile cabinet colleagues queued up to denounce him The denunciations continued even after Benn disappeared into hospital having been struck down with a mysterious illness (causing some to allege that he had been poisoned), later diagnosed as Guillain-Barré syndrome, a condition which causes numbness in hands and feet. All this was lapped up by a grateful Tory press, only too anxious for ammunition that proved to its readers that Labour – at this time still ahead in the polls – was in the grip of an extremist conspiracy. Even the *Guardian*, which could generally be relied upon to report fairly all sides of an argument in the Labour Party, abandoned any sense of balance. The paper's usually sensible political editor even went so far as to remark that *Tribune* staff would be more at home chucking bombs rather than cricket balls.

By September it began to dawn on some of those who had not, thus far, contemplated the possibility, that Benn might actually win. Members of the miners' union, against the advice of their leaders, came out for Benn. Immediately the miners' leader, Joe Gormley, went on television proclaiming the inevitability of Benn sooner or later leading the Labour Party. Gradually, imperceptibly, the middle ground began to shift. I received a call at home from the political correspondent of a respected national newspaper, offering me a job as his assistant. 'The Labour right is all washed up,' he said. 'I realise that I've been talking to the wrong people. I feel like a journalist in South Africa whose only contacts are with the white regime.' A Labour frontbencher, later a prominent member of the Blair government, rang to say that he just wanted me to know that he would be voting for Benn and that he thought he could bring one or two others with him. Suddenly, I began to realise what life would be like if we won. The entire centre ground would shift in our direction. MPs not previously fans of Tony Benn would suddenly discover in him virtues that they hadn't previously noticed – and many would end up in his government, if there was one.

By the end of September it was neck and neck. At which point Neil Kinnock wrote a long article for *Tribune* denouncing Benn and calling on Tribune Group MPs to abstain, which a number duly did. Healey won by a whisker. Arguably, Kinnock's intervention had tipped the balance. Passions ran high. At the *Tribune* rally a few days later, where Kinnock traditionally made the fund-raising speech, Margaret Beckett, later to become one of New Labour's most impressive ministers, remarked: 'I thought I was soft left, but I'm not so soft that I can't tell the difference between Denis Healey and Tony Benn.'

The 1981 deputy leadership election was the most intense power struggle I have ever witnessed. The final days were electrifying. The office itself was trivial but there was a widespread feeling that some real power was in danger of changing hands. It is hard to believe now, but at the time, before the Falklands factor entrenched her in office, the Thatcher government was deeply unpopular. In the space of two years they had doubled unemployment and collapsed a quarter of manufacturing industry. Riots were breaking out in the inner cities. Labour was well ahead in the polls. Benn, then at the height of his powers, appeared to be sweeping all before him. There was a possibility, however unlikely it may now seem, that he could become prime minister. 'No Longer *If*, But *When*', screamed a headline in one of the Harmsworth newspapers over a full-page picture of Benn. This being so, it would not be at all surprising if the 'guardians of all we hold dear' were taking a close interest in the outcome. We know from the memoirs of the former MI5 officer Peter Wright, that some of his colleagues, apparently under the illusion that the prime minister Harold Wilson was a Soviet agent, were conspiring to bring down the Labour government in the mid-1970s,* so it does not take a great leap of the

---

* *Spycatcher* (Viking, 1987), pp. 368–9.

imagination to think that they may at least have taken an interest in, or even tried to influence the outcome of, the struggle for control of the Labour Party in the early 1980s.

There were two occasions during the course of the campaign when I sensed an unseen hand at work. The first was when Denis Healey, interviewed on a Sunday lunchtime political programme, accused Benn's supporters of orchestrating heckling at meetings of his supporters in Birmingham and Cardiff. Pressed, he identified Jon Lansman, one of Benn's henchmen, as the culprit. Indeed, he claimed personally to have seen Lansman trying to shout him down. Immediately, while Healey was still on air, I rang Jon's home in Greenwich only to be told by one of his flatmates that he was staying with his girlfriend's grandmother in mid-Wales. I asked for the telephone number and was given it. I advised the flatmate that a media feeding frenzy was about to break and that under no circumstances should he impart to anyone Jon's telephone number or any details of his whereabouts. I rang Jon in Wales and asked if Healey's accusation was true. He denied having been at either event. On one of the dates in question he had been on holiday in Sicily. I advised him to stay where he was and talk to no one. I then put out a short statement to the Press Association repeating his denial and the fact that he had a cast-iron alibi and demanding that Healey apologise. Within two hours a photographer in the pay of the *Daily Mail* was staking out the house in mid-Wales. How and where the *Mail* got the address is a mystery. Could someone have been listening to his phone? Or mine? There may well have been a simple explanation, but I am unable to think of it.

The second incident was more curious. A week or so before the election, on the day that the executive of the Transport and General Workers' Union (which had the biggest say in the outcome) was due to decide how to cast its vote, *The Times* published profiles of the three candidates – Benn, Healey and John Silkin. Each profile was divided into sections: a potted biography, views on key issues and so on. Incongruously, in the middle of each, there was a section setting out the assets of the candidates. The assets of Healey, who was not poor, were disposed of in a single sentence. Likewise those of Silkin, who was probably the richest of the three. The section on Benn's assets, however, contained the following sentence: 'City sources speak of a Stansgate trust, registered with the Bank of Bermuda, the beneficiaries of which are members of the Benn family.'

This was obviously deeply damaging. Indeed, it leapt off the page. As soon as I saw it I rang the Bank of Bermuda to be told not only that there was no such trust, but also that no one from *The Times* had been in touch even to inquire about it. I then rang Julian Haviland, *The Times'* political correspondent and a man of great integrity, whose name was on the article. Much embarrassed, he told me that the crucial sentence was not in the copy he had filed. It had been inserted without his knowledge. I eventually traced the culprit, a journalist on the financial section of the paper, who refused either to apologise or to reveal who had supplied him with his falsehood. Eventually, a grudging apology was wrung out of *The Times*, in those days edited by Harold Evans. Again, it is difficult to think of an innocent explanation.

In the years that followed, Labour's prospects went from bad to worse. Margaret Thatcher, her popularity boosted by the successful outcome of the Falklands war, triumphed in the 1983 election. The Opposition vote was hopelessly split between Labour and the SDP. Michael Foot resigned as Labour leader to be succeeded by Neil Kinnock, who immediately set about purging the party of alleged Trotskyites and dumping unpopular policies. The year-long miners' strike sowed yet more division and provided yet another triumph for Mrs Thatcher. At *Tribune*, which by this time I was editing, we had a number of memorable run-ins with our new leader. That in a nutshell explains why Neil Kinnock was, to put it mildly, not best pleased to see me pop up in Sunderland, deep behind the lines.

CHAPTER TWO

The Deep North

Neil Kinnock was by no means alone in his disappointment at my selection. Not everyone in Sunderland was overjoyed either. Sunderland, like much of the north-east, was a one-party state and, as in many one-party states, those who ruled were intolerant of dissent and suspicious of outsiders. The prospect of an MP who had been widely portrayed as a left-wing bogey-man and a southerner to boot was enough to induce apoplexy in some quarters. Ordinarily, I ought never to have stood a chance of selection in such a place. In those days Labour parliamentary candidates were chosen not by a ballot of members, but by the local party management committee composed of delegates from the ward and trade union branches. The process was eminently manipulable. What would usually have happened in such a seat is that an MP thinking of standing down would quietly tip off the local oligarchy who would flood the management committee with trade union delegates, many of whom had to be signed-up into the Labour Party in order to qualify (such was the depth of their commitment that the union would often pay their membership subscription and sometimes even an allowance for attendance at party meetings). Once the management committee had been flooded, the sitting MP would then announce his intention to retire, at which point membership would be frozen until after his successor was selected. A new candidate (often a union appointee) would then be chosen. Membership would be unfrozen and the new 'delegates' would then melt away, leaving the local party saddled with a candidate most of them had not voted for.

Since these were safe seats, he (and it invariably was a he) would be there until he chose to retire.

This is what should have happened in Sunderland. The sitting MP was Gordon Bagier, a former railwayman who in his twenty-three years in Parliament had made scarcely a ripple on the nation's consciousness. The one occasion he had come to national attention was in September 1968 when he had taken part in a trip to Greece, at the expense of a public relations agency employed by the Greek government, at a time when Greece was under military rule. He was lucky to survive the furore that followed. Bagier did not live in the constituency, he had held no surgeries for many years and, by the time I came on the scene, his appearances in Sunderland were rare. By 1983 (admittedly a bad year for Labour) he had honed the Sunderland South majority down to 5,500, a considerable achievement in what ought to have been a safe seat. As a result he found himself increasingly at odds with the active members of his constituency party and, in 1985, announced his intention to retire. To the chagrin of the local oligarchy, however, he failed to tip them off in advance, which meant that the composition of the management committee was frozen before it could be flooded. Result: for the first time in living memory a free selection was permitted.

I owed my presence in Sunderland to Bob Clay, the MP for Sunderland North who had been elected in 1983. Bob was already making waves locally. He could be, as I was later to discover, a difficult colleague, but he was a formidable organiser and in most respects an outstanding MP. He was anxious that the nomination for Sunderland South should go to someone on (more or less) the same political wavelength as himself. I was not his first choice, but the candidate he had earlier favoured had dropped out, and so he turned to me. The economy of Sunderland in those days was still dominated by heavy industry. Two and a half thousand miners still worked at Wearmouth colliery. Shipbuilding was in decline, but the two surviving yards – Pallion and Austin & Pickersgill – still employed several thousand men between them. There was a glass industry which traced its roots back 300 years, a brewery and a swathe of engineering in factories, mostly based along the River Wear which cuts a deep gorge through the centre of the city. As late as 1997 there were still around a thousand textile workers employed there making shirts and suits for Marks & Spencer. Today they have all gone, replaced by gleaming new call centres, a vibrant university and the Nissan car plant. Thank heaven for Nissan. Goodness knows where Sunderland would be without it.

Bob Clay introduced me to local miners and shipyard workers and I quickly secured the support of their union branches. I then won the nomination of the biggest of the eight ward branches and before long I had built a modest base in the local party. At which point the oligarchy began to panic. Bert Twigg, the old fixer who was the Labour Party's north-east organiser, in a clear breach of the rules, instructed the party secretary not to circulate applications from candidates outside the region. Jean Corston, the Labour Party national organiser, promptly ordered him to rescind this instruction, but Twigg refused. When challenged, he blurted out, 'But you know what will happen, if I do.'

'No,' said Jean. 'Tell me.'

'Chris Mullin will win.'

There were seven short-listed candidates, of whom I was one. The only other outsider was Albert Booth, a decent Tribunite and former Cabinet minister who had lost his seat four years previously. Albert and I ended up in the final ballot where I defeated him by just four votes.

A few days later a *Daily Mail* columnist wrote, 'Poor Sunderland. After the relegation of its football team ... the town has now suffered another blow.'

Later, the *Sun* published a list of 'Kinnock's Top Ten Loony Tunes'. I was number eight.

The oligarchy were not good losers. A campaign for my removal began immediately. One or two of them began ringing round regional and national trade union leaders trying to persuade them to object to the outcome on the grounds of some unspecified irregularity. Albert Booth, bless him, refused to co-operate. In the weeks that followed, local unions began to flood the management committee with 'delegates'. An extra forty were added. Serried ranks of grim-faced men of a certain age, most of them strangers. They rarely spoke, raising their hands in unison whenever a vote was taken, usually on a nod from one of the oligarchy. At the annual meeting they turned up with lists instructing them who to vote for and systematically took control of the party. Not one of my supporters was allowed to remain in even the lowliest office. The implication was clear. I was next.

For the first eighteen months of my candidacy I walked on eggshells. I moved into the constituency immediately. As has been my habit throughout my life, I talked to anyone who would talk to me and gradually extended my circle of friends. But it was not easy. The party was riven by bitter factionalism. The local Labour headquarters was an elegant but dilapidated house in an early-Victorian terrace close to the town centre. Monthly meetings took place on an upper floor. The room was L-shaped. Key members of each faction sat at opposite ends, from where they could hurl imprecations at people they could not see. The chairman, a volatile councillor who was subsequently jailed for sexual harassment, sat in the middle from where he had a good view of both factions and was ideally placed to stoke up tension whenever it looked like dying down – an opportunity of which he took full advantage. At my first meeting I had to come between two members, both councillors, who were threatening fisticuffs. It was awful, and what went on bore little or no relation to the lives of the people we affected to represent.

I did my best to raise their eyes to the bigger picture. In order to by-pass the oligarchy, I established a campaign committee on which each of the ward branches was represented. We set up an election fund. Members were invited to take out a standing order for a pound or two a month and many did so, with the result that I wasn't dependent on funding from the regional trade union barons. Gradually I found out who my friends were. I appointed an agent, Kevin Marquis, who had played a leading part in reviving a previously moribund ward branch. A brilliant organiser, Kevin was to remain my agent for the next four general elections. His only failing was that he didn't have a driving licence, so the candidate had to drive the agent. There was no shortage of willing helpers, though they tended to be concentrated in the branches that were in friendly hands and which often contained the fewest Labour votes. From the party branches controlled by the oligarchy, there was a surly indifference, although, even in the most hostile terrain, there were people who quietly made it known that they were on my side. About a year before the election, in an attempt to kick-start the campaign, I produced a leaflet introducing myself as the candidate and was immediately ordered (on some spurious technical ground) to pulp it. Even after the election was under way, with only a week or two to polling day, at least one branch was still debating whether or not to take part.

From the outset Kevin and I made clear that there was going to be a vigorous election campaign, whether the rulers of Sunderland liked it or not. The only decision for the oligarchy was whether they were going to participate. It was many years since there had been a decent election campaign in Sunderland South. In some wards no canvassing had taken place for decades. The habit of putting up posters had more or less died out. It didn't help that there was very little opposition. The local Tory Party was dead outside of the two or three wards they controlled and the Liberals were virtually non-existent. In the absence of serious opposition, Labour had simply taken the electorate for granted. This was especially true of the pit villages and the vast council estates. I proposed to challenge that. There would be no no-go areas. If local members weren't willing to participate – and some were militant in their indifference – I would bring in people from outside.

Our strategy was simple. Voters in most of Sunderland were not sitting around agonising whether to vote Tory or Liberal. The issue for most of them was whether or not to vote. Voter turnout in local elections in the most disaffected parts of the borough was as low as 10 per cent. Even in the former pit villages, where there was still a sense of working-class solidarity, the numbers voting in local elections rarely exceeded 30 per cent. In general elections it was not much more than double that. Our task, therefore, was to push up the turnout in the knowledge that almost every extra vote was likely to be a Labour one. We focussed on the areas where the turnout at elections was traditionally low. Since these were precisely the areas where there was a shortage of active members, I brought in people from the middle-class wards. Our reception on the doorstep was friendly. Over and over people remarked that they had not been visited by anyone from the Labour Party in living memory. 'I'll write this in my diary,' one woman said. Another left a message on the answerphone in our election office saying that she would not be voting Labour until we got rid of the three 'useless' councillors in her ward. One of them was still there when I retired from Parliament twenty-three years later. There were pockets of resistance, but these were easily overcome. Sam Glatt, a respected local GP, knocked on a door in the Silksworth ward to be greeted by a small boy who called upstairs to his dad that there was a man from the Labour Party at the front door. 'I'm not voting for that IRA-loving extremist,' came the reply, accompanied by a number of expletives. Sam went on his way and a few minutes later the man, pulling on his trousers, came running after him. 'Sorry, Dr Glatt. I didn't realise it was you. Don't worry, I'll be there.'

Red-and-white posters which read simply MULLIN LABOUR started going up in windows that hadn't displayed an election poster in years. The habit, once common in working-class areas, of display-ing the Labour election address in porches and front windows revived. As soon as one went up, others would follow. One of the great pleas-ures in the days immediately before the election was driving round the estates handing out posters to households that were displaying my election address. The beauty of it was that they had self-identified. We were assured of a warm welcome at every door we knocked on. After a while it dawned on me that many of those in three-up, two down post-war council houses, where support was particularly strong, were people whose lives and those of their children had been shaped by the achievements of the 1945 Labour government and they had not forgotten. Sadly, those days have passed. The triumph of the market, rampant consumerism, mass unemployment, the sale of public assets and the passing of the post-war generation has diluted the sense of social solidarity to the point where it is in many places non-existent. By the time I left Parliament the habit of displaying election addresses and posters had almost died out. In 1987, however, it was alive and well. We had no problem engaging with the public. The only resistance we encountered was from half a dozen key members of the local Labour Party. No posters appeared in their windows. We resolved this by plastering the houses of their neigh-bours with posters in the hope of embarrassing them. They eventually responded by sticking up identical pictures of Neil Kinnock over a small sticker which said simply, 'Vote Labour'. For the rest it was MULLIN LABOUR. So great was demand that we had to order several reprints.

With a week to go we had canvassed all the big estates. A huge task, inconceivable before or since. Micky Joyce, a shipyard worker, was in charge of operations in the Thorney Close branch, which was dominated by a vast estate of post-war council houses. His organisation was scientific. The results for each polling district were displayed on the wall of his front room. By the eve of polling day he had accumulated around 5,000 promises when he came across a lone Tory canvasser. 'You're wasting your time round here, mate,' said Micky in his thick Wearside accent. 'There's ninety-four Tories in this ward and, if you come home with me, I'll give you their names and addresses.'

On election day the sun shone. We hired the colliery band and toured the constituency on an open-top bus fitted with loudspeakers, blasting away the apathy. In the evening we poured people into the estates, driving up the turnout. It was an exhilarating experience. We had fought the seat as though it were marginal and it had paid off. The result was a swing to Labour more than double the national average. The only people not happy were the rulers of Sunderland, or some at least. My victory speech, at the count, was actually heckled by several local Labour Party members. Some years later Gerry Steinberg, elected for the first time at Durham on the same night as I was returned at Sunderland South, told me that on arriving at his count, which took place after mine, he came across a forlorn-looking refugee from Sunderland South Labour Party.

'Great result,' said Gerry and was astounded to be greeted by the response, 'That's the last time that bastard gets elected round here.'

Once the election was out of the way I thought the friends of the oligarchy would soon get tired and melt away, but they didn't. As promised, I opened an office in the constituency. I held regular surgeries. I asked more questions and took part in more debates in my first year in Parliament than my predecessor had done in the previous five. In short, I provided a level of service hitherto unknown in the Sunderland South constituency. None of this made much difference. The campaign to unseat me began almost at once. It was led by a local councillor, Les Scott, an intelligent man with a burning desire to represent the area in which he had been born and bred and a slight overestimation of his own undoubted talents. Although on the original shortlist, he had been eliminated after the first ballot in which he received only 3 out of 76 votes, well below both his ability and his expectations. Despite the margin of defeat he managed to convince himself that he had somehow been cheated and at once set to work to organise a rematch. I was not helped by the fact that at the time I was heavily involved in the campaign to rescue the innocent people convicted of the Birmingham, Guildford and Woolwich bombings, which enabled my critics to present me either as a friend of terrorists or at the very least as wasting my time on an issue that had nothing to do with Sunderland. Anonymous letters to this effect began to appear in the local newspaper. Although some undoubtedly came from local Tories, it was apparent that others came from rather closer to home. At the 1987 Labour Party conference in Blackpool, a few months after the election, I was approached by a delegate from the General and Municipal Workers Union, slightly the worse for wear. He didn't beat about the bush. 'We're going to deselect you,' he growled. Immediately, I wrote to the regional secretary, asking if the man was speaking for himself or for the union and, in order to ensure that I received his full attention, I copied my letter to the union's general secretary. The reply focussed on the fact that I had had the temerity to copy my letter to the general secretary, but did not address the question. So I wrote again, once more copying my letter to the general secretary. This time I received a response grudgingly denying that they were planning my removal. Evidence, were any needed, that attack is usually the best form of defence.

Much of my first two years in Parliament were spent looking over my shoulder. No week passed without someone calling me up to report what was going on behind my back. At one point Kevin Marquis, my agent, was approached by a senior councillor and told that local authority support for the co-operative agency which Kevin ran was conditional on his not trying too hard to get me reselected. The councillor added that, if the conversation leaked, he would deny it had ever taken place. Meanwhile my management committee remained packed with surly, dubious 'delegates'. A branch of the

Transport and General Workers' Union consisting mainly of milkmen appointed a ferociously hostile local councillor, a teacher by profession, as their delegate. Slowly but surely, however, I was making friends. It is not easy to get rid of a sitting MP, especially one who was so obviously doing his job. A number of members who had not supported me at the outset made clear that they were not willing to be involved in a coup. In the autumn of 1989, the tide began to turn. The Guildford Four were suddenly and sensationally released, their convictions quashed. Overnight what had begun as a lonely cause was now a popular one. Joe Mills, one of the more amiable of the regional union barons, was later overheard to remark, 'If only the Guildford Four had been kept inside for another six months, until we got Chris Mullin's reselection out of the way.'

The reselection process commenced in the autumn of 1989. My wife, Ngoc, was heavily pregnant with our first child, Sarah. Les Scott won the nomination of his own ward branch and a number of union branches. I picked up six of the other seven wards, including to my pleasant surprise two which were allegedly 'enemy' strongholds. The eighth ward, Thorney Close, which I had been unable to attend, decided not to nominate. Several local trade union branches, defying pressure from regional officials, also nominated me. Shortly before the final showdown Carol Roberton, a journalist on the local paper, was telephoned by a *Sunday Times* reporter. I didn't appear to be taking the reselection very seriously, he asserted. A local source had informed him that I had failed to show up to the Thorney Close branch meeting.

'Did your informant say why?' asked Carol.

'No.'

'Because he was attending the birth of his daughter.'

'Ah ...'

'That will give you an idea of the sort of people you are dealing with,' Carol added, replacing the phone.

The final showdown took place one November evening in the assembly hall of the former Bede grammar school where, two years earlier, the election count had taken place. About 200 party members attended and others voted by post. Les Scott spoke. I spoke. A vote was taken and I won by a margin of two to one. It was a cathartic experience. Les accepted the outcome with good grace, as did (most) of his supporters. From that moment on I was the undisputed representative of the Sunderland South Labour Party and would remain so for the next twenty years.

At the count on the night of the 1992 general election, I found myself standing next to my Tory opponent, a man of impeccable local origins (of which he made much). As we stood watching my votes pile up while his remained static, he remarked gloomily, 'I was born at the wrong end of the country.'

To which I, an Essex man, replied, 'So was I.'

CHAPTER THREE

'Your mummy has gone
to the angels'

My mother's family came from Ireland. Refugees from the Great Famine. My late uncle Peter recalled that, when he was young, an ancient Irish great-uncle with a long white beard ('we called him Santa Claus') used to come to stay. This was John Owen McCarthy. Born at Bandon in Co. Cork in May 1848, he and his family had landed on the beach at Penarth near Cardiff, where he lived for the rest of his life. Pause here for a moment and consider. Uncle Peter, alive and well as recently as 2008, could clearly recollect having known a man who, as an infant, was a refugee from the Irish famine, 150 years earlier.

My mother, Teresa, was born in July 1920 into a large, happy, Catholic family, presided over by a genial patriarch. She was one of nine children. Everyone who remembers Grandpa Foley does so with a smile. No one has a bad word to say about him. A stockbroker by profession, he worked with his brother Charles for a firm in the City. These days mention of the word stockbroker conjures up images of seven-figure bonuses and grand houses in the better parts of London or the Home Counties. Grandpa Foley wasn't in that league. Comfortable, but never wealthy, he and my grandmother, Roselyne, settled for a terraced house at 44 Ripley Road, Ilford. They moved to Ripley Road in July 1906 and one hundred years later, my mother's older sister, Maureen, was still there. Ilford has long since been engulfed by the advancing suburbs, but before the Great War it was almost rural. There were fields with grazing cattle at the end of the road from which, if you climbed on the gate, you could glimpse above rooftops the distant masts of Thames barges making their way up- and down-river.

There were not many Catholic families in Ripley Road, but those who lived there were devout. Between them they produced two priests, one bishop and a cardinal. The bishop was my uncle Brian. The cardinal was John Heenan, who became the archbishop of Westminster. Heenan's father, Jim, was Grandpa Foley's best friend. He was also a local character. He owned a dog called Pike and had a little trick with which he used to entertain visitors. 'Die for Ireland, Pike,' he would say and the dog would lie down, not moving a muscle. Then, in an entirely different tone, 'Die for England,' and Pike would stand there cheerfully wagging his tail. Once Mrs Heenan, a saintly, much put-upon woman, came home to discover that her husband had traded her treasured sewing machine for a carpentry workbench which he had parked in the middle of the living room. She simply sighed and said, 'Oh, Daddy.' That was as near as she was ever heard to uttering a cross word. The Heenans and Foleys were forever in and out of each other's houses. Jim had fixed a large bolt to the front door, but everybody in the street knew that to gain entry all you had to do was put your hand through the letter box and pull on the string which he had attached and the bolt slid aside.

Like all the Catholic children in the area, my mother was sent to St Peter and Paul's School in Ilford High Road. The headmaster was Mr Saurin, about whom the children made up a little rhyme:

> Mr Saurin's a very good man
> He goes to church on Sunday,
> To pray to God to give him strength,
> To cane the kids on Monday.

My mother was a shy child who would not ordinarily have said boo to a goose, but once – not long after starting at St Peter and Paul's – she was provoked beyond endurance. Mr Saurin was delivering his daily homily to the morning assembly, ending with an injunction that they should always go to church on Sunday and say their bedtime prayers. 'Don't be like the heathens,' he said, 'Don't be like the *heathens*.' Whereupon young Teresa Foley ran out in front of the entire assembly shouting, 'It's not true, it's not true, the Heenans are our best friends. They always say their prayers.'

Mum's mother, Roselyne, died in November 1932, of TB probably contracted from a neighbour she had been helping to nurse. Memories of her are sketchy. As a young woman she had assisted for a while at the Convent of Notre Dame, Southwark. A surviving programme from a school play lists her as a piano soloist. She was an accomplished pianist and fluent in Walloon French, in which she always said her prayers, a legacy of her Belgian education. Two of Roselyne's nine children died in infancy. The earliest memory of my mother's oldest brother, Terence, was of a little white coffin being carried out of the house at Ripley Road and placed under the driver's seat of a horse-drawn hearse which then pulled away down the street, followed by his weeping mother.

There is a photograph taken in a studio in Ilford, not long before Roselyne died, which shows the family as they were. Grandpa Foley, the patriarch, seated in the centre, surrounded by his children. My mother, nine years old, crouched by his side. Terence, by then in his twenties, is seated next to her, handkerchief protruding from a breast pocket, a carnation in his buttonhole, very much the man about town – my mother always looked up to Terence. Then Maureen, still at school, white socks, best dress. To Grandpa Foley's left is Peter, the youngest, then only about six, a plump little fellow in short trousers looking as if he is about to burst into tears; then Eileen, the oldest, also in her twenties, staring intently at the camera, unsmiling. Behind, gripping the back of Grandpa's chair, is Roselyne, tense, a large flower in her buttonhole. She is flanked by Brian, who by this time must have been home on leave from Ushaw, the Roman Catholic seminary in County Durham where he was studying for the priesthood; on the other side, leaning slightly, Cyril, the most handsome of all, three-piece suit, tiepin, breast-pocket handkerchief.

With the hindsight afforded by the intervening years we know what became of all of them. Roselyne had just three years to live. She was fifty-one when she died. Grandpa Foley lived to see all but one of his children married and settled, dying peacefully of pneumonia and heart failure in 1953. Handsome Cyril, like his mother, was struck down by TB and spent his teenage years in and out of sanatoria – he married, had a son who became a judge and died in 1974, aged sixty. After Cyril there was a twenty-year intermission at the end of which the others died more or less in chronological order. Terence, everyone's favourite uncle, enjoyed good health into his mid-eighties before dying slowly and bravely of cancer in 1994. Brian, as we have seen, became a bishop, passing peacefully at the ripe old age of eighty-nine. Eileen lived into her nineties, ending her days frail and barely able to see, but with her mind intact. Maureen died aged ninety-one, still living at Ripley Road, in the house in which she was born. Peter, the youngest, was the last to go – in January 2010. To the end he lived in a modest flat, just round the corner from his childhood home. A gentle, kindly, otherworldly man who never had two pennies to rub together, Peter was a poet and local historian. A walk around Ilford with him took you back to the time when farms, fields, estates and manor houses covered the land which has long disappeared under the concrete of Edwardian suburbia. And my mother? The little girl in the picture. As we shall see, she lived to a good age, but ended her life a frail, bent, forgetful old lady shuffling along with a walking frame.

A little ritual attended Grandpa Foley's daily departure for the City. Every morning, regular as clockwork he caught the 9.05 a.m. from Seven Kings to Liverpool Street, arriving in good time for the opening of the Stock Exchange at 10 a.m. Roselyne and the younger children would gather at the front gate to watch him depart. Dressed in the then de rigueur uniform of the City (bowler hat, three-piece suit), Grandpa would progress slowly up Ripley Road, a furled umbrella over his arm, passing the time of day with neighbours as he went. When he reached the top he would turn and wave the umbrella before disappearing in the direction of the station. At Liverpool Street, always from the same stall-holder, he purchased a shiny red apple. 'I saved this one just for you, sir,' the stall-holder would say.

Each evening at around six, when Grandpa Foley returned, the same ritual would be repeated in reverse.

My mother was twelve years old when Roselyne died. Until the end of her days she vividly remembered that night. 'It was foggy, a real pea-souper. We were sent home early from school. When Peter and I got home my father and Terence were there. I wasn't surprised; sometimes when there was fog they came home early from work in case the trains stopped. We were told that Mother was in bed with a cold. I was told not to do piano practice in order not to disturb her.

'In the middle of the night somebody came into my room. I was terrified, trying not to breathe. I heard a drawer open. Then a match struck, a candle was lit and I could see that it was Eileen. I called out to her, but she didn't respond; instead, she hurried out of the room. I thought, "What's Eileen doing here?" Eileen had married two months earlier and no longer lived with us. She hadn't been there when I went to bed. I opened the door and Mrs Heenan came in. She said, "Your mummy has gone to the angels."

'I went and sat on Peter's bed until he woke up, then we got dressed and went downstairs. It was still early in the morning. Uncle Errol, mother's younger brother, appeared, and Peter and I were taken to his house. Errol and his wife had no family. She was a socialite with lots of fine clothes; they had no children. It was a totally silent house; no toys or children's books.'

Later they were taken to stay with wealthy friends of Errol and his wife at a big house in Eltham. They had a telephone and car, both at that time unheard of in Ripley Road. There was also a maid in a black dress and white pinafore. 'At night we left our shoes outside the bedroom door and she cleaned them. We were very impressed. One day Eileen arrived, all dressed up. She said, "At eleven o'clock I want you and Peter to kneel down and say a prayer," and then she went away, saying she would be back later. We thought this was very peculiar. Of course, that would have been the moment of Mother's funeral.'

Mum left school at fifteen and, after completing a secretarial course, went to work at the headquarters of Marconi at Temple Bar. On the first morning she was delivered to the main entrance by her brother Cyril, by this time the proud owner of the only car in Ripley Road, a Hillman Minx. The doorman, assuming that she must be related to one of the directors, ushered her into the lift and sent her up to the principal floor where she was treated royally until someone realised that she was the new office girl, whereupon she was abruptly informed that in future she must use the staff entrance, round the corner in Arundel Street.

Even so, she was well treated. The 1930s was an age of innocence.

As the office junior, a vast age gap separated her from those for whom she worked, who were mostly older men. 'In those days a girl of sixteen looked as a thirteen-year-old would today and men in their forties dressed as sixty-year-olds would today. They made a great fuss of me, bringing back iced cakes from Fullers, a nearby baker. At lunchtimes I used to go up to the roof to eat my sandwiches and watch the boats going by on the river. Once I saw the Queen come by on a barge.'

Mum was one of the first people in the world to view television. Marconi had acquired the rights to develop the world's first television. There was great excitement. Head office staff were invited in small groups into a basement room where they were allowed fifteen minutes each to view this new miracle technology. Mum was unimpressed. 'It just consisted of pronouncements by an upper-class woman with a posh voice. I couldn't wait to get back upstairs. I thought, "This will never catch on."'

One Friday in September 1939, the staff at Marconi's head office were told that, if war had broken out by Monday, they should report to the company's factory at Chelmsford. That Sunday, at about 11 a.m., Mum and a friend, Bridie Neelan, were on their way home from Mass. Through an open window they spied half a dozen people gathered around a radio and then the words of Chamberlain, '… consequently we are at war.' They walked on through South Park when suddenly an air-raid siren sounded. 'This was within five or ten minutes of the declaration. We had all been practising putting on gas masks and we were told a siren would sound if there was an attack. We ran to Bridie's house only to find her mother in a terrible panic, soaking a blanket in the kitchen sink. She took us down the garden, ordering us into an air-raid shelter, and hung this blanket across the entrance. After about five minutes, the all-clear sounded.'

On the Monday, as instructed, Mum reported to Marconi's in Chelmsford, where, in due course she met the man she was to marry.

My father, Leslie, was a Scot, born in 1920 at Eldersley in Ayrshire in a terraced house backing on to a golf course. An aunt of Captain Scott, who not long before had perished in the Antarctic, lived next door. My paternal grandparents were a dour, stubborn couple, not big in the sense of humour department and not at all keen on Catholics. Somewhere in the distant past the family had migrated from Ireland. The late Irish cardinal Thomas O'Fee once told me that Mullin was a Presbyterian name. My father's grandfather had been a factor on Lord Elgin's estate.

Grandpa Mullin had been a naval engineer in the First World War. He was remarkably lucky: every ship he served on was torpedoed soon after he left it, and he emerged from the war unscathed. Later he was an engineer at the vast J & P Coats textile mill at Paisley, but when my father was about seven, Grandpa fell out with his boss at Coats, upped sticks and moved south to Enfield in Middlesex. He became chief engineer overseeing the construction of the Brimsdown B power station. The contractors cheated by not putting steel reinforcing rods in the concrete floor, except at the ends, where they were visible. Grandpa refused to sign off on the work and complained to his bosses, but they didn't want to know. Instead they offered to promote him out of the way, but he refused to go quietly and so they sacked him. 'Grandpa was an engineer,' said my father, recounting the incident with watery eyes many years later, 'not a politician or a diplomat. He didn't understand there was no point in just shouting at the bosses.' As a result he was blacklisted and, despite being highly qualified, out of work for two years. He was eventually taken on as chief engineer of the power plant at the Ford car plant at Dagenham, where he remained for the rest of his working life.

Some people might have been pushed leftwards by the experience, but not Grandpa Mullin. Brimsdown B was a public sector project and, so far as he was concerned, it embodied all the incompetence and indifference that he came to associate with the public sector. Ford, by contrast, was efficient and dynamic. If he said something needed doing, it was done without argument.

Both my father and his brother, Jack, inherited the scientific gene and both won places at Imperial College London to study engineering. They might have qualified for a grant towards the cost of their education, but for the fact that Grandpa resolutely refused to disclose his income on the grounds that it was no one's business but his. My father graduated in 1940 and went to work for Marconi's in Chelmsford, where he was to remain for the next forty-five years. He spent the war helping to devise direction finding equipment for bombers. Later he would do the same for civil aircraft. In evenings during the war he worked as a volunteer driver for the ambulance service, in which capacity he spent three days and nights helping to pull bodies from houses around Hoffmann's ball-bearing factory, after a failed German attempt to bomb it in December 1944. Hoffmann's was close to the crematorium where, sixty years later, we said goodbye to Dad. There is a memorial to the victims of the bombing just by the exit gate. I glimpsed it from the back of the funeral car.

The news that my father wanted to marry a Catholic went down like a lead balloon with his parents. 'So you want to marry our Leslie?' was all Grandpa Mullin said to my mother when they broke the news. He was a man given to long silences and would sit for hours by the fire, puffing his pipe, without uttering a word. In this case the silence was a very long one. The invitation to the wedding was declined, though he and Grandma did put in an appearance at the last moment. Thereafter, my parents saw little of them. Although they gradually became reconciled, Grandpa Mullin remained a man of few words. My mother once remarked, 'I would spend ages thinking up something to say that required more than a "yes" or "no" answer. He would move his pipe from one side of his mouth to the other and say in broad Scots, "Aye".' Grandpa dropped dead on 15 May 1955, while washing his car. Grandma lived into the 1970s, though by the end her mind had long gone. Which was fortunate in a way since she ended her days in an Essex nursing home, run by Roman Catholic nuns.

CHAPTER FOUR

'We will either make you or break you'

My mother gave birth four times. Disaster attended each birth save mine. On the day my sister Elizabeth was born, I – then aged twenty months – fell from top to bottom of the stairs in pursuit of a greengage. We had no telephone. My mother, heavily pregnant, rushed to the front gate in search of help, but the street was empty and there was no sign of our immediate neighbours. I, meanwhile, lay unconscious at the foot of the stairs.

At this point a small miracle occurred. No sooner had my despairing mother retreated indoors than there came a knock at the door from an elderly lady with snow-white hair who introduced herself as Sister Fletcher, a retired midwife standing in for the district nurse who had been due to attend my mother. Sister Fletcher soon had an ambulance organised and I was whisked off to hospital, returning a few days later with a broken leg encased in plaster. Elizabeth was born that night.

My brother David, born four years later, was way overdue. The family doctor was consulted and advised a bumpy car ride, a suggestion my father took rather too literally. That Sunday we climbed into our little Ford Prefect and set off for a spin around the lanes of Essex. At some point we became stuck behind a car driven by an elderly man who, each time my father tried to overtake, veered to the right, forcing us to retreat. At the third or fourth attempt we ended up on the verge, upside down. I have only the vaguest recollection of the incident: sudden darkness, followed by us all lying or squatting on the grass next to our upturned car, my sister screaming, my mother's leg bleeding, her blue dress torn. The ambulance crew, when they arrived, took one look at Mum and decreed that she should be taken straight to hospital but she, not wishing to leave her children, resisted. In the end they took us all home. Our GP, Dr Pirie, was contacted and agreed to meet us at the gate. I was claiming to have hurt my arm and Dr Pirie invited me to test the proposition by punching him. I hit him so hard that his head ricocheted off the wall. David was born that night. He weighed a terrifying ten pounds thirteen ounces.

On the day my younger sister Patricia was born, Sister Fletcher arrived to look after my mother only to find all three of us children in bed with whooping cough. Recalling the disasters that had attended the two previous births, she remarked, 'This must be your bad luck this time round.' It wasn't. A few hours later my father rang to inform his parents that they had another grandchild, only to be told that minutes earlier Grandpa Mullin had dropped dead.

We lived at number 36 Dorset Avenue, a street of identical 1930s pebble-dashed, bay-windowed houses. In those days, before most people had cars, we didn't so much go to the shops. The shops came to us. Mr Hurrell in his little van, from his grocery at the top of Baddow Hill. Mr Morgan, the fishmonger and his assistant, Jimmy. They called on the day King George VI died. My mother broke the news. ''Ere, Jimmy, the King's dead,' Mr Morgan called, as though he were ordering a pound of haddock. The window cleaner I observed with fascination as he sat on our front doorstep, supping his tea from the saucer. And Bundles, the old tramp who lived in a ditch behind the Marconi club. Occasionally I was dispatched to Mr Whiting's shop at the end of Beehive Lane to buy five Woodbines for our neighbour, Mrs Martin.

In those far-off days Dorset Avenue backed on to a field of grazing cattle. The field also contained two large oak trees, one of which was hollow. At one end of the road there was a gate leading into more fields, soon to be concreted over to house Marconi workers. The first black man I ever saw, Mr D'Souza, lived on the Marconi estate. Every day Mrs Speakman, an extremely aged lady who lived in Chelmerton Avenue, was wheeled to the top of the street by her carer. A relative of Lord Haw Haw, aka the traitor, William Joyce, hanged after the war, was also reputed to live in Chelmerton Avenue. The war was not long over, so Lord Haw Haw was fresh in local minds.

Our next-door neighbours, Georgina and Charlie Martin, had lived in Dorset Avenue since the 1930s. Charlie was a production controller at Hoffmann's ball-bearing factory. Each morning, punctually at 7 a.m., he set off to work on his bicycle, returning at 12.15 sharp for his lunch and departing again exactly half an hour later. I would wait for him by the front gate and he would offer his hand through the slatted fence, saying, 'Put it there if it weighs a ton.' For years I translated this as, 'Put it there for a waste of time.'

Mrs Martin was a diminutive Scots woman while Mr Martin, not much taller, was an Essex man, from Colchester. A small watercolour of Colchester castle hung on their wall above the dining-room table. Mrs Martin left it to me when she died.

The Martins' house was named Craigellachie, after a village in the Cairngorms. Although she had lived many years in England, in both accent and vocabulary Mrs Martin was still very Scottish, always referring to her shopping as 'messages' and inviting visitors to 'come away in'. Her daughter, Jeanie, was several years older than us. There had been another girl, too: Christina. A photograph of Christina occupied pride of place on the sideboard in the dining room. An angelic child with fair, curly hair, she had died in a fall from a bedroom window aged eighteen months, not long before my parents moved in next door.

I loved Mrs Martin. We all did. She was the grandmother we never had. I was in and out of her house just about every day from the time I first walked; even after we moved away, we never lost touch. She was an inveterate gossip. Nothing went on in the street that she didn't know about and, whether they were interested or not, the neighbours and the ladies at the Co-op were kept regularly updated with bulletins of our doings. My mother, for all that she was fond of Mrs Martin, was wary of divulging any family business that we were not prepared to have broadcast to the entire neighbourhood. Mrs Martin was generous, too. No one, not even Bundles, was turned away empty handed from her doorstep.

Until October 1952, 38 Dorset Avenue had another resident, Mrs Martin's elderly father. Grandpa Saurel (although we always knew him as Grandpa Martin) was a local legend, occasionally returning home the worse for wear, on one occasion bent double, delivered by schoolchildren after he had gone pea-picking and couldn't straighten his back. A relic of the 1860s who in his youth worked out of Aberdeen on trawlers, he entertained all and sundry with tales of voyages to the freezing Arctic ('so cold that we chipped the ice off our hands'). According to local legend, he was one of the last prisoners to be sentenced to the treadmill, for jumping ship. Stone deaf, or at least claiming to be, all communication with Grandpa Martin was by writing on a little grey tablet which erased on being pulled out of its cover. Even then he frequently chose not to understand messages that were not to his liking. He was an old rogue and tales of his villainy abounded. One night, during the war, when sugar was rationed, Mrs Martin crept downstairs to find her father using a penny to scoop sugar into a paper bag. He had been stealing her sugar for months and selling it for beer money. One day a workmate of Charlie's, a Salvationist, commented on what a remarkable old man his father-in-law was. It transpired that, unknown to his family, Grandpa Martin had joined a local chapter of the Salvation Army where, to the delight of the brethren, he had publicly repented his many sins and vowed from that moment on to live a life of rectitude.

'I hear you've given up drink,' Charlie teased him.

'You what?'

'Drink. You've given it up. You can't drink if you are a member of the Salvation Army.'

That, needless to say, was the end of that.

Grandpa Martin was the same age as Queen Mary and used to complain that she would outlive him 'with all those people looking after her'. He was right, but only just. He died peacefully in his sleep, a few months before his royal contemporary. Tales of his exploits kept us entertained for the next thirty years.

Only on looking back have I come to appreciate how hard my mother's life must have been. She nursed us through all the usual childhood illnesses – chicken pox, measles, whooping cough. There were no washing machines, dishwashers, disposable nappies or any of the other modern conveniences that we now take for granted. It was the same for everyone, of course, but Mum's life was made more difficult by the fact that there were no nearby grandparents to help out and Dad's work took him away to America and the Far East for weeks, sometimes months, during which time she was in effect a single parent.

I was a sickly child. Scarcely a birthday passed in my first eight years when I wasn't laid up with some illness or other – ulcerated colitis, meningitis, pneumonia – necessitating long periods in hospital. Hazily I recollect lying in a little glass cubicle with worried-looking adults peering at me through the glass. I seem to recall a homemade red-and-white patchwork quilt. Once, when I wet the bed, a nurse hit me.

One autumn day, when I was four years old, my parents came to visit me in hospital. 'Daddy has to go away,' they said. This was devastating news. I adored my dad.

'When will you come back?'

'Not for some time.'

'Next week?'

'Er ... No.'

'Next month?'

'Not exactly.'

Tears began to well. 'You'll be home for Christmas, won't you?'

'Afraid not.'

'When?'

'In spring, when the flowers come out ...'

By now I was screaming, inconsolable. 'You must leave,' a nurse advised my parents. 'Just walk away.'

In due course we became used to Dad's absences. 'I'll wave,' he said, 'when the plane flies over our house.' And at the appointed hour we used to go into Mrs Martin's back garden and wave a tablecloth at any passing plane on the assumption that it contained our dad.

I was almost a year late starting school, on account of illness. In the early years there were long absences, too. Later it dawned on me that this late start and the months of sickness that followed might be the reason why, against expectations, I failed the eleven-plus. Dimly, I still recall being delivered on my first day to the Catholic primary school, behind the Church of the Immaculate Conception on London Road. I remember only two things about my short time there. First, a girl called Judith putting up her hand and asking to go to the toilet only to be told to 'sit on it'. Second, a Christmas lunch at which we were told that the pudding contained silver sixpences and anyone lucky enough to find one should report to the teacher in charge who would change it into coppers, since a sixpenny piece was far too large a sum for a small person to have charge of. After about six months it was decided that the Immaculate Conception was too rough for a child of my delicate sensibilities and I was transferred to the allegedly more respectable St Philip's Priory, a private school half a mile up the road.

St Philip's was run by nuns who, while not among the Stasi of the Catholic Church, were not averse to a bit of violence.

What else do I recall about the 1950s? The coronation, of course. At school we were issued with mugs and pencil boxes emblazoned with the Union Jack and a picture of the young Queen. The coronation was my first glimpse of television. The Martins acquired a set long before we did. On the big day Mr Martin's relatives came from Colchester and we sat in their living room munching sandwiches and watching the great event on their twelve-inch black-and-white TV. Oh yes, and the hangings. It was through Mrs Martin that I developed an unhealthy interest in murderers. Hawley Harvey Crippen, the doctor who poisoned his wife and fled to America with his lover, Ethel le Neve, who was disguised as a man. Crippen owed his downfall to Dad's employers, having had the bad luck to travel on the first transatlantic liner to be fitted with radio by Marconi. Edith Thompson and Freddie Bywaters, lovers convicted of murdering her husband. Neville Heath, whose last words were reputedly, 'Give me a whisky, make it a double.' John George Haig, the acid-bath murderer. The sinister John Reginald Halliday Christie, who hid the bodies of his victims in the walls and under the floorboards of his terraced house in Notting Hill. Ruth Ellis, who gunned down her lover outside a pub in Hampstead. These last two were sensations still fresh in the popular memory when I was young. But it wasn't just the famous. I remember the little murderers, too: twenty-one-year-old John Vickers, who killed an old lady during a burglary, hanged at Durham on 23 July 1957. Guenther Fritz Podola, a pathetic little German who shot dead a policeman – hanged at Wandsworth on Guy Fawkes Day 1959. Flossie Forsyth, an eighteen-year-old Teddy boy, part of a gang who kicked a young engineer to death – hanged at Wandsworth on 10 November 1960. They all took the short walk to the gallows as we wolfed down our cornflakes before setting out for school. Their last hours – 8 a.m. was the hanging hour – would be graphically recounted the next day in Mr Martin's *Daily Herald*. Mr Martin took the *Herald* until it closed in 1964, after which he began taking the *Telegraph*. I suspect his politics may have changed around that time, too.

In 1955 the Mullin family took a step up in the world. We sold our house in Dorset Avenue and moved to Manor Drive, a cul-de-sac of newly built detached four- and five-bedroom houses with, oh wonder of wonders, *central heating*. Our new home cost £5,500, an enormous sum at the time. My mother said later that she didn't like to say we lived in a house with central heating for fear of being thought boastful. No sooner had we moved to Manor Drive than I climbed on my tricycle, crossed the busy Baddow Road and raced back to see Mrs Martin, vowing never to desert her. Our house in Dorset Avenue remained unoccupied for a long time, enabling me that summer to raid the Victoria plum tree at the end of the garden. At Manor Drive we again had fields at the bottom of our garden, stretching away more than a mile to the River Chelmer. A little to the left there was a copse. As children, we whiled away many happy hours building dens in the woods and roaming the fields. Before long, they, too, disappeared under concrete. The copse in which we built our tree houses was bull-dozed in a single afternoon while I was away at school, the land com-pulsorily purchased. Reg Spalding, the elderly farmer who had also owned the fields behind Dorset Avenue, received little in the way of compensation. He was left with only a few acres near the river which were too damp to build on. When I last looked, his old farmhouse had been engulfed by a 1960s housing estate, bounded by the Baddow by-pass.

Failing the eleven-plus was a seminal event in my life. It was a close-run thing. I had been expected to pass and the nuns lodged an appeal with the result that I and another boy were granted an interview for the one remaining place at Maldon Grammar School. He was accepted, I was not. For many of my contemporaries the eleven-plus was an event that determined the course of their lives. A lottery, the outcome of which was fixed by the number of places available at the local grammar school, which varied greatly, depending on where you lived. Nearly fifty years later I was invited back to St Philip's Priory to present the prizes. During the course of my speech I remarked that in my day we had the eleven-plus which marked you for life. It may have been my imagination, but at that moment I felt a slight chill in the air. 'We still have it,' whispered one of the teachers, after I had sat down.

Before the coming of comprehensives, those who failed the eleven-plus were destined for the Sandon Secondary Modern School. Several of my friends ended up there. Not a bad school as secondary moderns went, but like all such schools sadly lacking in investment, good discipline and, above all, ambition. Only the fact that my parents could afford (though it must have entailed sacrifice) to pay for me to be sent away to boarding school saved me from this fate. Thus it came to pass that I ended up at St Joseph's College, Birkfield, Ipswich.

St Joseph's was centred around an early nineteenth-century mansion on a hill outside the town. It was run by the De La Salle Brothers, a religious order founded in the seventeenth century to educate the children of the poor, although somewhere along the line the mission had changed and they had ended up educating the children of the prosperous. Like many such schools, St Joseph's was managed on a mixture of inspiration and terror. Most of the Brothers had a good side, but some were prone to outbursts of violence and at least one was a paedophile. On what was for many of us our first night away from home, as we stood shivering in our pyjamas, Brother L assembled us in the dormitory and delivered a little homily, the nub of which was, 'We will either make you or break you.' He repeated the phrase several times. In later years I noted with satisfaction that St Joseph's broke him before it broke most of us. He went off to study at Essex University and never came back.

If I learned one thing at St Joseph's it was how to work hard, a habit that has stayed with me all my life. I am grateful for that. Not a moment was left unaccounted for. Four days a week (seven if you were particularly pious – as I was) we rose early for Mass. There were classes on Saturday mornings. On Saturday afternoons those of us not in school rugby teams, were required to be on the touchline to support those who were. Sunday mornings after Mass, were reserved for homework and writing letters home (envelopes to be left unsealed). After lunch on Sunday those not in school teams had to assemble in a classroom where two teams were picked. Since I was useless at rugby, nobody wanted me on their team. Among The Useless there was much competition to be one of the two or three who were surplus to requirements. Our fate, infinitely preferable to the rough and tumble of the rugby pitch, was to be appointed linesmen or sent off on cross-country runs. This I didn't mind since long-distance running and table tennis were the only sports at which I was any good. Thus I devoted seven years of my life to avoiding rugby. In later years I developed a talent for painting portraits with oils. My greatest work, a large painting featuring eight popes – from Pius IX to Paul VI – led to my being exempted from Sunday afternoon rugby. Later I diversified into painting young, lightly clothed women which led to murmurs that perhaps I was needed on the rugby field after all, whereupon I went back to popes.

The academic regime, though not of a particularly high standard, was rendered fiercely competitive by a system of testimonials. Every week our marks in each subject were aggregated and we were awarded a total out of a possible 200. These were then recorded on coloured paper: gold, red, blue, white. Gold was a rarity, achieved only by the brightest. The only regular recipient of a gold was a very clever boy whose first name was Gervase. I often wonder what became of him. Most of us received reds. A blue was a minor disgrace. A white, catastrophic. I recall only one white being awarded and terrible retribution followed. The boy concerned disappeared shortly afterwards. He was so badly mistreated that I wouldn't have been surprised to hear that his body had been found in the Orwell, which flowed nearby. Each Saturday morning we waited in trepidation as Brother Director toured the classrooms handing out the testimonials. He started at the top and worked down. Gold attracted a round of applause so we could hear the director coming from a long way off. Our names were called in order of ranking. To begin with I was usually in the last half dozen, but by the fourth form I had worked my way up to about halfway. At which point there was an unfortunate development.

Until then classes had divided into streams: A, B and C. A for those who had passed the eleven-plus, B and C for those who had not. There was no distinction between the last two. Now, however, it was proposed to divide B and C according to merit. The best fifteen boys from each class became the Alpha stream and the remainder went into the B stream. I just scraped into the upper half and was, therefore, allocated to 5 Alpha, which meant that I was again near the bottom of the class, back where I had been four years earlier. To crown all, class 5B, despite having a high concentration of ne'er do wells, was given most of the best teachers. Drastic action was called for. I made what was probably the best decision of my life: I asked to be relegated to the lower stream. Overnight, I went from bottom to top of the class, which did wonders for my morale. True, there was a downside. I was bullied mercilessly, but I knew I would outlive the bullies. And sure enough, come GCEs, I was vindicated. I was one of only a handful (perhaps the only one) of the class 5B students to make it into the sixth form and from there to university.

Many years later I returned to St Joseph's, to address a local book club which held its meetings in the school library. A few ghosts still linger. The dormitory in the '51 Wing where, in full view of all of us, Brother L had administered what he called 'a medium caning' to the unfortunate recipient of the white testimonial. The place by the '55 Wing where, in my first year, a boy called Phillips blew himself up on Guy Fawkes day with a home-made firework. Brother James's room outside which we queued to reclaim lost property at a price of one whack with a plimsoll per item (all our clothes were labelled so the penalties could not be evaded). The dormitory in the '55 wing where an obese Kuwaiti youth celebrated his hundredth coupling with a prostitute.

Today the mansion is still more or less intact, though the huge cedar tree which once dominated the park is long gone. Likewise Belstead woods, in which in later years we trespassed, is now a housing estate. Even Lord Belstead's house has fallen to the bulldozer. The Brothers, too, are gone. The school, though still Catholic, is now run entirely by lay persons. At the time of my last visit, the head was a woman and, oh wonder of wonders, St Joseph's now takes girls – a dream beyond our wildest imagining. The establishment is well down the league table of independent schools. Many of today's students (far more than in my day) are foreigners, children of the Russian and Chinese nouveau riche, one or two of whom have been known to pay their fees with a bag full of cash.

As for my contemporaries, most have disappeared without trace. Every so often, at a book-signing or a literary festival, I am approached by someone who was at St Joseph's with me. I am still in touch with a couple of veterans from my schooldays. Frank Nelson, whose ancestor stands atop the column in Trafalgar Square, emigrated to New Zealand where he became a local newspaper journalist. And my good friend David Fraser, who came late to the school (thereby missing the Great Terror), became a successful commercial lawyer. Perhaps the best known old boy is the musician, Brian Eno, whose works include *Music for Airports*.

I earned my first pocket money selling blackberries, venturing as far as Little Baddow to a field by Riffham's Wood which only I knew about. For a week or two in late August I would cycle daily up Danbury Hill, returning with a wicker basket brimming with blackberries which I sold to neighbours. Those were the hardest few shillings I ever earned. The road up Danbury Hill rises steadily for more than a mile and my bike had no gears. Later summers were spent picking peas and potatoes and budding trees on Seabrook's fruit farm near Boreham. This last was back-breaking work. I was paired with an old country-man who spent the day bent double astride a row of young fruit trees which seemed to stretch to the horizon and beyond. His job was to slit the bark and insert a bud; mine was to come along behind, binding the slit. My partner was a man of few words. 'How many do you think we've done?' I would ask after hours of silence. To which, in his thick Essex accent, he would reply, 'The better part of a tidy few.'

Later, in the year I left school, Frank Nelson and I worked as waiters at Pontins near Lowestoft. Our job was to serve a three-course meal to thirty-two happy campers in forty-five minutes in a dining hall that accommodated 1,500 people. Speed was of the essence. If anyone asked for so much as a teaspoon, the hapless waiter would be thrown completely off course. The trick was to get near the front of the soup queue so that you would be ahead of the pack for the rest of the meal, a feat I rarely, if ever, achieved. There was a merchant sea-man's strike that summer and many of my fellow waiters, strikers from the *Queen Mary* and other big ocean-going liners, ran circles around the rest of us. My campers were almost invariably among the last to be served. To complicate matters the campers were divided into teams who, egged on by zealous bluecoats, had to outshout rival teams. Each section had a slogan. It was not easy serving a three-course meal with a bluecoat standing on your hotplate bawling 'Ziggy zaggy, ziggy zaggy, oi, oi, oi.' Pontins was my first encounter with the working classes. By and large they were cheerful, decent people, toler-ant of the poor level of service I offered and invariably sympathetic as I raced between tables, sweat pouring down my face.

Pontins was also the place where I first kissed a girl. Her name was Nancy and she worked in reception.

CHAPTER FIVE

Something to Write Home About

At university I studied law, but since I was spending more time working for the student newspaper, it seemed logical to become a journalist rather than a lawyer. I applied to join the Mirror Group training scheme and was initially rejected, but someone dropped out and I was offered a place at the last minute.

The scheme was based around a group of local newspapers in South Devon. In years to come prominent graduates would include Alastair Campbell (destined to become a key player in the rise of New Labour), Andrew Morton (whose works include *Diana: Her True Story*) and David Montgomery who went on to edit the *News of the World* and later became chief executive of the Mirror Group. The idea was that, after a course in the basics of journalism, we would be apprenticed to one or more of the half-dozen weekly newspapers owned by the group. I must have been particularly insufferable because I ended up being shunted around all six.

While still a trainee journalist I was selected as the Labour candidate for North Devon in the 1970 general election. At the grand old age of 22 I was far too young and immature to represent anyone, not that there was the slightest danger of being called upon to do so. Even in those days Labour voters in the constituency numbered little more than 5,000, and it has been downhill all the way since then. The sitting MP, clinging on by his fingertips against a strong Conservative challenge, was the Liberal leader Jeremy Thorpe. Thorpe impressed me for several reasons. North Devon was a classic rural seat. Most of his constituents were opposed to what was then known as the

Common Market; he was in favour. They were strongly anti-immigrant (although there were virtually no foreigners in Devon at that time), but he was liberal on immigration. Most of his constituents were keen on the death penalty (though murders in North Devon were rare); he was opposed. At the count, when I was found to be a few votes short of holding on to my deposit (which in those days required 12.5 per cent of the total votes cast rather than the present 5 per cent) he graciously insisted on a recount to see if the extra votes could be found.

In those far-off days, before misfortune overtook him, Thorpe had galvanised political life in North Devon, holding meetings in every village, sometimes as many as four or five a night, in addition to a gruelling schedule of national events. The electoral turnout was 85 per cent and a crowd of several thousand attended the final hustings and the declaration of the result. Much of that was down to his extraordinary magnetism. I might have been young and impressionable, but I prefer to remember Jeremy Thorpe as I knew him when he was at the height of his powers, rather than the tragic figure he later became.*

In March 1970, three months before the election, I obtained the first scoop of my career. I wangled an interview with the prime minister, Harold Wilson, on behalf of *Student*, a glossy magazine founded by the young Richard Branson, his first step on the way to billionairedom. I was with the prime minister for about forty minutes. A shadowy photograph of our encounter, me a long-haired youth, Harold puffing on his pipe, hangs on the wall of my study. We were standing by the window in the Number 10 drawing room. It would be another twenty-seven years before I stood in that spot again. A few days later the *Daily Mirror* printed an extract from the interview across two pages. This did not go down especially well with many of my fellow trainees or the Fleet Street old hands who taught us. They, after all, had been trying to teach us the proper use of full stops, commas, quotation marks and

---

*In 1978 Thorpe, who had resigned as Liberal leader in 1976, was charged with conspiracy to murder a gay lover who was allegedly blackmailing him; although acquitted, his reputation never recovered and he lost his seat at the 1979 general election. In later years he suffered from Parkinson's disease.

short paragraphs with the promise that, if we applied ourselves dutifully, we might one day be blessed with a by-line at the foot of an inside page in the great *Daily Mirror*. Now some insolent young upstart, who hadn't been on the scheme for ten minutes, had gone and landed a double-page spread. It was not long after this that the managing director of West of England Newspapers (the Mirror Group's local subsidiary) was overheard referring to me as 'that fucker Mullin'.

Towards the end of our two-year apprenticeship we trainees were attached for a couple of months to one of the Mirror Group's national publications. In my case this was the *Sunday Mirror*, where, at the end of my first week, my expenses were rejected by the person who was supposed to vouch for their accuracy on the grounds that they were so low they would embarrass everyone else in the office. At which point an old hand took pity on me and offered a short course on how to construct fraudulent expenses which, needless to say, I ignored. Many years later, at the height of the furore over MP's expenses, I was telephoned by a journalist from the *Sunday Mirror* who was proposing to write a story along the lines of 'they are all at it'. I took pleasure in pointing out to him that the only place I had ever worked where they were 'all at it' was the *Sunday Mirror* in the early 1970s.

In the summer of 1971 I secured a visa to visit China as one of a party of young people on a tour organised by the Society for Anglo-Chinese Understanding. At this time China under Mao Zedong was still a closed country. The Cultural Revolution may have burned itself out, but Nixon was yet to visit and visas for journalists were seldom granted.

Looking back, this was one of the seminal moments in my life. It awakened in me a lifelong interest in Asia and I made friendships that have lasted to this day. It was also potentially my first big break as a journalist. I was given eight weeks' leave of absence from the training scheme and Tony Miles, the then editor of the *Daily Mirror*, agreed to pay my expenses. The *Mirror* also provided a Pentax camera and many rolls of Tri-X film. My, so-to-speak, fellow-travellers, were mainly students at Oxford or Cambridge, several of whom spoke rudimentary Mandarin. There were also two Americans: Gael Dohany, a film-maker; and Gil Loescher, an academic who many years later would lose both his legs in the explosion that killed the UN representative in Iraq.

We flew to Moscow and from there caught a train to Beijing. The journey lasted six days and seven nights, across Siberia, past Lake Baikal and then south across Outer Mongolia and northern China. We were the only Western passengers apart from two Queen's messengers who joined us at Ulan Bator. Other travelling companions included a number of mysterious North Vietnamese, a Mongolian general and a Czech engineer bound for a cement factory in northern Mongolia who remarked that the ice on the Selenga river, on the border between Siberia and Mongolia, froze to a depth of several metres in winter. We were told at the border that the Americans in our party were the first ever to cross the Mongolian–Chinese frontier by train.

The train was Chinese. Each carriage had a Chinese steward and the walls were decorated with pictures of the Great Helmsman; unseen loudspeakers played 'The East is Red' as we pulled out of Moscow's Yaroslavl station. The engine and the dining car, however, changed according to which country we were passing through. For the first five days the dining car was firmly in the hands of the Russians, which meant we had to make do with a diet consisting mainly of cabbage soup and meatballs, supplemented by whatever tinned fruit and fish we had brought with us. When the train reached Mongolia it was replaced by a local dining car that travelled across the country virtually unused since the stewards stoutly refused to accept anything but Mongolian currency. Only when we reached China, and a Chinese dining car was attached, was there a marked improvement in the quality of the cuisine.

From the outset our party, eighteen persons in all, divided broadly into two ideological camps. On the one side was a group I christened the Rave Babes, who thought that everything about Maoist China was wonderful and adapted effortlessly to the slogans of the hour. The other faction I tagged Capitalist Roaders. They were only about 95 per cent signed up to the glories of the Chinese revolution and from time to time expressed mild scepticism about some of what we were told. I was in the second camp. Although by no means a Rave Babe, I firmly believed at that time that the Chinese revolution was the greatest advance in human history, an opinion acquired from a hasty perusal of the works of sympathetic Westerners such as Edgar Snow, Jack Belden and Felix Green. We knew a little of the devastating famine that followed Mao's Great Leap Forward and the excesses of the Cultural Revolution, but tended to dismiss the most lurid reports as capitalist propaganda. Now I know different, although, to be fair, it wasn't until many years later – when the Chinese themselves began to write their memoirs and official archives were opened – that the full horror became known. Anyone who is under the slightest illusion about Mao or the Communist Party of China should read the works of Jung Chang, Frank Dikötter and Mao's doctor, Li Zhisui.*

Young, impressionable and ignorant, we marvelled that great order prevailed under heaven, and in a country of more than a billion people which had known decades of civil war, famine and chaos this seemed no small achievement. There were no beggars on the streets and no shortage of food in the markets (in contrast to the half-empty shelves we had seen in Russia, supposedly a wealthier country). One statistic above all spoke volumes: in 1949, the year of the revolution, average life expectancy in China was just twenty-eight years; by the 1970s it had almost doubled. Whatever their sins, the Communists must have done something right.

Even so, there were small incidents from which I should have drawn larger conclusions. On our first night at the Beijing Hotel, just off Tiananmen Square, we were treated to a banquet. In those days it was common for even the lowliest officials to be invited to sit at the top table in a spurious show of equality. Under the surface, however, all was not as it seemed. I attempted to strike up a conversation with the man sitting next to me, but when we had scarcely got beyond pleasantries perspiration began to roll down his forehead and he began to shake. He turned out to be not an official, but one of the stewards who had accompanied us on the train from Moscow, now in his best bib and tucker, and I had failed to recognise him. Of what was he afraid? Later, visiting a coal mine in southern China, I rounded a

----

* *Wild Swans* (Simon and Schuster, 1991); *Mao's Great Famine* (Bloomsbury, 2010); *The Private Life of Chairman Mao* (Random House, 1994), respectively.

corner slightly ahead of our party just in time to see a brutal looking cadre roughly push an old man out of the way. Back in Beijing two or three of us tracked down Rewi Alley, an old New Zealander who in the 1930s had come to China as a fire inspection officer and stayed. On his wall he had a black-and-white photograph of Chairman Mao, taken some years earlier at the airport. The face of the man standing next to Mao had been crudely obliterated. 'Who was that?' I asked. 'Ah,' he replied cheerfully, 'that was Liu Shaoqi, the former president. We had to rub him out during the Cultural Revolution.'

Our chief guide was a genteel, middle-class woman who, one felt, had known better times. No doubt she had suffered during the Cultural Revolution. Though she talked vaguely of having spent time in the countryside she treated us warily – as well she might, for there was a spy in our midst, a commissar we nicknamed the Mandarin, who spoke not a word of English but who spent most of the trip making notes. On the first night I spent a lot of time chatting to a young male guide who was much more sociable than the others. The Mandarin must have noticed, because after a couple of days the guide disappeared without explanation. Another guide, Mr Li, a thin, tense man from Guangdong in southern China, told us that he had lost most of his family to famine. We were given to understand that the famine in question was prior to the revolution, but knowing what I do now, I can't help wondering whether they were really victims of the devastating hunger that followed Mao's catastrophic Great Leap Forward.

We travelled the length of China by train and bus – south to the cradle of the revolution in the lush Jinggang mountains, east to the great cities of Shanghai and Nanking, north to the barren province in Shansi, where we stayed two nights in the homes of peasant farmers in Sha Shih Yu, a model village where the peasants had the unfortunate habit of applauding whenever we went near them, thereby rendering impossible any hope of sensible dialogue. Foreigners at the time were a rarity in China and we attracted huge, curious crowds wherever we went. In Shanghai the crowds were so great that we had to board a bus to keep ahead of them. '*Waigoran, waigoran*' (Foreigner, foreigner), we could hear the children whispering. Gil Loescher, six feet eight inches tall, was of particular interest. He and I wandered the back streets of Nanking, attracting crowds of children who would disappear down alleyways as soon as we tried to take a photograph. In the end it became a game. One of us would walk a little way ahead and then suddenly spin round and take a photograph. If you look carefully at their faces, you can see the children, caught on the hop, are just getting ready to run.

We knew nothing of the terrible tensions below the surface at the highest level of the Communist Party of China. No one did. Three weeks after we departed a plane containing Mao's designated heir, Lin Biao, mysteriously crashed in Mongolia. Allegedly, Lin had attempted a coup, presumably in protest again Mao's decision to make friends with America, but as always the truth was opaque. In August I photographed a class of young Chinese schoolgirls, dressed identically and all with regulation pigtails, rehearsing in Tiananmen Square for the great national day parade due to take place on 1 October, the anniversary of the revolution. That year, however, the parade was cancelled as a result of Lin Biao's disappearance.

After five exhilarating weeks we returned the way we had come – on the train across Mongolia and Siberia. Unfortunately, I blew my chances with the *Daily Mirror*. The copy I turned in was hopelessly naive and the editor wisely declined to use it. I avenged myself by negotiating a toe-curlingly embarrassing centre-page spread in the *Mirror*'s great rival, the *Sun*, then recently acquired by Rupert Murdoch. The opening line reads 'The first thing you notice about China is the girls …' (Aaaagh …) All was not lost, however. The *New York Times* magazine bought my account of the train journey from Moscow to Beijing and the *Telegraph* magazine ran a feature on our stay in the village of Sha Shih Yu. I thought I was made, but I was wrong. Nothing I ever wrote subsequently proved of interest to the *New York Times*. The *Telegraph* magazine, however, proved more promising.

In January 1972, on graduating from the Mirror Group training scheme, I was offered a job at the *Sunday Mirror*'s Manchester office which I declined. Instead I paid £81 for a one-way ticket to the Far East, having made little or no preparation and having only the vaguest idea of where I was going. I hoped to fund my travels by writing about them, which, in the end, I more or less succeeded in doing, though I had no commissions and few contacts. In those days there were no

Lonely Planet guides, no internet and no mobile telephones. I simply disembarked at Bangkok airport, caught a bus into the city and ended up in a doss house-cum-brothel near the railway station. Later, I made my way up to Laos, a beautiful but tragic land which had been sucked into the Vietnam war and as a result had the unenviable distinction of being the world's most bombed country. There I did something extraordinarily foolish. I caught a bus north up Highway 13 in the general direction of the war. I was the only foreigner on the bus and inevitably the other passengers assumed I was an American. When they started calling me a bomber I decided it was time to get off. I spent the night in a temple at Vang Vieng, a town surrounded by jagged limestone hills, before returning to the capital, Vientiane.

Undaunted, I then set off down Highway 13 in the opposite direction. A few hours out of Vientiane, just before Paksan we came to a bridge which had been recently dynamited. A small boat ferried us to the far bank, where a fleet of pick-up trucks waited to take us south. The only other foreigners were two French nuns who worked locally. After a while, as the light was beginning to fade, we came to a tree which had been felled to block the road. What was this? An ambush? We held our breath. The driver hesitated and then, spotting a gap between the upper branches and the verge, managed to steer us through. On the far side there was a burned-out car, still smouldering, the fate of the occupants unknown. That evening in Paksan I was sitting outside a restaurant on the main street when from the outskirts of the town there was a burst of gunfire. Instantly, the lights went out, the street cleared and I found myself alone. My abiding memory is of a one-legged man, using his crutch like a pole-vaulter as he disappeared round a corner.

The next two days were less eventful. I continued south on a series of buses and trucks. It was the hot season, the road was unpaved and we bounced along throwing up a great cloud of orange dust as we passed. Much of the Royal Lao Army consisted of boy soldiers who would occasionally hitch a ride. They would clamber aboard, clutching their M16 rifles, which they would sometimes pass round for other passengers to admire. Each had a belt full of hand grenades which would swing back and forth unnervingly as we bounced through potholes. It was a relief to reach the safety of Pakse.

In Pakse there was a South Vietnamese consulate. My plan was to apply for a visa and then catch the weekly flight to Saigon. Once again, I had not done my homework. I duly called at the consulate only to be firmly told by a courteous official that he was unable to issue me with a visa, only the embassy in Vientiane – from where I'd just come – could do that. Despairing, I set off down the street, hotly pursued by the man from the consulate brandishing my wallet. I had left it, stuffed full of dollars, on his desk. Without it I would have been stranded. The man could easily have kept it and disclaimed all knowledge had I returned. That was the moment I realised that, despite all the tales of corruption in South Vietnam's military regime, there were good people on both sides of the conflict. Later I came to realise that there were bad people on both sides, too.

Once again I was foolish. Instead of taking the sensible course and spending a few extra dollars on a direct flight back to Vientiane, which would have taken less than two hours, I once again set off on the three-day journey by road. On the second day, after Savannakhet, the buses and pick-up trucks ran out. I sat all day in the great heat by the dusty highway and not a single vehicle passed. Eventually, a soldier appeared, an officer in the Lao army. He spoke little English, but his message was unmistakeable. This was not a safe place for a foreigner. He indicated the scar from a bullet wound on the back of his neck. I went with him to a nearby village, where I was put up for the night, and the following day a place was found for me on a truck heading north. Eventually, I made it back to Vientiane in one piece.

I spent eight months bumming around Asia, through Burma, Bangladesh, Nepal and across northern India, through the Khyber Pass into Afghanistan, a beautiful, primitive land of arid deserts, rugged mountains and feuding tribes. This was in the days before the earth changed places with the sky. Before the coming of the Russians, the Taliban, Osama Bin Laden, the warlords and NATO. The market stalls were laden with luscious fruit, King Zahir was in his palace and the great Buddhas still occupied their alcoves at Bamiyan. In those days a Westerner could go anywhere unmolested. After exploring Kabul and Bamiyan, I took a ramshackle bus south to Kandahar and from there across the desert to Quetta in Pakistan. The bus had been bought second-hand from Germany and still displayed its original destination – Munich railway station. It was manned by a couple of fearsome-looking brigands, one of whom chewed all day on a single piece of gum which, from time to time, he took out of his mouth and placed on the choke button to rejuvenate. From Quetta I went by train to Karachi, from where I took a boat to Bombay. It was the dry season and the heat was unrelenting.

In those days more than 80 per cent of Indians lived in the countryside (today it is more like 50 per cent), but an invisible barrier separated urban India from the surrounding countryside. For hour after hour the rural people could be glimpsed ploughing their fields, tending their crops. When the train stopped they would lay siege, attempting to sell bananas, cashew nuts or mangoes through the barred windows, but none of the city-dwelling passengers knew how to make contact with them. They might as well have lived in a foreign country for all the contact they had with their urban brethren. I wanted to spend time in a village and asked my Indian acquaintances if they could put me in touch with anyone who lived in the countryside. They scratched their heads, consulted their friends, but no one had the slightest idea. Eventually, I was given the name of a Catholic priest in Poona (now called Pune) and he put me in touch with a local official who agreed to accompany me to a village and interpret while I chatted to the villagers.

'Sir, what is your memo for breakfast?' he asked as I turned in on the first night.

Later I was passed on to an Irish priest in Andhra Pradesh, and from there I went south to Tamil Nadu to visit Joe Homan, once a teacher at my school. Ten years earlier, with just £200 in his pocket, Joe had disappeared to southern India to set up a village for destitute children. Fifty years later, he was still there. I visited him again in January 2012. By then he had established half a dozen children's villages and other projects designed to lift rural children out of poverty and provide a better life for them and their families. Joe Homan led one of the most useful lives of anyone I have known.

I returned home in the autumn of 1972. There followed four or five months of unemployment. Like many a freelance journalist, I never quite admitted, either to myself or to my friends, that I was unemployed, but for all practical purposes I was. No one who hasn't been out of work can truly understand what a debilitating experience it is. Gradually your self-confidence evaporates. One day blends into another. There is no distinction between weekends and weekdays. You can't bear to see friends because there is so little to talk about.

Eventually, I got a job as a reporter on the *Hampstead & Highgate Express*, a remarkable local newspaper edited for decades by the redoubtable Gerry Isaaman, a man who knew his patch inside out. I wasn't much good as a local reporter since my mind was often elsewhere and never quite adjusted to reporting the finer points of Camden Council committee meetings or controversial planning applications on the fringes of Hampstead Heath. There was, however, one great bonus. I struck up what became a lifelong friendship with the paper's news editor, Liz Forgan, a wonderful woman who went on to achieve great things in public life.* During the course of my life I have come across a handful of people who I look upon as life enhancers, merely to spend time in whose company is to come away refreshed. Liz is one of them.

After a few months at the *Ham & High* my fortunes began to look up. I was asked by John Anstey, editor of the *Telegraph* magazine, to write a lengthy piece on 'the future of South East Asia, dear boy'. Under Anstey, the *Telegraph* magazine was widely considered to be the best of the weekend supplements. One of his strengths was a willingness to encourage young writers and, briefly, he took a shine to me, but there was a downside. Anstey was a tyrant and, as with all tyrants, those who worked for him were at the mercy of his whims. He rarely emerged into daylight, preferring to operate from behind a wall of secretaries, bombarding the underlings with often contradictory memoranda. Features editors came and went, some lasting only a matter of weeks. This posed the added difficulty that whoever held the post when copy was commissioned was rarely the person who received the finished work, and their replacement might have entirely

---

*Senior Channel 4 and BBC executive during the 1980s and 90s; chair, Heritage Lottery Fund 2001–8; chair, Arts Council 2009–13; chair, Scott Trust (which owns the *Guardian*), 2003–16.

different ideas. Anstey was especially hard on women. Marina Warner, now a successful author and academic, worked for him around that time. She says, 'Anstey was a bully. He enjoyed giving his female colleagues a hard time. I was amazed by the number of us I found in the ladies loo, crying.' He liked to disparage work roughly and without explanation. 'He was difficult to gain access to – secretive, arbitrary, opinionated, heavy ... a sort of Middle Eastern dictator.'

Marina had her revenge. Unable to stand working for Anstey any longer, she departed for a job on *Vogue*. Soon afterwards she entered, under an assumed name, the magazine's Young Writer of the Year competition. It wasn't until the shortlist was announced that birth certificates were sent for, at which point her cover was blown. Of the several thousand entries, hers was easily the best and, inevitably, she won. Among the glittering prizes: a job on the *Telegraph* magazine. How did Anstey react when he discovered her identity? 'He took it quite well, as it happens. Rough justice of a sort, and he understood that.'

Byron Rogers, who worked for Anstey in the early 1970s, compared the *Telegraph* magazine under his editorship to Montenegro, 'the independent little mountain kingdom that somehow survived inside the Ottoman empire, a place where the central authorities never came ... There, in a brown felt-lined room, dark even at midday, a thin ray of intense light illuminating a few inches of his desk, John Anstey ruled absolute and withdrawn, a grand Turk among the women.' Rogers went on, 'the editor of the main paper which appeared six days a week, had one secretary. Anstey who edited the give-away magazine, had four. But then he needed them for he communicated only by letter, even with his own staff, and then usually to sack them.'*

I, too, had my share of difficulties. Early in 1973 I purchased a second-hand Citroën 2CV from a posh young car dealer in Fulham who was the proud owner of a top-of-the-range BMW and a Messerschmitt light aeroplane. 'Breakfast in Calais, dinner in Nice' was how BMW were advertising the car. In passing, the dealer remarked that the car would probably get him to Nice faster than the plane. I foolishly mentioned this to Anstey and he immediately seized upon it.

---

*Byron Rogers, *Me, The Authorised Biography* (Aurum, 2011).

So, there came a day when a party of us – the *Telegraph*'s motoring correspondent, two photographers, the owner of the plane and myself – assembled at a small hotel in Calais to put the proposition to the test. The car's advantage was that the pilot had to get to and from the airport, submit a flight plan and land at least once to refuel. To be sure, the BMW was a beautiful car, but the 775-mile journey was hair-raising. The French were yet to impose speed restrictions on their motorways. We would slow down to 100 mph to pour out coffee on the back shelf, causing scarcely a ripple. And yes, the car did reach Nice before the plane. That evening we all assembled for dinner at a château outside Nice. Anstey himself flew down for the occasion. He departed next morning, leaving instructions that he wanted a photo-graph of the car and the plane racing each other. It is, of course, illegal for planes to fly so close to a main road so, very early next morning, in the hope of avoiding both French air-traffic control and the gen-darmerie, we decamped to a stretch of motorway outside Nice, placed photographers on two bridges and at a prearranged signal the plane swooped.

Back in London I hastily knocked out my copy and submitted it. Almost by return came a note from Anstey with a list of impossible demands, one of which was that I was to make clear that this exercise had not been a race which, most assuredly, it was. (I guess he had received advice from lawyers.) The last line added maliciously: 'I do not want this copy taken out of the country' (he knew very well that I was due to depart for the Far East the following day). I ignored this last stricture, did my best to amend the copy on the flight and posted it back to him from Singapore. Later I heard that he had given it to the *Telegraph*'s motoring correspondent to rewrite and the man, bless him, had refused. The photographs weren't satisfactory either and the team was sent back to a disused aerodrome near Calais to repeat the exercise. In the end nothing appeared. The entire, ludicrous exercise must have cost thousands.

So, it was with distinctly mixed feelings that I accepted Anstey's commission to write about the future of South East Asia. On the one hand, it was too good an opportunity to miss. On the other, I knew this was the end. There was no way that my assessment of the war in Vietnam and its likely outcome would coincide with that of the *Daily*

Telegraph. My strategy was to string the trip out as long as possible, staying in cheap hotels and taking on as much other work as I could garner in the certain knowledge that, once I had handed in my copy, I was unlikely ever again to be invited to write for the *Telegraph*.

In Singapore I had half an hour with the prime minister, Lee Kuan Yew, who ruled the city-state with a rod of iron for more than thirty years. The Singaporean authorities in those days took a very dim view of long-haired males. At the airport there were posters indicating the maximum permitted hair length. Those whose hair was longer risked being refused entry. Aware of this, I'd had a trim before setting out. I passed unscathed through immigration and went to see the British high commissioner, Sir Sam Falle.

'Get your hair cut,' he advised.

'But I just have.'

'Not enough,' he said.

By the time I went to see Lee Kuan Yew I might have passed for a Buddhist monk. I remember little of the interview, except that we argued about Vietnam. 'You should join a monastery,' he said in response to my suggestion that if, as he claimed, we were defending freedom, perhaps we could do better than General Thieu.* One other thing: Mr Lee's desk was entirely clear. There was not a single piece of paper, a pen or even a blotter. Since that time I have noticed that the desks of the powerful are almost always free of clutter.

From Singapore I went to Indonesia to interview the country's foreign minister, Adam Malik, then up to Laos to do what really interested me. The destruction of Laos was one of the great unreported crimes of the twentieth century. A remote, picturesque, rural backwater with its own royal family, Laos had the misfortune to find itself caught between the warring parties in Vietnam. Officially it was neutral, but the veneer of neutrality could be maintained only by turning a blind eye to the activities of both sides. The North Vietnamese, under heavy American bombardment, had established a network of trails through the sparsely inhabited forests of eastern Laos, along which they supplied their soldiers in the south. They also armed and

---

*President of South Vietnam, 1965–75, who came to power following a series of military coups.

trained an indigenous Lao insurgency, the Pathet Lao. For their part the Americans armed the hill tribes and began bombing what became known as the Ho Chi Minh trail. As the war intensified, it spread inland, engulfing and annihilating everything in its path. By 1970 the Americans had dropped an incredible one ton of bombs per citizen on Laos and a quarter of the country's population were refugees. Officially they were 'refugees from Communism', but if you talked to them, most said that aeroplanes had destroyed their homes – and only one side had aeroplanes.

As the bombing spread, so did Pathet Lao control of the countryside. By the time I came on the scene in the early 1970s, the communists controlled two-thirds of Laos, leaving the government with only the towns along the Mekong valley and the lowlands around Vientiane. The American strategy (similar to that employed in South Vietnam and later in Cambodia) was to render uninhabitable territory captured by the communist insurgents. The clue lay in the type of bombs they dropped: so-called 'Area Denial Ordnance' – millions of bomblets about the size of hand grenades, designed not to explode on impact but to scatter over as wide an area as possible, turning once-fertile land into a huge minefield. Even today, forty years after the end of the war, Lao rice farmers and their children are being killed and maimed by cluster bombs buried in scrub and mud which, on contact, explode into hundreds of steel splinters. In 1980, eight years after the bombing ceased, I visited the Plain of Jars, one of the most beautiful and fertile areas of Laos, which, with Russian help, the Lao government was trying to rehabilitate. Up to that time 65,000 pieces of live ordnance had been recovered.

Even by the early 1970s very little had been written about what was going on in Laos, a sideshow compared with Vietnam. Little by little, however, the lid had been lifted. In February 1970 a group of journalists had stumbled upon Long Tieng, a vast CIA-run airbase in the mountains of northern Laos, the existence of which was until that time a closely guarded secret. At the time of its discovery Long Tieng was one of the largest US overseas military bases. It had a three-quarter mile long runway and was one of the busiest airports in the world, with a population of around 40,000, making it the second largest city in Laos, and yet it appeared on no map and very little was known

about what went on there. In addition to several hundred CIA opera-
tives and other American advisers, it housed several thousand Thai
mercenaries and a secret army which the CIA had set up under the
Hmong warlord Vang Pao, into which tens of thousands of hill-tribe
youths had been pressganged. The war was run from the US embassy
in Vientiane under the control of successive US ambassadors who
were, in effect, proconsuls. Of these the most notorious was George
McMurtrie Godley. A fellow ambassador who knew him well said of
Godley, 'He was a super-hawk, going far beyond his brief and revelling
in the kill-ration. He was coarse, insensitive and behaved more like a
governor general than an ambassador.' On one occasion, at a British
embassy party in honour of the Queen's birthday, Godley (known to
fellow diplomats as 'Almighty' Godley) had a disagreement with the
Indian ambassador and grabbed him by the lapels. Until the late
1960s, the war in Laos had been a secret, even from the US Congress,
which, by the time I came on the scene, was beginning to take an
increasing interest in what was being done in their name in Laos.

Vientiane, the capital of Laos, was an unusual city. A backwater in
which, uniquely, all sides in the conflict were represented, on account
of the Lao government's theoretical neutrality. Americans, Russians,
Chinese and the North Vietnamese all had embassies. They occasionally met at diplomatic cocktail parties where they eyed each other
warily from a safe distance. Even the communist Pathet Lao were
represented, in a large house near the main market, a stone's throw
from the ministries of the government with which they were at war.
And just to confuse matters, the nominal leader of the Pathet Lao was
Prince Souphanouvong, half brother of the prime minister, Prince
Souvanna Phouma.

In the summer of 1973 I returned to Laos and teamed up with a
young Australian photographer and adventurer, John Everingham,
who lived in Vientiane and spoke the language. He stayed on there
after the communist takeover and rapidly became disillusioned, eventually helping his Lao girlfriend to escape by swimming the Mekong,
an event which brought him brief international fame and was made
into an excruciatingly bad film starring Priscilla Presley. But all that
lay in the future. In the early 1970s Everingham was one of the very

few people who had managed to cross over into the parts of Laos controlled by the communists, where he had taken some remarkable photographs. On his first visit to the Pathet Lao zone, in December 1971, he had visited Long Pot, a valley of hill-tribe villages. The head man was extremely worried. The war was getting ever closer and he was under pressure to send younger and younger boys for the army to feed into the Pathet Lao meat grinder. Lately he had refused and had been warned that, if he persisted, his villages would be considered communist controlled and bombed. When Everingham returned six months later he found the villages gone. His photographs showed the scene before and after. Each taken from more or less the same spot. One depicted a picturesque cluster of traditional thatched houses on stilts, set against a ridge of sharp green limestone hills. In the other, the same green hills, but no houses; just bare earth, charred remains and the tell-tale scum of napalm. They were incontrovertible evidence of what was happening and completely undermined the repeated assurances of successive US ambassadors that civilians were not being targeted.

In the countryside north of Vientiane we visited camps where a succession of so-called 'refugees from communism' described how their homes had been destroyed by aerial bombing. They were simple people, mainly illiterate rice farmers who, until the bombers came, had never left their hills and valleys. Few had ever met an American and none knew where America was or why America had bombed them. They described their plight in simple terms. It was impossible not to be moved. This was the head man of Ban Muang, a village on the Plain of Jars:

> Life was good in Ban Muang. We grew paddy rice, corn and vegetables. There were wild cattle and deer in the forest and also tigers and bears. When the Pathet Lao came in 1964, life went on as usual. They brought their own rice and did not take ours. But before the Pathet Lao had been in the village for a month, the planes came. They shot at us and dropped bombs. Much of the village was burned. The planes came back many times, they came day after day. Even after the village was destroyed they came back ... After the first day we never lived in the village. We went to the forest where we built huts and dug tunnels beside them. We

slept in the huts and, when the planes came, we hid in the tunnels. For five years we lived in the forest. We could only work in our fields between 5 a.m. and 8 a.m., then the planes came.

A second man said, 'It wasn't just the village. If the planes found anyone in the open they bombed him. If they saw a buffalo in a field, they bombed it.'

From Laos I went on to Vietnam, a country that would come to play a large part in my life. Somewhere in the chaos of Saigon there was a young student, Nguyen Thi Ngoc, who would later become my wife. But that was many years in the future. For now I was just another journalist observing a war that, by the time I came on the scene, was in its final throes. The Paris Peace Agreement had been signed and America had withdrawn its troops, leaving behind a network of 'civilian' advisers (many of them military men who had merely swapped their uniforms for suits). The aim was to create a decent interval between US withdrawal and the collapse of the artificial regime in the south, a collapse which, although regarded by most observers as inevitable, when it came eighteen months later was far quicker and more dramatic than anyone had anticipated. For the time being, an uneasy truce prevailed. Taking advantage of this, I caught a series of public buses north up Highway One a journey of several days via the coastal cities of Nha Trang, Quy Nhon, Quang Ngai and Da Nang, ending up in Hue, the former imperial capital which five years earlier had been captured by the Vietcong and held for twenty-eight days against relentless bombardment. At Hue, the road ran out. The zone north of the city had been the scene of recent heavy fighting and was closed to civilians. By a stroke of luck, however, I ran into one of the ubiquitous American advisers who typed out on a piece of official notepaper a request that I be allowed to make 'a reportorial visitation' to the town of Quang Tri just south of the 17th parallel which divided North and South Vietnam. This got me past the military checkpoints and on to the road known to veterans of a previous conflict as The Street Without Joy. Destroyed tanks and other military vehicles littered the roadside and not a single house was intact. A year previously Quang Tri had been captured by the North Vietnamese in the offensive that preceded the signing of the Paris Agreement. Once in enemy hands it was declared a free-fire zone and subjected to a terrifying onslaught by B-52 bombers. The town itself had been annihilated. Not one structure had survived. Camped in the ruins were soldiers of the southern army and across the river, clearly visible from their corrugated-iron dugouts, were the tents of the North Vietnamese. Next time, in the absence of American air power, they would not be stopped.

Back in Saigon, I made a remarkable discovery. The *Daily Telegraph* correspondent whose reports appeared in the paper under the by-line John Draw was not John Draw at all, but Nguyen Ngoc Phach, an officer in the army of the southern regime attached to the staff of General Cao Van Vien, the chief of staff. It wasn't that his reports bore a resemblance to the official version of events. They *were* the official version. So blatant was the arrangement that Lieutenant Phach used to appear in uniform at the Reuters office to tap out his dispatches. This unusual arrangement was known to most other Saigon correspondents, but such was the reluctance of dog to eat dog that no word of it had leaked out. When I got home, I offered the information about John Draw's real identity to the editor of the *Guardian* diary column, but he declined to use it on the grounds that it was 'a bit so-whattish'. I doubt the *Guardian* would take the same view today. I took the matter up with the *Telegraph* editor, Bill Deedes. He confirmed that John Draw was indeed Nguyen Ngoc Phach, but obfuscated as to whether Phach was an officer in the army of the southern regime.

From Saigon I flew to Cambodia, where the situation was a great deal more precarious. Phnom Penh, the capital, was surrounded. In places the enemy were within ten miles of the city centre. Only the bombing was reckoned to be holding them at bay and the US Congress had finally forced President Nixon to order a cessation from 15 August. I flew in on 8 August. No one knew what would happen when the bombing stopped. Even as we took off from Saigon there were doubts as to whether it would be possible to land at Phnom Penh's Pochentong airport, which was already under sporadic rocket attack. On arrival I went to see the British ambassador, who advised that the fall of the city was imminent and that I should leave immediately.

When I declined, he suggested I buy a supply of tinned food and retreat to my hotel room.

Phnom Penh in those days was a sad place, but little did its hapless residents know that there was much worse to come. Once an elegant colonial city on the bank of the mighty Mekong, it was now crowded with refugees from the countryside. The government of Marshal Lon Nol had come to power in a military coup two years previously which had ousted the hugely popular Prince Sihanouk. Sihanouk had done his best to keep his country out of the war engulfing his neighbours, even turning a blind eye to American bombing of the Vietcong enclaves on the border with Vietnam. But neutrality was not enough and the Americans had connived at his overthrow. The result was disastrous. Sihanouk immediately flew to Beijing and joined up with the insurgents with whom, until that moment he had been at war. Almost overnight they went from being a minor insurgency to a credible alternative government.

The Paris Peace Agreement had put an end to the bombing of Vietnam and Laos which left the US free to massively increase the amount of ordnance they were pouring onto Cambodia. As the deadline approached so the bombing intensified. At night the city shook as the B-52s plastered the countryside around Phnom Penh. As in Laos, the war seemed to be controlled from a windowless annex attached to the American embassy. US diplomats were actually burning down the country to which they were accredited. This only became apparent when a journalist, twiddling with the dial on his transistor radio, found himself listening to a dialogue between the pilots and their command centre and noticed frequent references to 'the embassy'. Thereafter the radio was left hanging in the office of the Reuters news agency, permanently tuned to the channel linking the embassy and the bombers. Many bombs went astray. On 6 August a B-52 accidentally dropped twenty tons of bombs on the centre of Neak Luong, a small regime-controlled town on the Mekong, about forty miles south-west of Phnom Penh. This was the biggest accident of the war. More than 400 people were killed or injured and much of the town was destroyed. One man lost his wife and ten of his eleven children. The cover-up began immediately. The town was sealed off and, when challenged, official spokesmen in Phnom Penh obfuscated.

They might have got away with it but for Sydney Schanberg, a coura-geous *New York Times* reporter who managed to hitch a ride on a barge and floated down the Mekong into Neak Luong, where he became the first outsider to witness what had happened. With several other jour-nalists, I had dinner with Schanberg soon after he returned from Neak Luong. He would later become famous as the American journalist characterised in Roland Joffe's film *The Killing Fields*. The bombing of Neak Luong is the opening scene. An official report later blamed the incident on 'a computer error in Honolulu', the navigator had his pay docked by 700 dollars and, by way of compensation, the families of the dead were offered a hundred dollars a head, which at that time represented a new high for the value of a Cambodian life.

Incredibly, even at this late stage in the war, the Americans had no idea who they were fighting in Cambodia. Little or nothing was known of the dreaded Khmer Rouge who eighteen months later would emerge from the countryside and wreak a terrible revenge on the urban population. The official line, carefully explained to me by an American diplomat, was that they were facing a Vietnamese inva-sion: 'Yes, there may be a handful of Cambodians involved, but they were primarily a front for the Vietnamese.' As for the Khmer Rouge leaders – Khieu Samphan, Hou Yuon and Hu Nim; 'the three ghosts', as they were known – at least two and perhaps all three had been murdered years ago by Sihanouk and their places taken by imposters, said the American. This nonsense continued to be spouted with an entirely straight face even after Sihanouk had travelled to the so-called liberated zone and had fun filming himself with the men he was supposed to have murdered. Even the name of Brother Number One – Saloth Sar, aka Pol Pot – was unknown until Sihanouk blurted it out at a press conference in Pyongyang. How was it possible for a government with the vast intelligence and military resources of the United States at its disposal to be so mind-bogglingly ignorant?

On my second day in Phnom Penh, with the congressional dead-line for the end of the bombing fast approaching, I witnessed a bizarre little ceremony at Pochentong airport at which the US ambassador made a show of handing over an ancient DC3 to the chief of staff of the Cambodian army, General Sosthène Fernandez. It was intended to symbolise a transfer of responsibility to the woefully inadequate

Cambodian military, much of which existed only on paper. 'From now on you are on your own, good luck,' was the subliminal message. All concerned put on a brave face, even though by then contingency plans must have been in place for a sudden evacuation. The ambassador, Emory C. Swank, resplendent in a white suit, was helicoptered the five miles from the embassy to the airport (the roads being deemed unsafe). A podium had been erected, a military band played and all around columns of smoke arose as the bombers plastered the surrounding countryside.

By mid-August foreign correspondents from all over the world had assembled in Phnom Penh to see what would happen when the bombing stopped. Not everyone who claimed to be present was actually there. Jon Swain, the *Sunday Times* correspondent, opened a telegram addressed to a journalist from a prominent British newspaper. It was what is known in the trade as a 'herogram' from the man's foreign editor: CONGRATULATIONS YOUR EYEWITNESS ACCOUNT OF FIGHTING ON HIGHWAY TWO ... or words to that effect. The problem was, as we all knew, the journalist concerned was not there. He was safely in Bangkok or Singapore rewriting agency copy.

As is the way in such conflicts, most of the correspondents were billeted in the city's most luxurious hotel – in this case the Royale – from which they commuted daily to the war. The roads out of the city were like the spokes on a bicycle wheel. Depending on which one you chose, you could reach the front line in a matter of an hour or two. Highway Two was the shortest. There the war had reached Takhmao, a hamlet a few miles from the city centre. You could travel there after breakfast and be back in time for lunch by the swimming pool. On Highway Four you could get much further. I travelled about twenty-five miles in a convoy behind the prime minister, In Tam, who was anxious to demonstrate that reports of the regime's imminent collapse were exaggerated. We stopped at burned-out villages. 'Who did this?' we asked the locals. 'The communists,' they replied. At the time I was sceptical, but given what we now know about the Khmer Rouge, it was almost certainly the case.

As it turned out, reports of impending collapse were exaggerated. The bombing stopped at noon on 15 August 1973 and nothing changed. The foreign correspondents waited a week and then dispersed. It was to be another eighteen months before the regime fell. The end came on 17 April 1975, two weeks before the fall of Saigon. It was dramatic. US ambassador John Gunther Dean was pictured running for a helicopter with the embassy flag over his arm. The insurgents entered the city and began driving the population out into the countryside. No one was spared. Rich, poor, old, sick, they were all forced out of the city in temperatures of forty degrees centigrade. Thus began Cambodia's long dark night in which perhaps a third of the population perished at the hands of one of the world's most brutal regimes.

Back in London, I tapped out a 4,000-word account of the bombing of Laos, illustrated by John Everingham's graphic photographs, and delivered it to John Anstey at the *Telegraph* magazine. This was not what he had commissioned and it was not what most *Telegraph* readers wanted to read, but to Anstey's great credit he published without hesitation. My piece on the future of South East Asia met a less happy fate. As I feared, it was way out of line with the *Telegraph*'s world view. Anstey ran it past one of the paper's senior foreign correspondents, who duly shredded it. It was to be eight years before I wrote for the *Telegraph* magazine again.

CHAPTER SIX

Friends and Lovers

Until the age of about seventeen I firmly believed that kissing could result in pregnancy. It followed, therefore, that kissing was (a) dangerous and (b) immoral. No one actually told me that this was so, it was just something I deduced. I was by no means alone in suffering this delusion. Years later I walked out with a young woman educated at a Catholic school on the other side of the world and she told me that she had reached the same conclusion, though happily she had revised her opinion by the time we met. Until my final year at a strict Catholic boarding school in Ipswich, I had no contact with girls beyond the occasional glimpse of the matron's teenage daughter and the sisters of fellow pupils who visited on open days. There were just three boys in my school year who had desirable sisters. I remember their names to this day. The boys, that is. With one exception I never knew the girls. Once, during a school play, I managed to manoeuvre myself into a seat next to one of the said sisters, who paid me not the slightest attention. Not that I would have been capable of responding sensibly if she had. Although I got to know her well some years later, the prospect that she might one day favour me with her company, that we might hold hands and even embrace was at that time beyond my wildest contemplation.

No one ever told me the facts of life. Gradually and belatedly, with the aid of a biology textbook found discarded on a classroom window sill, I worked them out for myself. Even then it was some years before I fully grasped the basics of female physiology. Why should I? The subject was never mentioned. I recall only one attempt at any form of sex education and it was excruciatingly embarrassing for all concerned. At short notice we older boys were assembled in the library to be addressed by Dr Moss, the school GP. Throughout, his eyes focussed on the floor. The purpose of the exercise seemed to be to alert us to the dangers of venereal disease, which, he suggested, could easily be caught from contact with toilet seats. Goodness knows what prompted this, but looking back it may be that one of the Gulf Arab pupils, all of whom were enormously rich and boasted of consorting with prostitutes during school holidays, had contracted VD and that the powers-that-be had suddenly panicked. In any case, the exercise was not a success and was never repeated.

By the time I was in my final year at St Joseph's a more relaxed regime prevailed and sixth formers were occasionally allowed into town. Tenuous contact was thus established with girls from the local convent school, though this was strictly limited to hours of daylight. One day it was announced there was to be a school dance and that girlfriends would be welcome. For boys who lived locally and were in daily contact with the outside world this was feasible, but where were we boarders, who until very recently were forbidden to leave the premises without a good reason and express permission, going to find girlfriends? I look back in astonishment, but somehow or other I did come up with a partner. I remember nothing about her except that her name was Susan and she was the daughter of a local farmer. Exactly how I came by her, I have no idea. Indeed, were it not for the existence of a photograph taken at the dance, I would have dismissed her as a figment of my imagination. Anyway, although I hazily recall a visit to her family, she soon lost interest in me. I don't suppose it was a lot of fun walking out with a boy who had to be back in school by supper time and who believed that kissing caused pregnancy.

I was a lonely youth with an overwhelming sense of social inferiority. Back home in Chelmsford, I knew hardly anyone of my own age, the links to my home town having been severed when I was sent away to boarding school, aged eleven. Occasionally I was invited to parties where I knew virtually no one. I would hide in the shadows and leave early. By the time I was sixteen I had just two friends left at home – Clive and Richard, who, having gone to mixed schools, were considerably more worldly wise than I. Clive's father was dying of multiple sclerosis and his hard-working mother ran a boarding house in Springfield, near the prison. Richard was from a family of glove manufacturers with factories at Witham in Essex and Blaydon in County Durham.

Gloves were going out of fashion, demand was in steep decline and when the Witham factory closed the family moved north in order to be near to the remaining factory. In the summer of 1965 Clive and I hitch-hiked up the A1 to pay our friend a visit. It was my first visit to the north-east. Little did I know then that it would one day become my home.

Our first outing was to the Newcastle bowling alley, where Clive's attention was diverted by a one-armed bandit into which he proceeded to pump whatever coins he had in his pocket. Richard and I meanwhile had spotted two young women seated diagonally at a nearby table. Having established that they were unaccompanied and that the seats were vacant, we duly joined them. Their names were Karen and Shirley. Karen was blonde and well developed; Shirley thin and brunette. They were aged seventeen and fifteen, students at a smart private girls' school and they were very definitely interested in male company. Imagine Clive's dismay when he returned from playing with the slot machines to find that they were spoken for. The fact that he was altogether more at ease in female company than I was must have made it doubly galling.

We arranged to meet the girls again on the following evening in Durham, where we hired boats on the river. Clive, who was in an understandably surly frame of mind, went off on his own while Richard paired with Karen and I with Shirley. They were very forward young women. No sooner were we out of sight of the boathouse than Shirley took control of the oars and rowed us under an overhanging tree on the riverbank. She took a pack of cigarettes and a matchbox from her pocket, but for some reason the match wouldn't light and she tried instead to strike it on my trouser zip. Most teenage boys in such circumstances would have died and gone to heaven, but I was struck with terror. Back on dry land, in twilight, we took a romantic stroll along the river bank. Clive, on whom it was now beginning to dawn that all was not lost, trailed along behind humming 'You're Gonna Lose That Girl', a Beatles' song popular at the time. Richard and Karen disappeared into the undergrowth and before long Shirley, too, had steered us off the path and into the bracken where I lay paralysed with fear, resolutely resisting her advances. Needless to say the evening was not a success. We saw the girls back to their home in Low Fell, the posh part of Gateshead – to this day I remember the precise address – where I coyly bade farewell to Shirley with a peck on the cheek while Richard and Karen engaged in a rather more intimate dialogue. The three of us then made our way on foot through the Team Valley industrial estate, across the A1 and back up to Richard's home in Whickham, with me prattling on about the immorality of it all. What an ignorant, sanctimonious, little prig I was.

The next day, I hitch-hiked home, alone. So keen was Clive to see the back of me that he loaned me ten shillings to help fund the journey. For days afterwards Shirley's scent lingered on my jacket. As for Clive, in the following months he made several more journeys up the motorway, returning with tales of passion and debauchery. Thus it was that my initiation into the mysteries of sexual activity was delayed for some considerable time.

My early love life was disastrous. At university I did not have much difficulty attracting girlfriends, but I had great difficulty keeping them. In my second year I went out with a shy young woman from Derbyshire who studied languages. At Easter she came home to stay for a few days, the first girl I had ever introduced to my parents. That summer I persuaded her to come with me hitch-hiking through France and Spain to North Africa and back up through Italy. First, however, I had to earn money to fund the outing and off I went to a pea-harvesting plant in Norfolk, working twelve-hour shifts, seven days a week. She, meanwhile, went with a party of fellow language students to Austria to brush up her German. When the day came for us to set off on our adventure I met her at St Pancras station and immediately realised that all was not well. We got as far as Paris, where it emerged that in Austria she had had a brief relationship with another boy. After two nights in an unspeakably insanitary Paris hostel she decided to go home and I went on alone. She had made the right decision. Minimal planning had gone into the expedition; it was seriously underfunded and she could never have endured the hardship that followed. As for her little fling in Austria, I don't blame her. I was an inconsiderate, useless lover. She could do much better and I hope she did.

Towards the end of my time at university I struck up a close friendship with a young woman, a year below me, on whom I had had my eye for some time, but who for most of that time was spoken for. She was the first girl I can recall who made my heart race. Her parents lived in Africa. She was the daughter of a colonial judge who had stayed on after independence. By the third term of my final year she had separated from her long-term boyfriend and I espied a narrow window of opportunity. Our burgeoning relationship, however, seemed destined never to be consummated since I was about to leave for the big wide world while she faced another year of study. On my final day at university, as I was about to drive south with my chattels already loaded into the old Ford van I had purchased a few months previously for the princely sum of £85, I decided on impulse to stop off at her hall of residence to see if I could persuade her to come with me to Greece. To my utter joy she said yes. First, however, she had to visit her parents in Africa and I had once again to labour in the desolate pea vinery in Norfolk to earn the wherewithal to fund my half of our journey. I counted the days to her return, fearing all the while that she would change her mind.

But she didn't. Sure enough, at the appointed hour on the appointed day, she appeared at the railway station in Chelmsford and off we set in my old van. We took the boat from Harwich to the Hook of Holland and by nightfall we were camped by a motorway just outside Brussels. As before, planning had been minimal and, as before, from the moment she stepped off the train at Chelmsford I sensed that something had changed. This time, however, learning from previous experience, I decided not to press the matter until we were too far from home for her to turn back in the hope that time would heal whatever was bugging her. Alas, it was not to be. We got as far as Florence before she spilled the beans. In Africa, it emerged, she had had a brief holiday romance. Her disapproving parents had bundled her back to the UK in the mistaken belief that her trip across Europe would be as one of a party of young people and that this would soon take her mind off other matters. History repeated itself. In Rome she announced that she wanted to go home. I was mortified at the prospect of being abandoned once more. We spent a melancholy afternoon talking things over under the shade of a tree in the gardens of the Villa Borghese. I tried to persuade her to stay. The affair in Africa was a small matter that she would soon forget (as indeed she did), but she was adamant. I, too, should have turned back at that point, but decided to press on. So there came an awful day when we parted. She went north and I went south, tears streaming down my face.

In the years that followed I had an intermittent series of relationships, often with young women with whom I was hopelessly incompatible. Usually there was little commitment on either side and many disappointments followed. For all that I affected to be a man of the world I was selfish, emotionally immature and more often hurt than I cared to admit. Also, I had other things to do. Books to write, places to see, not to mention an enormous amount of time spent politicking. One by one my contemporaries married, had children, moved away. By the time I was in my thirties a lonely future beckoned, but all that was to change when, on a visit to Vietnam in April 1985, I met and fell in love with Nguyen Thi Ngoc.

CHAPTER SEVEN

Good Morning, Vietnam

The Vietnam war was one of the formative events of my life. Even in the isolation of my Catholic boarding school in Ipswich, with only *The Times* and the *Daily Telegraph* upon which to rely for information about the outside world, I managed to work out that there was something wrong with the official version of events. What had begun as a brutal colonial war, as the French fought to cling on to their empire in the Far East, had become an even more brutal attempt by the Americans to resist the advance of communism, which in those far-off days was thought by some to be a monolithic conspiracy bent on world domination (the fact that the Russian and Chinese communists hated each other was not yet apparent). In the long run, of course, the Vietnamese turned out to be natural capitalists who embraced market forces with an enthusiasm that not even Margaret Thatcher would recognise. Arguably the overall impact of ten years of slaughter and the squandering of billions of dollars (to say nothing of America's loss of moral high ground around the world) was to delay the advance of the free market by the best part of two decades. The very opposite of what the Americans thought they were doing.

In my boarding school in Ipswich, all I knew of Vietnam was what I read in the newspapers and occasionally glimpsed on television news. Most apparent was the massive disparity in firepower between the two sides. There was something particularly obscene about the richest and most technically sophisticated country on earth pounding a civilisation of rice farmers back into the Stone Age.* Night

---

*US Airforce General Curtis LeMay said in his memoirs that his solution would be

after night television news showed US warplanes carpeting Vietnam with napalm, defoliant and high explosive. Before long they were said to have dropped more bombs on Vietnam than were dropped by both sides in the Second World War. However just the cause, and it was far from clear that this was a just cause, how could this be justified? This was the first televised war and it wasn't possible to hide the consequences. The streams of refugees, the burned-out villages, the horrendous injuries and, in due course, the atrocities. One of the first images to make a lasting impression on me was a picture on the back page of the *Daily Telegraph*, of a little girl wearing only pyjama trousers, her arm bandaged, crying her eyes out. The image haunted me. I see her still. By the time I became conscious of the war, American bombers were already pounding North Vietnam. The suggestion that they were only targeting military objectives was obvious nonsense. How could they drop bombs from seven miles up on targets they couldn't see and claim to be hitting only military objectives? The North was a closed country and at first little was known of the impact, but in due course it became apparent that in the southern provinces of North Vietnam virtually no town or village remained intact. Farmers and their families were living underground, emerging only at night to plough their fields. Later the bombing extended to the larger cities in the North, Hanoi and Haiphong. Here foreigners lived and the Americans were more careful to target infrastructure. Nevertheless, thousands died, including the French consul general who was not, presumably, a military target.

As the scale of the horror became apparent, so the politics began to change. By the late 1960s US President Lyndon B. Johnson had sent half a million young men to fight in South Vietnam and still it was not enough. At home the Labour government came under pressure to dissociate itself from its American allies. The US embassy in London was besieged by crowds chanting 'Hey, hey LBJ, how many kids did you kill today?' In Washington veterans began throwing away their medals on the steps of the Capitol and in Chicago demonstrators laid siege to the Democratic Party convention. And then, on the eve of the

---

to 'tell the North Vietnamese communists to stop their aggression or we are going to bomb them into the Stone Age'.

Vietnamese New Year, in February 1968, came the Tet offensive. All over South Vietnam, the Vietcong emerged from hiding, capturing towns and cities deep behind the lines, even briefly occupying several floors of the American embassy in the centre of Saigon. In purely military terms the uprising was a defeat. The Vietcong were beaten back and suffered heavy casualties, but for the Americans the political price was high. The fiction that the war was winnable could no longer be maintained. Visibly worn down, Johnson announced he would not contest the 1968 presidential election. In his place came Richard Nixon and his sinister sidekick, Henry Kissinger, and the slaughter reached a new intensity as they attempted to bomb their way to the conference table. Four years later Nixon, cynically proclaiming that peace was at hand, was re-elected by an overwhelming majority. No sooner was the presidential election out of the way, than the bombing resumed. This was the background to my political awakening.

As a young journalist, I was determined to visit North Vietnam. Early efforts were frustrated, however. Along with a couple of other participants in the 1971 tour of China, I visited the Vietnamese embassy in Beijing in pursuit of a visa. We were courteously received, but politely rebuffed. Repeated efforts to apply in London were similarly unsuccessful. Britain did not recognise the North, which was represented by a couple of diplomats posing as journalists who lived at an address in Belsize Park and were not in a position to issue visas. It was not until 1980, five years after the fall of Saigon, that I finally gained entry to the newly unified Vietnam. By now Ho Chi Minh's dream of building a Vietnam 'ten times more beautiful' had foundered in the face of a litany of new disasters: floods, typhoons and new wars with China and in Cambodia. In the North each new disaster was met with dignity and stoicism by a people who had never known anything but a life of struggle. Hanoi was an exhausted city. The tiredness showed in the flaking paint and the crumbling French villas, in the ancient, rusting tram cars and in the pinched faces of the people. There were no fat people in Hanoi. None at all. But for all the poverty there were smiles and small courtesies that you would never find in any Western city. There were no cars in Hanoi except for the handful belonging to foreign embassies and government ministries; the bicycle was king. The flow was continuous. They moved at a lazy, stately pace, meandering only to avoid pedestrians. There were no traffic lights. At junctions the cyclists mingled, emerging on the other side miraculously unscathed. Today the bicycles have been replaced by motorcycles and they in turn are gradually being replaced by automobiles. Many of the old French villas have been demolished and replaced by high-rise monstrosities of concrete and steel. Before much longer Hanoi will resemble Bangkok, Manila, Taipei or any of the other polluted urban jungles that pass for capital cities in Asia. Attempts by foreigners to persuade the government to preserve at least the centre of the old city have been brushed aside in the scramble for development. Whenever I come across a Vietnamese of influence I say, 'It is not obligatory to repeat the mistakes of your neighbours. The only advantage of having been poor for so long is that you can look around and see what works and what doesn't.' This tends to be greeted with a helpless shrug, 'I am only the prime minister, what can I do?' I don't begrudge the Vietnamese their newfound prosperity, but I am glad to have seen Hanoi before the coming of market forces.

By 1980, in the southern cities which had once waxed fat on American aid, those unable to cope with the abrupt decline in their living standards were taking to the boats. To a large extent the disaster was self-inflicted. The old men who ran Vietnam were products of the Stalinist system. So, too, were the generations of young cadres who had been sent to the Soviet Union and eastern Europe to be trained in Stalinist economics. State ownership of the means of production, distribution and exchange was all they knew. It was to prove ruinous.

It was always inevitable that the southern economy would collapse once the Americans went home and US aid ceased, as it did, overnight in April 1975 when the communists entered Saigon. What was not inevitable was the stifling bureaucracy and paranoia so intense that it resulted in the strangulation of all productive activity. And with bureaucracy came endemic corruption, as officials tried to supplement their tiny salaries by demanding bribes for even the simplest services. The goodwill that greeted the arrival of the North Vietnamese army and their southern allies in the immediate aftermath of victory swiftly evaporated. Tens of thousands of soldiers and officials connected with the old regime were ordered to report for re-education. They were told it would be for only a few days or weeks, but many were held for years in remote labour camps. Property was confiscated, corrupt and incompetent northern cadres displaced managers and technocrats who would have been content to serve the new regime as they had the old. Agriculture was collectivised, leading to sharp falls in production which in turn led to prolonged rationing. Craziest of all, trade between provinces was banned, necessitating checkpoints on all the main roads and the payment of bribes. Before long just about everyone with a skill marketable in the outside world had taken to the sea in small boats. Some died and others languished for years in refugee camps before being granted asylum in the West, where many of them prospered. 'Our stupidity,' was the phrase Vietnam's foreign minister, Nguyen Co Thach, used repeatedly, when I met him some years later.

One story will suffice, told by the driver of a car that Ngoc and I once hired to take us on a visit to her relatives in the central highlands. It concerns Da Nhim, a Japanese-built hydroelectric power station in the hills between Dalat and Nha Trang. Da Nhim was managed by a competent technocrat who, come the end of the American war, wanted no more than to continue in his job doing what he knew best. But no. The new masters decreed that, as a former official of the old regime, he must be re-educated. So off he went to a re-education camp for a year or two only to find upon his return that his job had been taken by a new, ideologically sound (but not technically qualified) manager. He hung around for a while in the hope that he might be re-employed, but when it became clear that he was surplus to requirements, he used what remained of his savings to purchase a place on a refugee boat and flee the country. As luck would have it, he and his fellow refugees were picked up by a Japanese ship and taken to Japan, where he went to work for the very company that had built that power station at Da Nhim. Meanwhile, back in Da Nhim, under the ideologically sound (but technically incompetent) manager, things were going from bad to worse. Eventually an SOS was sent to the company in Japan that had built the plant. And who did they send to put it right? Yes, the man who had managed it under the old regime. He arrived at Tan Son Nhut airport and was chauffeured back to Da Nhim, where, no doubt to the amusement of his erstwhile colleagues, he set to work to make good the damage done by years of ideologically sound (but technically incompetent) management. This time, however, he was paid in precious dollars rather than the pittance in local currency that he would have earned had he been allowed to remain at his post. Some years later, when word of the disaster that was Vietnam's economy had finally reached the old men in the Politburo, I related this sorry tale to Foreign Minister Thach. He wasn't in the least surprised. 'I could tell you many such stories,' he said.

Mr Thach was an unusual communist. He had been ambassador to India and spoke English. He did not use jargon and was at ease in the company of foreigners – and he had a sense of humour. When I first met him Vietnam was isolated. The United States, still smarting from its ignominious defeat, had organised an aid and trade embargo. Many in the US were also pretending that Vietnam was still holding American prisoners of war, a claim the US government knew to be nonsense but refused to rebut. Vietnam's invasion of Cambodia – in response to repeated attacks by the murderous Khmer Rouge – provided a further excuse for revenge. With utter cynicism, America and its allies colluded with China and Thailand to provide covert aid to the Khmer Rouge and their allies with a view to stoking the civil war in Cambodia and keeping Vietnam bogged down and bleeding. 'Why didn't you ask for help from the United Nations, instead of invading?' I inquired at my first meeting with Mr Thach. His reply was devastating:

'We have a different view of the UN than you.'

'How so?'

'Because during the last forty years we have been invaded by four of the five permanent members of the Security Council.'

Earlier I had asked if I could travel south by train, instead of flying, only to be told that for security reasons no foreigners were allowed in Vietnamese trains. Now I repeated my request to Mr Thach.

'Conditions on Vietnamese trains are much too bad for foreigners,' he replied.

'No problem,' said I. 'I've travelled all over India by train and I'm sure that conditions on Vietnamese trains are no worse.'

On the contrary, said Mr Thach. 'I used to be our ambassador in India. I, too, have travelled on trains in India and I can assure you that conditions on Vietnamese trains are much worse.'

I persisted and he gave in. Before my eyes he scribbled a note to the relevant authorities, *Give this foolish foreigner a railway ticket*, or words to that effect. A day or two later came the answer. Request refused. Mr Thach had been overruled. In what country in the world, I asked myself, was it necessary to go to the foreign minister in order to obtain a railway ticket and in which country in the world was the influence of the foreign minister insufficient? That was how it was in 1980s Vietnam.

My wife, Nguyen Thi Ngoc, was born on Christmas Day 1954 in a refugee village of mud and straw huts in the coastal province of Quang Ngai in central Vietnam. She was the third of nine children, six girls and three boys, and the fortunes of her family mirrored those of her country. Her father's parents were subsistence farmers from the coastal province of Binh Dinh. In the 1920s they migrated to Kontum, a settlement in the central highlands, in search of a better life. In the early years they lived in a shack by the Dakla river, on which Ngoc's grandfather earned a precarious living ferrying people across in a sampan. The family were poor, hungry and often ill. Of her grandparents' seven children only three survived to adulthood. Because he was so often ill Ngoc's father frequently stayed away from school and was eventually told not to return. Such was the determination of Ngoc's grandfather to educate his children that he changed his family's names three times in order to reregister them in school.

Kontum at that time was sparsely populated. The countryside was mainly inhabited by hill tribes who scratched a living from slash-and-burn agriculture. In order to encourage people from the coastal belt to migrate to the malarial highlands the French, who needed labourers for their tea and coffee plantations, allowed migrants to claim as much land as they could clear and cultivate. As luck would have it, the land claimed by Ngoc's grandfather was close to the centre of what was to become Kontum city and, as the town expanded, so the value of the land increased. Grandfather eventually sold most of his land, retaining only a plot near the town centre on which he started to construct three houses, one for each of his surviving sons, with the aim of keeping the family together whatever the uncertainties that lay ahead. Sadly he died before the houses were complete, leaving Ngoc's father, Nguyen Tang Minh, then aged sixteen, and his older brother as breadwinners for the family. Minh noticed that several local Vietnamese of Chinese origin made a good living making sweets and pastries so he loitered around their shops, learning their recipes, to which he added a few of his own, and within a couple of years he and his older brother had earned enough to complete the construction of the houses.

In 1945, following the retreat of the Japanese, Kontum was occupied by the Viet Minh and as a result soon came under attack from the French. The family had no choice but to abandon their new homes and flee. Ngoc's father and his two surviving brothers, Uncles Three and Eight,* together with Uncle Three's wife and her sister set off on foot through the forest towards the Viet Minh stronghold of Ba-To in Quang Ngai province, ninety miles north of Kontum. The journey lasted fifteen terrifying days and nights. On the way they were harassed and shot at by French war planes. Many of those who fell by the wayside had to be abandoned. For a while it seemed they would be reduced to beggary, but the Viet Minh were well organised and, with help, the family managed to avoid starvation and once again survived by making pastries which they sold around the villages and refugee camps. Twice they had to relocate, once when French warships shelled their camp and once when it was napalmed by French warplanes. Conditions were basic. They lived in houses of mud and thatch, barely eking a living. Nine years passed. Grandma had a stroke and, after three days without speaking, died. Minh married Uncle Three's wife's sister. He possessed only the shirt he stood up in, which he wore only when he went out to sell his pastries, walking up to ten miles a day. Ngoc's mother's only blouse was a quiltwork of patches. They subsisted on a diet of sweet potato, manioc, salted fish and occasionally rice, supplemented with wild berries. Three children, including Ngoc, were born while they were refugees

---

*Vietnamese households with large numbers of children often referred to their children in numerical order rather than by name.

in Quang Ngai and, miraculously, all survived. Uncle Three and his wife were less fortunate. They had sixteen children, half of whom died in infancy.

After the defeat of the French, the family made their way back to Kontum, where they were pleasantly surprised to find their homes intact, although occupied by squatters who refused to budge. The middle house was being used as a vehicle repair workshop. A long struggle followed. It took the best part of two years to regain their homes, for part of which time they camped amid the noise and dirt of the vehicle workshop. Again they survived by making biscuits and Ngoc's mother opened a small grocery at the front of their house. They might have remained poor for ever, but for one giant stroke of luck. A boy selling lottery tickets came to the door. Minh never usually bought lottery tickets, but the hour was late and the boy had only one ticket left so he took pity on him. That ticket changed his life. He won 100,000 piastres, the equivalent at the time of about $15,000, a huge sum in 1950s Vietnam. Minh used the money to buy land on which he cultivated a coffee plantation. Between the rows of coffee bushes he planted fruit – pineapple, banana, mango, durian, lemon, longan. By the mid-1960s the family were prosperous. Minh purchased a van to transport his produce to neighbouring towns. Once, driving home in darkness, he was ambushed by the Vietcong, who had mistaken his van for an army vehicle, despite the fact that it had XE NHA (private car) painted prominently on each side. It was a lucky escape. The van was riddled with bullet holes, some of which had missed him by millimetres. After that, he stopped driving at night.

Minh's coffee became well known in and around Kontum. By the mid-1960s many of his customers were soldiers from the military base just out of town. He was sufficiently wealthy to be able to afford to send all his children to private schools. Ngoc's oldest brother, Hung, was sent to a Catholic boarding school in Hue; his older sister, Hong, to a boarding school in Quy Nhon. Ngoc and her remaining siblings went to local Catholic schools. Uncle Eight also prospered, building up a successful tailoring business which at its height employed ten people. He, too, fathered nine children.

But the war was never far away. At night the distant rumble of bombing could be heard from the Ho Chi Minh trail which ran down the nearby border between Vietnam and Laos. Beyond the town most of the countryside was controlled by the Vietcong, and come the Tet offensive in February 1968 the war spilled into the town.

Tet, the Vietnamese new year, is a big event. Measured according to the lunar calendar, it might fall anywhere between the end of January and mid-February. Tet is the time by which all debts must be settled, disputes resolved and fortune tellers consulted about what lies ahead. Houses are decorated with sprigs of cherry blossom, a symbol of prosperity. Midnight on New Year's Eve is greeted with a huge outburst of firecrackers (easily mistaken for gunfire). The first person to cross the threshold can bring either good or bad luck. Much to their frustration, Ngoc and her siblings were under strict instructions to stay indoors on New Year's Day for fear that, were they to be the first to visit neighbours, they might be blamed for whatever misfortunes followed in the year ahead. New Year in Vietnam is also a time of presents: new shoes, a new dress and, for each child, cash in a little red paper envelope. Ancestors, too, are included in the celebration. Offerings of food are placed on the family altar. The children went with their father to visit the family graves, clearing weeds and planting incense sticks. The dead are well cared for in Vietnam. Their spirits linger long after they have departed. Ngoc's father had created a little cemetery in his plantation where late grandparents, uncles, aunts were gradually assembled, lying together in a shady corner, each grave marked by a small headstone. In years to come, when the plantation lay derelict and earmarked for development, the ancestors would again be unearthed and moved to a more agreeable location.

Tet 1968 was different from any other new year before or since. At about 8 a.m. Ngoc, then thirteen years old, heard the sound of what she thought were firecrackers coming from the direction of the central market, a block or so away. If not firecrackers, then it must be soldiers of the southern army, still celebrating, loosing off shots into the air. Then her aunt from next door appeared, saying that the Vietcong were occupying the market. 'At that time I was very naive,' she says. 'I did not know that the Vietcong were Vietnamese like us. I thought they were foreigners.' By now there was no mistaking the sound of gunfire. Soldiers appeared in the street outside. Ngoc's father managed to lay hands on a supply of sand and sacks. The day was spent building a makeshift bomb shelter in the store room next to the kitchen. Several layers of sandbags were placed over the corrugated iron roof and these were covered with sacks of coffee beans.

On the second and third day, relays of soldiers took turns to advance up the street, pouring gunfire and tossing hand grenades into the market. The fighting continued day and night. 'Very loud. We hardly slept.' And to no avail. The VC remained entrenched. On the fourth day the soldiers were ordered to flush them out by burning down the entire market. A huge conflagration ensued, lighting up the horizon. 'We lay down at the front of the house, peeping out to see what was happening.' For a while there was fear that the fire would spread. Residents with buckets formed a line, pouring water over the houses nearest to the market in a desperate attempt to stop the flames spreading. When it was over a handful of charred bodies were found in the ruins, one of them an elderly Chinese night watchman who had been trapped throughout the siege. Several hundred shop owners had lost their livelihoods, including Ngoc's aunt (the wife of Uncle Three), who wept hysterically on learning that her shop was destroyed. She had no savings. There would be no compensation.

Four years later the war came again to Kontum. The government ordered that the town be evacuated, but Ngoc's father, fearing that they would lose everything, refused to go until the last moment. By this time the town was empty and the roads were cut. The only way out was by a military plane. The family set out for the airport in their van, each child carrying a bag with his or her name on, made from a sack cut in half on to which a strap had been sewn. Ngoc and her sisters had sat up late making them. Each bag contained a birth certificate, rice, canned food and medicine. Ngoc's father drove the three miles to the airport, dropped off his family, then drove the van home and walked back. Uncle Three and Uncle Eight and their families were also assembled. The three families, in all about thirty children and adults, waited by a trench. Shelling was intermittent. At each new outburst everyone would dive into the trench. Their great fear was being split up. Ngoc, who spoke a few words of English, was deputed to ask the American officers in charge of the evacuation to put all three families on the same plane and was reassured that they would all be going to the same place: Pleiku, about thirty miles south.

Eventually, one of the massive American C130 transport planes landed, triggering a renewed bout of shelling. It stood waiting for them, ramp lowered, rear doors open, engines running. The refugees, urged on by the soldiers who feared that one of the shells would soon find its mark, ran towards the plane. In the chaos several people were blown over by the draught from the propellers. Ngoc's mother, frail and tiny, was almost blown away altogether. They just managed to scramble aboard before the plane started moving, rear doors still open. Hong vomited and almost fell, Ngoc pulled her back. Several people were left behind.

In Pleiku they camped in a Catholic church, along with many other refugees. They had food, but no money. For years Ngoc's father had ploughed all his profit into either the plantation or the children's education. He had no savings. This had long been a source of friction between Ngoc's parents. Secretly Ngoc's mother had siphoned off income from the shop and used it to buy gold. Only when they got to Pleiku did she whisper to the children that they were not destitute after all. 'She made us promise not to tell Dad. She wanted him to suffer a little,' says Ngoc. 'But Dad was so depressed at the prospect of not being able to feed his children that we felt guilty not telling him, so Hong and I broke our promise. "Oh Dad, you don't have to worry. Mum has gold." Mum said to him, "Now perhaps you will listen."'

After a few days, Minh hitched a ride on a helicopter back to Kontum. His stock of recently harvested coffee was stored, unguarded, in the family house and he was afraid of losing it. The family, meanwhile, remained in the church in Pleiku. After several weeks, Ngoc's mother chanced across a wealthy acquaintance who offered her the use of one of several homes she owned. They were now well housed, but still short of money. Younger brothers, Chau and Nga, aged twelve and fourteen, earned what they could, getting up at 3 a.m. to buy bread from a bakery in the market and resell it at a small profit.

After several months in Pleiku the war receded and it was safe to return home, but the schools in Kontum were still closed and so Ngoc, Chau and Nga remained registered in Pleiku, which meant that Ngoc had to return to Pleiku to sit her baccalaureate. The road was still unsafe. At Chu Pao bridge, a particularly dangerous spot about halfway between the towns, there were occasional ambushes. As they approached the bridge the driver would urge passengers to keep their heads down. On the day Ngoc travelled to Pleiku to sit her exams, no sooner had her bus crossed the bridge safely than she heard an explosion. A bus a hundred yards behind had suffered a direct hit with many dead and injured. 'My family thought I was in that bus. It was several days before they discovered I was alive. Yes I was scared, but when you live in a country at war you have to accept what happens to you.' She passed the exam.

The following year Minh made what turned out to be a wise investment. He bought a house in Saigon. It was tall and narrow, like a birdcage, on Le Van Sy, a road leading from Tan Son Nhut airport to the city centre. Oldest brother Hung, an engineering student, had been conscripted into the air force and was stationed at the airport, which was also a huge military base. Hong and Ngoc were now of university age. The house in Saigon was a place for them to live and would become a base for other members of the family when life in Kontum became impossible. It would be the family's salvation.

The war ended in the spring of 1975. One by one the towns along the central highlands – Buon Me Thuot, Pleiku, Kontum – fell to the advancing North Vietnamese army. Resistance was minimal. By this time all Ngoc's family had decamped to the house in Saigon, by now overflowing with cousins, aunts, uncles, friends. Only Ngoc's father refused to leave Kontum. He was afraid that the country would be repartitioned and that, were he to flee, it would be years before he could get back, by which time the family would have lost their home and the plantation that was the source of their wealth. Besides, the prospect of living in the communist zone held no terrors for him. After all, he had lived nine years under the Viet Minh. Life had been hard, but they had treated people fairly.

After the highlands, it was the turn of the coastal cities. Hue and Da Nang fell in quick succession. By the end of March only Saigon and the Mekong Delta remained in the hands of the regime. All communication with Kontum had ceased. One day brother Hung telephoned. He was now stationed at Phan Rang, about a hundred miles north of Saigon. Since the house in Le Van Sy had no telephone he called the next-door bookshop. 'No more studying,' he said.

'Everything is about to change. You have to find a way to earn money.' That was the last time Ngoc spoke to him. Three days later he was dead, killed by shell fire.

Gradually the noose around Saigon tightened. The huge airbase at Bien Hoa, a few miles to the north-west, came under attack. The city was swollen with refugees. The house at Le Van Sy was crammed to bursting, at one point sheltering thirty-five people sharing one small bathroom and a tiny kitchen. At Saigon's Catholic Minh Duc University, where Ngoc studied, attendance by students and teachers dropped off to the point where lectures were abandoned. Many of the students came from wealthy families who were preparing to leave. There were rumours of an impending bloodbath. Following Hung's advice, Ngoc managed to find a clerical job with an advertising company. 'Come back in ten days,' they said, but she returned to find the office closed, the owners having fled.

As the end approached, neighbours began to melt away. Without a word to anyone the family from the bookshop next door shut up shop and left. Mr Minh, vice president of the lower house of the National Assembly, lived in a large house across the street. From the roof Ngoc could see into his compound. Each evening the telephone would ring and the family would pack their belongings into their car and head off in the direction of the airport, only to return a few hours later. This little ritual was repeated half a dozen times until one day the family did not return. When next heard of they were living in America.

Ngoc's family had no intention of leaving. Having no connection to the southern regime, they had nothing to fear. 'All we wanted was for the war to end.' Incredibly, as life around them disintegrated, Ngoc's mother decided to open a shop in their downstairs room in order to generate some badly needed income. They sold pastries, wine, groceries and for a while did good business. People, fearing the collapse of the currency, were stocking up.

In the last days of April the airport came under attack. People living nearby, many of them Catholics who had fled south in 1954, began to stream down Le Van Sy, seeking refuge in churches near the city centre. By now the house was occupied only by Ngoc's family and several cousins, the friends from Kontum having found refuge elsewhere. Ngoc's mother wisely insisted that everyone stay on the lower floors for fear a stray shell would hit the house. Her fear was justified. On the final day of the war a passing North Vietnamese tank, on the lookout for snipers, put a shell clean through the upper storey.

Ngoc and her family knew exactly when the war had ended. Lying flat on the ground floor, they could see beneath the closed metal shutters that the leather boots of the southern army had given way to the rubber sandals of the *bo doi*, the army of North Vietnam.

The newcomers and the citizens of Saigon eyed each other warily. First impressions were surprisingly upbeat. The city had fallen with a minimum of bloodshed. The occupying army were well organised and highly disciplined. Looting and disorder were kept to a minimum. Long-lost relatives who had 'regrouped' in the North reappeared, reuniting families that had been divided for thirty years. Before long, groups of idealistic young people were volunteering their services cleaning the streets and sweeping away the detritus of the old regime.

Once liberation euphoria had worn off, however, a new reality began to dawn. The new authorities brought with them a vast security apparatus which operated on the basis that all foreigners were spies and anyone who had ever had contact with foreigners, Americans especially, was a potential spy. Soldiers, police, politicians and civil servants of the old regime were ordered to report for re-education. Some never returned, dying of malaria or dysentery in remote labour camps. Mr Quang, Ngoc's teacher of English in Kontum, a kindly man who had worked as an administrator for the local police, disappeared for six years, returning with one arm paralysed from a stroke only to find that his wife had abandoned him. He ended up sleeping on the pavement in Saigon and eventually fled the country by boat. One of her schoolteachers, a member of the ruling party of the old regime, disappeared for ten years. A neighbour in Saigon, a lieutenant in the army of the old regime, was gone five years. During this time, families who had lost their main breadwinner struggled to survive. One of Ngoc's university classmates was a daughter of a former mayor of Hue. He was arrested within hours of the fall of Saigon and detained for ten years. Meanwhile his daughter, excluded from university on account of her background, ended up making mats. 'I spent three years studying English,' she said, 'and ended up making mats.')

Loudspeakers appeared on every street corner, blasting out from dawn to dusk patriotic music interspersed with propaganda – claims of ever-rising production, increased output per hectare and so on, claims belied by the fact that, day by day, life for most people was getting worse.

Technocrats in positions of responsibility were initially encouraged to remain in post and to provide training for less experienced northern cadres. Little did they know that they were training their replacements. An American-trained senior air-traffic controller at Tan Son Nhut airport who had been sent to Hanoi to help train his opposite numbers in the North, found himself redundant after a couple of years. He ended up running a soup stall where, ironically, his less experienced colleagues came to consult him about problems at work. Such was the state of the economy by this time that he was soon earning more making soup than he had earned as an air-traffic controller. Likewise Mr Minh, who ran a thriving soup stall opposite Ngoc's house in Saigon. He had been one of the country's leading meteorologists, but soon found that he could earn more selling noodle soup. In Dalat, the former French hill station north-west of Saigon, the French-trained manager of the Palace Hotel (where Ngoc and I spent our honeymoon) was dismissed and replaced by a Soviet-trained apparatchik. Unsurprisingly, the quality of the service nosedived. Everywhere the story was the same.

In Kontum, where representatives of the new order were even more narrow-minded than those in Saigon, assets were confiscated. Anyone providing employment was deemed an exploiter. Le Ngoc Thanh, a former Viet Minh soldier in the war against the French and best man at our wedding, was the owner of a thriving transport business. He was allowed to keep only one of his trucks, on condition that he drove it himself. Uncle Eight, who had been running a successful tailoring business, was ordered to hand over all but one of his sewing machines and his entire stock of textiles. Overnight he was ruined. In years to come, when word of the disaster reached the old men in the Politburo, former businessmen were invited to reclaim their assets, but the change came too late for Uncle Eight. He died, impoverished, of TB. Money he should have spent on medicine was used to keep his family afloat.

Ngoc's father was determined to keep his plantation. It was his life's work and he had long dreamed that it would provide security for his family after his retirement. He soon came under pressure to hand over his van and the tools he used, but he refused. Eventually he sold the van and, hoping to appear less conspicuous, bought a motorcycle to which he attached a small trailer to carry his tools. This got him into trouble with the guard stationed at the bridge over the river on the edge of town, who asserted that towing the trailer was not good for his motorbike. 'What's that got to do with you? It's my bike,' said Minh, and was duly fined. In the end he took to travelling before the guard came on duty at 6 a.m. and returning after the guard had left. His efforts were in vain, however. Like all farmers he was obliged to sell most of his produce to the state at an artificially low price. Supplies of fertiliser and spare parts for equipment dried up. The coffee bushes became less productive with age, but there was no money to replace them. The plantation had become a drain on the family's fragile finances. Under pressure from his wife, he eventually sold it – for just $3,000 – and the family went back to making pastries, just as they had done as refugees in Quang Ngai twenty-five years earlier.

In the countryside farmers were organised into co-operatives and obliged to sell most of their produce to the state at prices well below the market rate. The result was a big fall in production and the growth of a flourishing black market. City dwellers without jobs were rounded up and removed to 'new economic zones', huge swathes of land reclaimed from scrub, swamp and forest. Life in most of these zones was so hard that many of those relocated there soon drifted back into the cities, preferring life on the streets.

The new authorities brought with them a plethora of new laws and regulations. Every household was provided with an internal pass-port, known as the family book. Only those members of a household whose names were registered in the family book were entitled to live there. Friends or relatives who migrated to Saigon from elsewhere risked arrest or removal. If the designated head of the household went abroad (legally or illegally) his remaining family were at risk of losing their home unless they could come up with the hefty bribe that might be necessary to reregister the house. The house in Le Van Sy was registered in Ngoc's name on the grounds that, being a government employee, her name might offer her and her siblings greater security. When she and I married in 1987 and she was preparing to join me in England, she dared not leave until she had succeeded in transferring the house into the name of her sister and brother-in-law, making certain that her family would be allowed to continue living there.

Corruption became endemic. Any successful business was at risk from predatory tax collectors. Even the simplest transactions required 'presents' for officials. Official salaries were so low that it was virtually impossible for an honest official to survive. Transactions that had once been simple now became complex. The purchase of a bus ticket, for example, could involve having to queue all night, with no guarantee of eventual success. There were two queues: one for officials and one for the *nhan dan*, the people. In theory, everything was for the people, but in practice the Party always had priority. The people were the prisoners of the Party. Documents were checked at every turn. There were frequent baggage searches. Bribes had to be paid to pass security posts. A bus journey from Saigon to Kontum that once took twelve hours now took twice as long.

There seemed to be no end in sight. Runaway inflation and a series of devaluations wiped out savings. People who were once prosperous faced ruin. Seeing no prospects for themselves or their children, anyone with a skill marketable in the outside world began to look for a way out. Many left legally, sponsored by relatives in America or Europe; others took to the boats, selling whatever they possessed in order to finance the journey. Preparations had to be made in great secrecy. Friends and neighbours disappeared overnight without a word to anyone. A vast underground network of people smugglers developed. The risks were high. Detection meant imprisonment. Many of the boats were unseaworthy and disappeared in the Gulf of Thailand. Others were attacked by pirates. Unknown thousands perished, among them two of Mr Thanh's much-loved children. Ngoc's father, who had hitherto been adamant that, whatever happened, the family should stick together, no longer withheld his consent when younger brother

Nga asked to leave. He now lives in Canada. In due course the disillusion spread to many lifelong communists. Colonel Bui Tin, famous throughout Vietnam as the officer whose tank had smashed through the gates of the presidential palace and who had accepted the surrender of the southern regime, ended up living in exile in Paris.

Ngoc was lucky. A few months after liberation she was permitted to resume her studies. Minh Duc University was closed and amalgamated with the University of Saigon. Students were divided into groups and underwent a programme of political education which proved surprisingly interesting. 'At first we didn't like it, but the lecturers were good. They were mainly southerners whose families had gone north in 1954 and who had now returned. We asked why, if Vietnam was now democratic, there was only one party. They replied that, since 90 per cent of the population was made up of workers and peasants, only one party was needed.' The students were required to spend time in the countryside doing manual labour. Ngoc and her friends went twice, once to help dig a canal at Thu Duc, a few miles out of Saigon, and once to Tay Ninh, near the Cambodian border, to clear land and build houses for a new economic zone. The work was hard, although a spirit of camaraderie initially prevailed, but the mood soon soured as reality set in. More than half Ngoc's fellow students in the English language faculty ended up living abroad.

Ngoc and I first met in the spring of 1985. By that time she was working for Saigontourist, the state travel company. I was the courier for a party of British visitors and she was our guide. I was thirty-seven years old and she was thirty. We chatted and flirted surreptitiously. Opportunities to be alone together were few and far between. Our first kiss was in the lift of Doc Lap Hotel. We managed to prolong the experience by going to the top floor and back half a dozen times without stopping. It should have been a doomed relationship. In a few days my party and I would travel north to Hanoi. A few sweet memories and that would be that, but when the time came to say goodbye I broke down in front of everyone on the bus. Our secret was out. From Hanoi I sent her a postcard with the message *I love you and I will return.*

I did so in the autumn, though not without difficulty. At that time unofficial contact between Vietnamese and foreigners was strictly forbidden, so a good deal of subterfuge was required. Ostensibly the purpose of my visit was to negotiate further tours on behalf of the travel company I had worked for. That could only be done in Hanoi, so I had to go there first so that my cover story would appear plausible, if challenged, before making my way south. When I finally made it to Saigon, by now rechristened Ho Chi Minh City, Ngoc had arranged for her close friend Kieu to be my guide, and Kieu conspired to bring us together as often as possible without attracting attention. One evening, in twilight, we managed a trip to a local amusement park, where we mingled inconspicuously, chaperoned at a discreet distance by her younger sister, Oanh. Visiting Ngoc at home was out of the question. The nearest I got was to sit in a car on the opposite side of the road while her brother-in-law, Vuong, came over and shook my hand. I wrote to her father, who was then in Kontum, saying that we wanted to marry and promising that I would take good care of her. It was a big step. Marriage between a Vietnamese and a foreigner was almost unheard of.

Having gained the family's approval, we now had to convince the authorities. The first move was for Ngoc to break the news to her employer. The odds were that this would mean instant dismissal. Her manager was deeply upset at the prospect of losing one of her most experienced guides and did everything she could to talk her out of going. In the end Ngoc was not dismissed, but demoted to domestic tour guide, in which capacity she would have no contact with foreigners. This was actually to our advantage, since she was now able to travel far more widely than if she had continued guiding foreigners. It also meant that she could pursue in person the progress of our application to marry with the authorities in Hanoi.

Our petition moved at a snail's pace through the thickets of Vietnamese bureaucracy. There was, as Ngoc used to say, a great deal of 'procedure to proceed'. Documents had to be completed, copied, witnessed, translated; approvals sought at many levels. Ultimately the decision would be taken by the Council of Ministers, no less. The best part of two years passed with no apparent progress. Communication with Vietnam from the UK was difficult. Hardly anyone had a telephone in their home. An exchange of letters could take weeks, not least because all foreign mail was censored, at least in theory. In practice, since Vietnam's vast, paranoid but inefficient security service lacked the resources to translate all incoming foreign mail, I suspect it simply languished in the post office for a few weeks until someone got round to authorising its delivery. (As one of our ambassadors remarked, 'I was briefed to expect East Germany, but when I arrived I found Mexico.') Rather than put a letter in the international post, I resorted (with the help of my friendly travel agent) to finding someone about to visit Vietnam and asking them to post the letter internally, thereby avoiding the censors. Ngoc, meanwhile, had found a reliable foreigner willing to post her replies in Bangkok. This worked well until one day I received a letter containing the sentence 'I now ill', the code phrase that meant she was in trouble. Worried, I scoured the world for an inbound tourist willing to relay a message, eventually locating one in a Bangkok hotel at midnight. In due course he brought out a letter saying that our correspondence had been rumbled. The head of the local street committee had hinted that he had seen a copy of a photograph I had enclosed with a previous letter, taken together on the roof of the former presidential palace.

Growing increasingly impatient, I wrote the Vietnamese prime minister a letter which I delivered via his ambassador in London. 'Although I have been a friend of Vietnam for many years,' I wrote, 'I am not asking to be made a hero of the people. Only for permission to marry the woman I love.' Whether or not that did the trick, who knows, but soon afterwards word came that permission was granted. A date for the wedding was duly arranged and my ticket booked, but there was an added complication: I had been selected to stand for Parliament at the next general election. Rumour had been rife for weeks that an election was imminent. I could not risk being out of the country once a date had been announced, but what kind of impression would it make on my fiancée and her family if I were to cancel at the last minute? It went to the wire. The prime minister, Margaret Thatcher, was due to make an announcement a few hours after my flight departed. What to do? I consulted a couple of lobby correspondents, just back from the morning briefing at Number 10. 'Go,' they said. 'There won't be an election.' Off I went and, at a stopover in

Bangkok, listened carefully to the BBC World Service news. It was confirmed. There was to be no election.

Ngoc and I were married at her home in Ho Chi Minh City on 14 April 1987, she wearing a traditional Vietnamese costume, red *Ao dai* and white silk trousers, I in my only decent suit. A reception was held for friends and family on the top floor of the Huu Nghi Hotel, at that time Vietnam's tallest building. We honeymooned at the Palace Hotel in Dalat, a colonial relic with high ceilings and shuttered windows, opening out onto a fine view of the lake and the hills beyond. On 11 June I was elected Member of Parliament for Sunderland South, a seat I would hold for the next twenty-three years. Two months later, on 27 August, carrying all her possessions in a modest suitcase, my new wife arrived at Heathrow airport to join me.

CHAPTER EIGHT

Seven Days in Tibet

In the summer of 1975, on leave from my job as a subeditor in the newsroom of the BBC World Service, I travelled to Nepal. Ostensibly I was there to report the coronation of King Birendra, but my principal purpose was to investigate rumours that the CIA had a hand in the Tibetan uprising against Chinese rule. It did not take long to establish a link. In Kathmandu I stayed in a hotel owned by the Raja of Mustang, a remote valley in north-west Nepal where an army of Tibetan guerrillas was said to have been based, conducting occasional raids into China. The receptionist was a young Tibetan and I started questioning him about the Dalai Lama's flight into exile in March 1959, when both the Chinese army and the world's press were combing the Himalayas in search of him.

'Why don't you ask that man over there?' The boy indicated an elderly Tibetan sweeping the floor. 'He came out with the Dalai Lama.'

With the boy interpreting, I began to interrogate the old man. 'Did the Dalai Lama's party have a radio with them while making their escape?'

'Yes,' he replied.

'Who were they talking to?'

At this point an argument broke out between the boy and the old man. 'Don't listen to him. He is crazy,' said the boy.

'What does he say?'

'He says they were talking to the Americans.'

And so they were. Gradually it emerged that, since the late 1950s, the CIA had been smuggling young men out of eastern Tibet, training them in paramilitary warfare and parachuting them back from unmarked planes at dead of night. The training took place at a US military base on the Pacific island of Saipan and later at Camp Hale in Colorado. In great secrecy Tibetans were smuggled out of eastern Tibet, via India and East Pakistan (now Bangladesh). A great deal of cloak and dagger was involved. The earliest trainees were disguised as Sikh prisoners. In order that the operation could not be traced back to the US, they were given outdated weapons easily available on the international arms market – a source of resentment among some of the young Tibetan guerrillas who had been led to believe they would have the use of modern technology to resist the heavily armed Chinese. Like so many CIA operations of that era, it was a disaster. Most of the young men who received training were either killed, captured or ended up as refugees in India. The first CIA-trained Tibetans to be deployed, were dropped near Lhasa in September 1957. Their names were Lhotse and Athar and their orders were to make their way to the Tibetan capital, establish contact with the young Dalai Lama and persuade him to appeal openly for American help.

They did not get as far as His Holiness. Instead they were received by his chamberlain, Thubten Woyden Phala. Eventually, word came back that the Dalai Lama was not willing to appeal openly for military assistance, although his older brothers – Gyalo Dondhup and Thubten Norbu – were already deeply involved in the CIA operation. Lhotse and Athar, who had been trained as radio operators, then left Lhasa and joined the Tibetan resistance in Lokka, the region south of Lhasa. In March 1959 the uprising spread to the Tibetan capital and the Dalai Lama fled. The radio operators linked up with his party and helped escort him to safety in India, communicating with the Americans as they went. In 1975 I found Athar, running a tea shop in Darjeeling, where for the first time he told his story.

Altogether, over a period of several years, there were more than thirty drops of trained men and arms into eastern Tibet. Later, when it became clear that the uprising had failed, the guerrilla army was transferred to Mustang, from where they continued to receive CIA air drops of supplies and weapons and carried out occasional raids on Chinese truck convoys on the Sinkiang–Lhasa highway, the highest road in the world. One of the early raids yielded a cache of documents apparently confirming for the first time the failure of China's Great Leap Forward. In 1964 two British film-makers, Adrian Cowell and Chris Menges, made a remarkable documentary in which they accompanied a group of Tibetan guerrillas on a raid into Tibet and filmed them attacking a Chinese truck convoy. By the mid-1960s the Mustang operation had become ineffective. The guerrillas were ageing, raids into Tibet had all but ceased and complaints began to be received that the group's leader, a ruthless and brutal former monk Baba Gyen Yeshe, was allegedly siphoning off funds for his own purposes. A new leader, Wangdu Gyatotsang, was appointed, but by now CIA enthusiasm for the operation had waned. In 1969 the Tibetans were informed that American support was being withdrawn and plans were drawn up for a resettlement programme.

It was a painful process. The guerrillas were reluctant to disband. They had devoted their lives to the resistance and had nowhere else to go. Some resorted to banditry. Occasional skirmishes broke out between supporters of Baba Yeshe and the new leadership. Meanwhile the Nepalese government was growing impatient. In 1974 Wangdu was summoned to Kathmandu and told that he and his followers must disarm. A representative of the Dalai Lama toured the camps with a taped message from His Holiness urging them to comply. Some reluctantly agreed, although two committed suicide rather than back down. Wangdu and a small band of diehard followers refused to comply and set off through the border area, dodging in and out of China, with the Nepalese army in hot pursuit. Eventually, however, they found themselves trapped between the Chinese and Nepalese armies. Wangdu and a number of his followers were killed.

When I came on the scene in the summer of 1975, little was known about any of this outside the Tibetan exile community. The former guerrillas were mainly to be found camped around Pokhara, Nepal's second city. Baba Yeshe and his small band of followers, regarded by many Tibetans as traitors for having collaborated with the Nepalese, were living in a guarded compound near Kathmandu. For those with sharp eyes there were occasional clues as to their former occupation. Some were wearing shirts made of the parachutes that delivered the CIA drops of food and weapons. I bought one off the back of a man I spotted in the street.

Through Tibetan contacts I made contact with Baba Yeshe and he agreed to see me. His compound was guarded by snarling mastiffs. He was praying when my Tibetan interpreter and I arrived and we had to wait for some time until he had finished. I may have been the first Western foreigner he had ever met. By now he was a controversial figure in the exile community and anxious to get his version of events on record. During the course of several hours he described in detail the operation in Mustang. How it was organised and funded. What happened in the final years. He had a good memory for detail, recalling each drop of weapons and other supplies, often remembering exact quantities.

Once I had the details I set off back across India to see the Dalai Lama at his exile home at Dharamsala in the north-west province of Himachal Pradesh. Dharamsala is a former hill station to which the British Raj once retreated to escape the heat of the Indian plains. At that time, although largely colonised by Tibetans, it still had the feel of an English village. Shady lanes, pink and purple rhododendron, a nineteenth-century church, its graveyard filled with Englishmen. In the centre of the main street, a row of large prayer wheels, around which elderly and picturesque Tibetan ladies in traditional dress circulated, twirling their smaller, hand-held versions, mumbling their mantras, storing up merit in heaven for the next life. Dharamsala was a little Lhasa. There were cafes, restaurants, a couple of small hotels, a carpet factory – all run by Tibetans. At one end of the town, on higher ground, a monastery from which could be heard the clashing of cymbals, the blowing of conch horns and the endless chanting of the mantra, '*Om mani padme hum*' (Hail to the jewel in the Lotus).

Above the monastery, on a cool promontory, in a comfortable villa shaded by pine trees lived the Dalai Lama. I had met him once before, three years earlier while backpacking around India. On that occasion I'd teamed up with two French journalists, a reporter and photographer, and together the three of us interviewed him. We talked of his meetings with Chairman Mao in the mid-1950s, when he had spent eighteen months in Beijing. 'My discussions with Mao were very frank. He told me, "Religion is poison." That's frank, isn't it? But I think Mao was fond of me and, for my part, I had much respect for him and he gave me good advice on a number of occasions.' From time to time at that first meeting, our discussion was interrupted by fatuous questions from the French reporter.

'Your Holiness, I am a Frenchman. What do you think of France?'

To which His Holiness responded, 'France, great country.'

Our discussion resumed and no sooner was it back on track than the Frenchman piped up again. 'Your Holiness, what do you think of General de Gaulle?'

'De Gaulle, great leader.'

And so on.

This time I was unaccompanied and our discussion was a good deal more serious. The Dalai Lama listened patiently while I outlined where I had been and what I had learned. He would not go into detail, but confirmed the gist of what I had uncovered. At times he would lapse into Tibetan and his secretary, Tenzin Geyche, would say, 'There are certain matters it is inconvenient for His Holiness to comment on.' He was at pains to point out – and this is surely true – that the uprising was spontaneous and had not been instigated by the CIA, they had simply latched on to it. 'This kind of report is extremely dangerous because it implies that the resistance in Tibet was initiated by outsiders. This is not so. I want to emphasise that the whole policy was initiated by Tibet, whether we had CIA/United States help or not. With or without the CIA, Tibetan determination was there from the start.' He went on, 'It was not a question of whether I approved or not. Events were such that the resistance came into existence in any case. In the overall struggle we have nothing to hide.'

Later I published an account of the CIA's role in the Tibetan uprising in the *Far East Economic Review*. It was also reprinted in the *Guardian*. This was my first major piece of investigative journalism. For some years it was the only first-hand account of the CIA's Tibetan operation and I was visited by a trickle of academic researchers who duly acknowledged my contribution in their footnotes. My third novel, *The Year of the Fire Monkey*, is based upon my researches. In 1999, almost twenty-five years after my report appeared, John Kenneth Knaus, a retired CIA agent published a definitive account of the entire operation. Like many who have come into contact with the Tibetan exile community, he and his colleagues had fallen in love with their protégés and some shared the Tibetans' sense of betrayal when they were eventually abandoned as America made friends with communist China. The CIA's Tibetan operation was, Knaus wrote, a noble but imperfect cause. He went on:

> The genuine desire to help a beleaguered people regain their independence was noble and forms the moral basis for their continuing claim on the American conscience to this day. The united and enthusiastic efforts of the entire government to marshal and deliver help to the Tibetans was unprecedented. There were, however, political and geographical limits to America's ability to provide what was needed ... The altruistic motivation in lending this help was always secondary to other objectives. In the end the Tibetans were worthy, but hapless orphans of the Cold War.*

An interest in Tibet and the Tibetans is one of the consistent threads running through my adult life. I was and remain entirely sympathetic to the Tibetans and their cause. The Dalai Lama, with whom I have been acquainted for more than forty years, occupies a high place in my small pantheon of political heroes. Not because of what he represents historically, but because of the dignity, generosity and essential pragmatism with which he has devoted his life to keeping a small flag flying for Tibet and its people. Although, like many people, I was initially attracted by the romance of a unique and in many ways beautiful civilisation, cut off behind the Himalayas, that had somehow survived into the second half of the twentieth century, I am way beyond that now. Tibet was never the Shangri-La that some of its more naive and sentimental admirers like to imagine. One has only to read the accounts of early travellers to see that life under the old order for most Tibetans was far from Utopian.

The Dalai Lama, to his credit, has never attempted to justify the old order. Indeed, no doubt to the unease of some of his more conservative supporters both domestic and foreign, he describes himself as a socialist ('to some extent a Marxist'). Despite the isolation of his upbringing, from an early age he displayed a lively interest in the world beyond the frontiers of Tibet. Had he been allowed to govern, he would no doubt have been an enlightened ruler and almost certainly

---

* *Orphans of the Cold War* (New York: Public Affairs, 1999), p. 324.

have opened Tibet to the outside world. Whatever the shortcomings of the old order, however, it has proved vastly more attractive to most Tibetans than anything the Chinese communists have had to offer. More than fifty years have passed since the Dalai Lama was forced to seek refuge in India. Three generations of Tibetans have grown to adulthood. Most were not born when he last occupied the vast Potala Palace in the centre of Lhasa and yet their loyalty to him and to their culture remains undiminished, and years of communist bullying, repression and indoctrination have only strengthened their resolve. Each year a steady trickle of refugees, many of them children, brave the high Himalayan passes to make their way to India in order that they might enjoy a better life and one in which their culture is respected.

For most of the twentieth century Tibet remained hermetically sealed from the outside world. The only foreigners allowed entry were communist fellow-travellers such as Han Su-yin and Felix Green, who, needless to say, reported that all was well. With the end of the Chinese Cultural Revolution and the death of Mao, however, the curtain gradually began to lift. In September 1980 I was invited to lead the first party of British tourists. We were a mixed bunch, politically as well as socially. Our party included a former chairman of ICI, Sir Peter Allen, and his wife. Sir Peter, whom we nicknamed Sir Piju in recognition of his taste for Chinese beer, was a man of massive girth. So vast was it that an armchair had to be placed in the central aisle of our plane to accommodate him. He was also a man of strong views. 'Typical totalitarian chaos,' he boomed, as we stood in the lobby of our hotel in Sian waiting for the lift to come down from the top floor. But he was not without humour. When his wife fell on the steps of the Drepung monastery, cracking a rib, he was heard to mutter under his breath, 'Next year, Cannes.'

In those days, the railway had yet to reach Lhasa. We flew west from Sian, landing at dusk near Golmud on the Qinghai plateau, where we spent the night in a lonely, spartan guest house. The plane was parked nearby, as one might park a car near a roadside motel. We were awoken in the morning by the sound of its engines. Then the flight to Lhasa, not the ideal place to fly into since Lhasa starts at 11,900 feet and everything else is up. We were all looking forward to sampling the atmosphere of the capital at first hand, so there was a small mutiny when it was discovered that we were to be accommodated in a luxury hotel outside the city, rather than in a city-centre guest house. After a stand-off in which our party refused to dismount from the bus, I managed to negotiate a compromise – two nights in one and three in the other.

On our first night the only other tourists sharing our hotel were a group of wealthy and elderly Americans with, one suspected, only the sketchiest interest in or knowledge of Tibet. Their tour had been organised by the prestigious travel agency Linblad, and so we took to referring to them as the Linbladders. After dinner on the first evening one of them tottered out of the dining hall and collapsed. The Tibetan guide accompanying them said that this was his third group of elderly Americans and he'd had to manage two deaths and four pulmonary oedemas. The oldest, aged ninety-eight, had succeeded in climbing a section of the Great Wall. Later, we discovered they had brought with them videos of *Hello, Dolly* and *The Sound of Music*. I subsequently recounted this in an article for the *Guardian*, only to receive an indignant letter from Mr Linblad himself asserting, among other things, that the videos had been intended for the amusement of the Tibetans. 'In that case,' I replied, 'the situation is rather more bizarre than I thought.'

We spent seven days in Tibet, five in Lhasa and two in Shigatse, the second city, driving between the two across central Tibet, over a 15,400ft pass and past the Yamdrok lake. Seven days as a tourist in a land as vast and mysterious as Tibet is not enough to obtain any more than the most basic impression. Even so, it was obvious that change was in the air. The metal gates which until April that year barred entrance to the Jokhang, the holiest shrine in Tibet, had disappeared and it was now open eight hours a day. The altars were piled high with offerings. Pictures of the Dalai Lama were openly displayed. As word that the worship of the Buddha was again permitted seeped out over the high passes and into the lonely valleys, pilgrims had started to make their way to the great shrines. Wild-looking Khampas from the remote east of Tibet were camped out around the Jokhang. Many had travelled on foot, walking for weeks. In Shigatse we came across a ragged family who had been walking for more than a month. Their little daughter was dumb and they had come in the hope that the Buddha might restore her speech. It was impossible not to be moved by such blind devotion.

For a while hopes ran high. Tibet was more accessible than it had ever been. Exiles were permitted to visit families they had not seen for decades. Pilgrims from Tibet were allowed to travel to Nepal and India. Western backpackers were allowed to roam the country at will. Talks opened in Beijing between representatives of the Dalai Lama and the Chinese leadership. There seemed every prospect that an accommodation would be reached that would enable the exiles to return and end what, for the Chinese, had been a running sore in its relations with the rest of the world. And then, suddenly, it all went wrong. In January 1987 Hu Yao-bang, whose period as general secretary had led to a period of unprecedented economic and political liberalisation in China, was forced to retire following a series of student demonstrations which those who opposed the reforms used to discredit him. His death in 1989 and the show of public support at his funeral led directly to the Tiananmen Square protests which were brutally suppressed. In the years that followed, a chill wind blew through China. Talks between the Tibetans and the Chinese were abandoned. Although in Tibet there was no return to the bad old days, the brief period of relative tolerance came to an end. When the Panchen Lama, Tibet's second highest reincarnation, died in 1989, the communists nominated their own successor and the candidate chosen by the Tibetans disappeared. He has not been seen or heard of since. Lately, despairing of progress, Tibetan youths have taken to immolating themselves in protest against Chinese rule. The only effect has been to harden attitudes on both sides.

Sadly, the time for compromise is running out. It is not realistic to imagine that Tibet can ever be an independent country. Although historically it has enjoyed de facto autonomy at times when the Chinese state has been weak, the stark fact remains that no country in the world has ever recognised Tibet as an independent state. Any solution must, therefore, involve Tibetan acceptance of Chinese sovereignty in exchange for a high degree of autonomy. Acknowledging Chinese sovereignty would be a bitter pill for many Tibetans to swallow and, given the level of distrust between the two sides, cast-iron guarantees of non-interference would be required. Only the ageing fourteenth Dalai Lama has the moral authority to make such a compromise. After he is gone it is unlikely that any successor will have the weight to make a settlement stick. 'The Dalai Lama is an individual,' he once remarked to me. 'The institution is not something inseparable from the Tibetan people. Maybe I am the last.'

CHAPTER NINE

My Brief Career as a Novelist

In the first week of October 1980 I was on a train returning from the Labour Party conference at Blackpool with Stuart Holland, recently elected MP for Lambeth Vauxhall, Tony Banks and Peter Hain, both of whom subsequently became MPs. We were discussing how the Establishment would react to the election of a left-wing Labour government. In those far-off days the proposition was not as fanciful as it now seems. Margaret Thatcher was in office, but had yet to consolidate her grip on power. Labour was ahead in the polls and there was a possibility that, come the election, the party would be led by Tony Benn. To cap all, the announcement that the Americans were planning to install cruise missiles in their British bases had given the Campaign for Nuclear Disarmament a new lease of life.

'A good subject for a novel,' remarked one of my travelling companions. Whereupon Peter Hain revealed that he and a friend were in the process of circulating to publishers an outline for just such a story. Stuart Holland went one better. He revealed that during the summer, by the swimming pool in Greece, he had tapped out the opening chapters of a novel on exactly that subject.

In the event I got there first. *A Very British Coup* was published in the autumn of 1982, by which time the climate was even more propitious. Prompted by the imminent arrival of cruise missiles, CND demonstrations were attracting crowds in excess of 100,000. The Establishment was getting so twitchy that, as we later learned, the Defence Secretary, Michael Heseltine, had set up a special unit in the Ministry of Defence to counter the impact of CND.

The Americans were getting twitchy, too. Not long after Michael Foot was elected Labour leader I received an invitation to lunch with an attaché from the US embassy and we duly met at a restaurant called Bumbles in Buckingham Palace Road. The question that interested the American was what a government led by Michael Foot would do about the US bases. Later, I received another interesting invitation. By this time I was working for the political weekly *Tribune* and we were selling my book by mail order through the paper. A few days after it was first advertised, we were intrigued to receive a cheque from the American embassy. We dispatched a copy of the hardback and waited to see what would happen next. We did not have long to wait. An invitation arrived from the minister, the most important official after the ambassador. In due course a day came when he sent his bulletproof Cadillac to *Tribune*'s modest office in Gray's Inn Road to convey me to his mansion in Kensington.

At first I had assumed that I would be one among a number of guests, but no: there was just the minister, two of his colleagues, an Asian butler and myself.

'Why are you interested in a minnow like me?' I inquired.

'I reckon,' he drawled, 'that you are among the top one thousand opinion formers in this country.'

'Well,' I replied, 'I must be about number nine hundred and ninety-nine.'

'The other nine hundred and ninety-nine have been here, too.'

A year or two later I received from an anonymous source an envelope posted in Brussels. It contained an internal State Department memorandum addressed to US diplomats in London listing a number of questions they were to put to their 'authorized contacts' regarding the balance of power within the Labour Party and opinion regarding the US bases in general and the impending arrival of cruise missiles in particular – the very issues on which I had been sounded out at my two free lunches with the Americans. A number of my friends received similar invitations at around the same time. Although in retrospect we can see that the US had no cause for concern, there is no doubt that for a time alarm bells were ringing in Washington.

At the time of its publication *A Very British Coup* attracted a mild flurry of interest. It was helpfully denounced in the correspondence columns of *The Times* and, as a result, sales at Hatchards, the top people's bookshop in Piccadilly, briefly exceeded those at the left-wing Collets in Charing Cross Road. Since that time I have realised that when it comes to selling books, a good high-profile denunciation is worth half a dozen friendly reviews and I have always done my best to organise one. The first hardback print run quickly sold out and a modest paperback printing followed. Thereafter, the novel might have died, but for events conspiring to make it topical.

In August 1985 the *Observer* revealed that an MI5 official, Brigadier Ronnie Stoneham, was to be found in room 105 at Broadcasting House. His job? To vet applicants for employment or promotion at the BBC. He was stamping upturned Christmas trees on the personnel files of those he considered to be ideologically unsound. Students of *A Very British Coup* will know that my head of MI5, Sir Peregrine Craddock, was also vetting BBC employees. What's more, he had a spy in the office of the Campaign for Nuclear Disarmament and in due course a real-life MI5 defector, Cathy Massiter, revealed that there had indeed been such a spy. His name was Harry Newton. Finally, in 1987, Peter Wright, a retired MI5 officer, caused a sensation with his claim that a group of MI5 officers, of whom he was one, had plotted to undermine the government of Harold Wilson. The enormous lengths to which the government went to suppress the Wright book suggested that there was substance to his allegations. Suddenly, the possibility that the British Establishment might conspire with its friends in Washington to destabilise an elected British government could no longer be dismissed as left-wing paranoia.

Not long after I was first elected, along with half a dozen other parliamentary colleagues, I was invited to lunch at Broadcasting House with BBC director general Marmaduke Hussey. The purpose of the lunch was to bend our ear on the Broadcasting Act, then just a gleam in Mrs Thatcher's eye, but halfway through I inquired, 'Who works in Room 105 now that Brigadier Stoneham has retired?'

Around the table there was the sound of knives and forks hitting plates.

Marmaduke, choking on his smoked salmon, gestured towards a woman at the end of the table and said, 'This is one for you, Patricia.' Patricia Hodgson, a senior BBC executive, hummed and haa-ed and eventually said, 'I think he is special assistant to the director general.'

'Yes, but what's his name and what does he do?'

Although we had most of the BBC top brass around the table, no one seemed to know.

'Tell you what,' I said, 'we're only two floors up. Why don't I just nip down, knock on the door and ask?'

No, no, no, they said. We'll write to you. In due course, they did, and sure enough it was one Michael Hodder, whose previous employment had been with the Ministry of Defence. And while they were at pains to assure me that Mr Hodder's job description was very different from Brigadier Stoneham's, it sounded remarkably similar.

In 1988 Channel 4 broadcast a television series based on *A Very British Coup*. My prime minister, Harry Perkins, was brought to life by Ray McAnally, a wonderful Irish actor who sadly died not long afterwards. Alan Plater wrote the screenplay, Ann Skinner and Sally Hibbin produced and Mick Jackson directed. I am deeply grateful to all of them for the success they made of it.

The novel's publishing history is less glorious. It has been published by half a dozen publishers, including three of the main paperback houses – Coronet, Corgi and Arrow. Each printed a disappointingly modest quantity which soon sold, followed by a flat refusal to reprint, leaving me to reclaim the rights and look elsewhere. Meanwhile, in an effort to test the market, I started selling copies through a handful of London bookshops – Collets at each end of Charing Cross Road, Central Books in Gray's Inn Road and one or two others. Each shop sold a hundred or more copies. Some sold several hundred. Before long it was number one in the *Time Out* best seller list. 'Your publishers must be pleased that it is such a success,' the manager of one shop remarked.

'They don't know,' I replied.

Happily, *A Very British Coup* is still in print after thirty-five years. Since the election of Jeremy Corbyn as leader of the Labour Party, prompting rumblings among the military top brass and near hysteria in some parts of the media (not to mention the parliamentary Labour party), it is enjoying a new lease of life.

The television version was a huge success. It swept the British Film Academy's television awards and, in America, won an Emmy for the year's best television drama. The TV series sold in more than thirty countries and in America enjoyed huge acclaim, with cover stories in the entertainment sections of the *New York Times*, *Washington Post* and *San Francisco Chronicle*. Had the book been available it might have sold in large quantities, but unfortunately it wasn't. All the main American publishers stoutly declared that there was not likely to be any serious interest in the US. By the time they were proved wrong it was too late. I later received a letter from America asking if the book was actually banned.

In 1985 I received a letter from a London-based Russian journalist with whom I was slightly acquainted from my time at *Tribune*. His wife worked for a Moscow publishing house, he said, and he wanted to know if she could have the Russian rights. I replied agreeing, but heard no more. By this time I was living in Sunderland, having been selected as the prospective Labour candidate. I lodged in the house of a doctor in a Victorian terrace near the city centre. One morning I went out to buy a newspaper and noticed two men in a car parked nearby who appeared to be watching me. When I returned ten minutes later, they were still there. In the mirror I could see the driver's eyes on me as I approached from behind. A little later I took my washing to the laundrette in Villette Road, about three-quarters of a mile away. On the way back, I noticed the car following me. I ducked behind a hedge. It passed and then did a U-turn. Only when I got back to my lodgings and looked at the *Guardian* did I realise what had happened. This was the day the government announced that it was expelling alleged KGB agents. Mostly they were diplomats, but among the names listed was the Russian who had written to me. My reply to his letter must have been diverted directly into the post box of the security services, who no doubt put in a call to the local Special Branch and asked them to check me out. I saw no more of the two men who had been parked outside my lodgings. Hopefully, they eventually worked out that I was not a Soviet agent.

One other curious incident. Headland House, the office block on Gray's Inn Road where *Tribune* was based for many years, was owned by the Transport and General Workers' Union. During the April 1992 general election a group of trade union representatives fund-raising for the Labour Party were given the use of the first-floor boardroom. A few days after the election, two men presented themselves to the caretaker and said they had come to adjust the carpet in the boardroom. The caretaker was immediately suspicious because there was no carpet in the boardroom. When challenged to provide proof of identity, the men fled. Presumably they had come to remove some sort of bugging device. They may, of course, have been agents of the Tory Party rather than MI5. Over the years there seems to have been a fair degree of overlap.

My second novel, *The Last Man Out of Saigon*, is set in the final days of the Vietnam war. In the immediate aftermath, just about every portrayal of the war in literature or film was through American eyes. The Vietnamese were just bit players. My aim was to write something which, while saleable in the West, showed the war from a Vietnamese perspective. *The Last Man Out of Saigon* is about a CIA agent called MacShane who is sent into Vietnam in the last week of the war, posing as a journalist. His mission is to activate a network of stay-behind agents with a view to making life as difficult as possible for the incoming communist regime. Needless to say, his cover is quickly blown. He is arrested, taken north and eventually sent to work in the countryside while the powers-that-be decide what to do with him. There he falls in love with a local teacher and begins to see Vietnam in a different light. It is as much a tribute to the beautiful simplicity of Vietnam, in the days before the coming of market forces, as it is a story of love and war. It is also an attempt to illustrate the vast gulf that existed between the worlds inhabited by the bombers and the bombed – and how different the view was from the ground looking up, to that from the sky looking down, through the sights of a B-52.

I had high hopes for *Last Man*. The publisher sent the manuscript to Graham Greene (whose *The Quiet American* is the greatest Vietnam novel) and he obliged with a friendly endorsement for the front cover. Richard West, a right-wing journalist, duly obliged with a denunciation which the *Daily Mail* splashed across its op-ed pages. He launched another attack in the *Spectator* and yet another in the *Far East Economic Review*. With each review he grew more virulent. When we sold

Japanese rights I dropped the *Spectator* a note suggesting that, if Mr West would care to stick a carbon in his typewriter, he might earn himself a few yen. So far as I know, he did not take up the suggestion.

American rights were sold. However, the US publisher printed only a modest quantity in paperback and it went unnoticed. Also, for reasons best known to themselves, the publishers chose to target the psychopath market, which, I readily concede, is a fairly large market in the US, though not one among which I can expect a large following. The cover, clearly designed by someone who had not read the book, depicted a marine stumbling through a minefield, clutching his M16. Result: a lot of disappointed psychopaths, one or two of whom wrote to me expressing their disappointment. One envelope simply contained a photograph of a chunky redneck standing by the open trunk of his car, clutching an assault rifle. On the back he had written: 'Korea: 1950–3', 'Vietnam: 1965–72', 'No Regrets'.

An option was sold on the film rights. The cheque came from a bank in Sunset Boulevard. I was nervous about what the American film industry might do with my novel (a 1960s version of *The Quiet American* had twisted the final stages of the plot out of all recognition and was duly denounced by Greene). Fortunately, although the cheque came from Hollywood, the film was to be directed by that great British film-maker Chris Menges. Until that time Hollywood's treatment of Vietnam was almost entirely based on the American experience and involved a great deal of violence. Films such as *The Deer Hunter* and *Apocalypse Now* tended to be shot on location in Thailand or the Philippines with local farmers dressed up as Vietnamese. I suggested that *Last Man* be filmed in Vietnam. Why try to reconstruct Saigon or Hanoi when you could have the real thing? At this time – the mid-1980s – Saigon and Hanoi were pretty much unchanged since the end of the war. On a visit to Hanoi I called on representatives of Vietnam's struggling film industry, who, needless to say, were keen. Sadly, nothing came of it and the option lapsed. No one ever told me why but these were the days when the American government, still smarting from defeat, was enforcing a trade embargo and threatening those who broke it with prosecution and I guess the film-makers had difficulty finding a sufficiently famous American actor willing to risk his career by playing the lead. A few years later and there would have been no problem. The French *Indochine* became the first Western film to be made in post-war Vietnam. Later a new and faithful version of *The Quiet American* starring Michael Caine was also filmed there. With better luck I could have been first on the scene.

My third novel is set in Tibet It is about an attempt by the CIA to assassinate Chairman Mao using one of the young men smuggled out of eastern Tibet in the 1950s. I consider it the best of my three novels. This, I hoped, was the one that would make my fortune, but it was not to be. *The Year of the Fire Monkey* sank without trace. It was marketed as a thriller when in fact I regard it as a novel which, besides being a good yarn, has something to say about great events. Just about the only reviews it received were a few lines in the thriller round-up sections. The longest and friendliest review appeared in the *New York Times*. Unfortunately, however, the book was not published in America. In 2010, nearly twenty years after publication, a well-known British film-maker bought an option on the rights. He seemed confident that the film would be made. At the time of writing, however, his interest seems to have waned.

A small flame still flickers, however. In 2010, almost thirty years after it was first published, another British film company proposed a remake of *A Very British Coup*. The idea was for an updated TV series, appropriate to the very different political circumstances of the twenty-first century. As each version of the script progressed, however, it became apparent that it was going to be very different indeed from the successful earlier version. By draft four the prime minister was no longer even Labour, but a moderate conservative, overthrown by the Tory right in alliance with a corrupt multinational. Then one day I received a telephone call from a slightly embarrassed producer.

'Er, Chris, would you mind if we changed the title?'

'What are you proposing to call it?'

'Coup.'

In the end the film-makers did some research and discovered that most people understood the new title to mean coop, as in chicken coop. Eventually, they settled on *Secret State*, 'inspired by' rather than 'based on' *A Very British Coup*. I make no complaint, however. Indeed, I count myself lucky. Had the film-makers been less scrupulous they might have got away without having to buy the rights and I would have missed out on a substantial contribution towards the cost of my walled garden in Northumberland.

Secret State featured a galaxy of stars: Gabriel Byrne, Charles Dance, Rupert Graves and Gina McKee. By remarkable coincidence, Gina, the daughter of a Durham miner, once lived in Cairo Street, Hendon, in the heart of my former constituency. My only request to the film-makers was that I be allowed a walk-on part, in the manner of Alfred Hitchcock. I thought they might make me a backbench MP or even a minister, but instead they made me the vicar conducting a memorial service for the dead prime minister.

So, there came a day when I found myself on set in a leafy part of Cheshire, popular with Premier League footballers. The location was a fourteenth-century church, St Mary's, Nether Alderley. A note in the porch revealed that this was the constituency of our beloved Chancellor of the Exchequer, George Osborne. The vicarage, a substantial early-Victorian house, partly concealed behind high hedges, had once been the home of Neil and Christine Hamilton until they met their nemesis in the shape of Messrs Mohamed Al-Fayed and Martin Bell. The place was a scene of frenetic activity. Cameramen, soundmen, riggers, production assistants – assembling, dismantling, reassembling, adjusting. In addition to the lead actors, there were twenty-eight placard-waving protesters, twenty mourners, ten uniformed police, a twenty-strong choir plus an entourage of drivers and protection officers.

I, clothed in full vicar's outfit – cassock, white surplice, purple stole, dog collar – was allotted three small cameos. First, I was to stand at the church gate and greet the mourners. When the grieving widow arrived I had to accompany her to the church door. Then I was to greet Gabriel Byrne, the acting prime minister, and finally proceed to a lectern and commence a homily for his late boss.

The scene at the church gate was shot repeatedly and from many angles. Rupert Graves, standing next to me, was a senior member of the government, but he was unsure which. He buttonholed a passing production assistant, 'One question: am I the Chancellor or the Home

Secretary?' The grieving widow, an exceedingly beautiful woman, arrived, and I accompanied her to the church. This scene, too, was shot many times. Then I lingered, awaiting the arrival of the acting prime minister, Gabriel Byrne, who swept down the path, accompanied by a posse of stony-faced protection officers and the (female) head of MI5 with whom he was in a whispered, deeply serious conversation. The party was preceded by a camera crew walking backwards. When they reached me the scrum miraculously parted, conversation ceased and Gabriel looked at me meaningfully. At this point I uttered the first of my four humble sentences. 'Charles [the dead prime minister] always spoke highly of you.' To which Gabriel replied, 'Thank you, vicar,' and then moved into the church, still deep in conversation with the woman from MI5.

The weather was suitably funereal. Dark clouds hung heavily all day and from time to time there was a light drizzle. Underfoot it was muddy. My cassock was designed for a taller churchman than I, with the result that, to walk anywhere, I had (to use a suitably biblical phrase) to gird my loins. Occasionally I forgot and found myself entangled. Nothing was left to chance. At the first speck of rain, someone appeared with an umbrella and held it over my head. From time to time a young woman sprayed my hair with lacquer. Someone else stooped to brush the mud from my cassock. And yet another person – from continuity – snapped away at odd angles with a digital camera.

By afternoon we had progressed to the church interior. An encounter between Gabriel Byrne and his on-screen ex-wife Sophie Ward had to be shot many times before the director was satisfied and then it was my turn again. I waited until everyone was inside the church and made my way down the aisle, pausing to shake hands with a couple of mourners. I then found myself standing at the lectern, facing the congregation, directly opposite the grieving widow. The politicians were seated on the other side, Gabriel Byrne and Charles Dance at the front. This was the point at which I had to spout my remaining three lines. A tricky moment because, although I had learned them by heart, I was in fear of drying up in front of the entire cast and crew, thereby destroying what was shaping up to be a promising acting debut. Happily, however, the director slid the relevant page of the transcript on to the lectern in front of me. I delivered my lines with confidence – and without much more than a downward glance. It was over in a single take.

Everyone was kind about my performance, but later doubts begin to seep in. The hour was late and the director anxious to wind up. Perhaps he had already made up his mind to drop the scene, but couldn't bring himself to tell me. I had to wait several months to discover how much, if anything, has survived the cutting room.

In due course a preview arrived. I logged in with trepidation. Was I still there? Sure enough, there were my fellow actors: Gabriel Byrne, suitably grave and prime ministerial; Charles Dance, the chief whip, suitably sinister; Gina McKee, radiant as the whistle-blowing journalist. The plot rattled along at great speed. Soon we were at the memorial service. Sure enough, there I was in my vestments. The camera lingered briefly. And that was it. Gone was the much-filmed walk to the church door with the beautiful widow. Gone my exchange with the acting prime minister. Gone my address to the congregation. Vanished, too, the twenty-strong choir. So that was that. My acting career had lasted all of three seconds.

Actually, I was lucky. Just how lucky was brought home to me when, some years ago, I was asked to speak at a literary event in Ipswich. The audience included a former chief political correspondent of the BBC, Peter Hardiman Scott, once a household name. In retirement he had written thrillers. He said that when my novel was published, he was two-thirds of the way through writing one along similar lines – a left-wing government, overthrown by the Establishment. He took it to his publisher who told him that it wasn't worth pursuing since I had got there first. How fortunate I was. It could so easily have been the other way round. He, after all, was famous while I was an unknown. *A Very British Coup* might easily have been quietly shelved, and my career as a novelist might have ended before it had even begun.

CHAPTER TEN

Moderates and Extremists

In September 1973 I bought what estate agents call a garden flat (and most other people call a basement), in a Georgian house on Brixton Road, halfway between the Oval and Brixton centre. I say 'bought', but in those days building societies red-lined old houses in the poorer parts of the inner cities, so no sooner had I been offered a mortgage than it was summarily withdrawn. In the end, faced with a threat of adverse publicity, the building society backed down but would advance only two-thirds of the £12,000 asking price. To cover most of the rest I had to take a short-term loan, with the result that my two repayments consumed well over half my income. Only the subsequent runaway inflation (as a result of which my BBC World Service salary rose faster than the interest rate) saved me from years of penury.

The flat at Brixton Road would remain my home until I moved to Sunderland thirteen years later and even then I continued to lodge there, when Parliament was sitting, for a further eighteen years. Brixton Road in those days was a tough environment. Two sets of riots passed my door. As luck would have it, I spent the day of the first outbreak, in April 1981, using a hired drill to remove the concrete covering much of the front garden with a view to planting shrubs. Had I known that the concrete was eighteen inches thick, I would never have started. By evening, however, I had amassed a large pile of hand-sized lumps, ideal ammunition for those bent upon a night of mayhem. There was no way it could be speedily removed so I spent the evening, until darkness fell, nervously keeping watch over it as rioters streamed towards the centre of Brixton.

The 1981 riots were essentially anti-police and it was possible for a middle-class white male to move unscathed amid the chaos even as Brixton burned. The second bout of rioting, in September 1985, was triggered by a police raid on a house in Normandy Road, a hundred yards from where I lived, in which the mother of the youth they were hunting was shot and paralysed from the waist down. In the riots that followed, West Indian youths ran amuck, burning and looting. I saw one group launch an assault on a coachload of terrified pensioners only to be talked out of it by a group of West Indian girls. That same evening I was attacked by a posse of youths encountered in a nearby street (although one was kind enough to pick up my glasses from the pavement and hand them back to me). Later, a few yards away, a young white woman was raped. Earlier I had stood on the balcony of a neighbour's apartment watching as the looting and burning spread from the centre of Brixton towards the Oval. Outside the house next door, parked under a large overhanging lime tree, was a gleaming white Mercedes with German number plates, a veritable provocation to any passing arsonist. By now the looters had reached the shops at the end of our terrace. The Mercedes apart, the only cars in sight were those heaped into the centre of the road and set alight. Our fear was that if the Mercedes burned, the fire would spread to the tree and from the tree to our terrace. I raced downstairs and frantically knocked on neighbouring doors in an unsuccessful attempt to find the owner. Then, a miracle. Just as the first youth hovered, a man with a child on his arm strolled coolly out of a nearby house, exchanged light banter with the predatory youth and drove away. Years later, when a young woman from the BBC German Service came to interview me, I recounted this incident. 'Oh,' she said, 'that was my uncle.'

The politics of Lambeth were sometimes as chaotic as life on its streets. In the late 1960s and early 70s Lambeth Council had been home to local politicians who would later become national figures – Tony Banks, Ken Livingstone and John Major. The late 1970s saw the rise of council leader 'Red Ted' Knight, and with him many of the fifty-seven varieties of Trotskyists who would come to plague inner-London politics. The result was that the ruling Labour group, absorbed in its own internal battles, lost touch with the people it was supposed to be serving. Instead of concentrating on reducing the backlog of council house repairs, keeping the streets clean and costs down, they went instead for gesture politics – declaring the borough a nuclear free zone, flying a red flag from the town hall, supporting revolution in Nicaragua and refusing to implement cuts in local government spending, with the result that many of them were surcharged and banned from holding office. Meanwhile, many of the services the local authority was supposed to be providing were dysfunctional and often appeared to be run for the benefit of those who provided them rather than the public they were supposed to serve.

But it wasn't just Trotskyists. The old guard had stayed too long. Many of the drastic slum clearance projects of the 1950s and 60s resulted in the sweeping away of streets of Victorian terraces which were replaced in some cases with years of dereliction and in others with brutalist concrete estates, which often won awards before they had to be knocked down. Those responsible, meanwhile, tended to live in converted windmills in Surrey or their equivalent. By the mid-1970s the tide began to turn against brutalist architecture and, thanks to popular resistance and some determined groups of squatters, many of the derelict period houses on and around Brixton Road were rescued from the path of the bulldozer and eventually refurbished to a high standard. With luck they will still be standing a hundred years from now, long after the monstrous carbuncles of the 1960s, 70s and 80s have been bulldozed. 'What's the secret?' I once asked the foreman of a construction company restoring the late-Georgian houses opposite mine.

'Simple,' he replied. 'No architects. These old houses were pattern-built.'

No doubt an oversimplification, but there is a germ of truth.

Anyway, back to the old guard. Many of the elderly machine politicians who dominated inner-city politics up to the 1960s were swept away in the local election meltdown of 1968 (when the Tories briefly and improbably took control of such places as Glasgow, Sheffield, Sunderland and Lambeth). Unfortunately, however, no such cathartic process had occurred so far as Parliament was concerned. Many of the Labour parliamentary strongholds in the inner cities were occupied by elderly MPs who had been in place since the Second World War – and, in one or two cases, earlier. Some had been big figures in their day, but their day had long passed. Many had become indolent and indifferent while their constituency parties rotted around them.* The Lambeth Vauxhall constituency, where I lived, was one of the most extreme examples. The sitting MP, George Strauss, had been in place since the 1920s. His personal secretary was also the party secretary, so it was difficult to join. He owned the party offices, an elegant Georgian house on Kennington Road which he had purchased for a song in the late 1930s. He always made clear that he would take it with him when he went (and he was as good as his word). Of all Britain's Labour MPs, Strauss was the Labour MP in the whole country with the least excuse for not living in his constituency (on the grounds that it could be seen from the terrace of the House of Commons), and yet he lived at Number One Kensington Palace Gardens, one of the grandest addresses in London. You didn't need to be a Trotskyite to see that there was something wrong with this set-up.

Only three other people attended my first meeting of the Vassall Ward Labour Party – two councillors and an eighty-two-year-old man called Sam Cosham. Of the secretary, there was no sign. Indeed he was rarely, if ever, seen again. On paper there were several dozen members, but most were elderly and had not been seen or heard of for years. In any case, why would you want to attend a meeting where absolutely nothing happened? The solution was to make Labour Party membership interesting again. Being so close to central London, the Vauxhall constituency contained no shortage of idealistic, intelligent young folk – people who worked for think tanks, trusts, charities and the public sector – only too keen to find an outlet for their political energies. It wasn't rocket science, merely a question of circulating some half-decent literature with the contact details of a membership secretary who could be relied upon to follow up applications. After that, all that was necessary was to meet regularly and make meetings sufficiently interesting to hold the attention of new members, often by inviting guest speakers. By the time I departed, the Vassall branch had 140 members and a regular attendance of thirty-plus. A similar process was under way elsewhere in the constituency. A hundred flowers were

*There were notable exceptions, such as Ian Mikardo in Tower Hamlets and Marcus Lipton in Brixton.

1. My mother, Teresa Foley (front row, third left) *was born into a large, happy Catholic family presided over by her father, Frederick, a genial patriarch.*

2. Grandpa Mullin, a man of few words.

3. My parents on their wedding day.

4. *In my Sunday best, aged about seven.*

5. *Aged 18-months with my broken leg – I fell downstairs on the day my sister was born.*

6. *Our neighbours, Charlie and Georgina Martin, substitutes for the grandparents we never had.*

7. March 1970: with prime minister, Harold Wilson, my first visit to Downing Street.

9. The declaration of the result: I am standing between the defeated Conservative candidate, Tim Keigwin and the narrowly re-elected Liberal leader, Jeremy Thorpe, Liberal leader. Thorpe's wife, Caroline, in the white coat, was killed in a car crash ten days later.

8. Labour candidate in North Devon, June 1970. I had hair in those days.

10. In the back streets of Nanking, China, July 1971: foreigners were such a rarity that we attracted huge crowds.

11. Schoolgirls rehearsing in Tiananmen Square for the national day parade which was cancelled following an attempted coup.

12. Cambodia, August, 1973: soldiers on their way to the front. The machine gun is pointed directly at me and the soldier with his finger on the trigger does not look happy.

13. The author in a bomb crater on Highway 2.

14. Children playing on a pile of shell cases look up at the sound of an explosion.

15. A little cigarette seller, Saigon, 1973.

16. *Quang Tri, Vietnam, 1973. From his outpost on the Thach Han river this soldier could see the tents of the North Vietnamese army.*

17. *With the prime minister of Singapore, Lee Kuan Yew.*

18. *My South Vietnamese press pass.*

19. *Savang Vatthana, the last King of Laos; crown prince, Say Vongsavang, and prime minister Souvanna Phouma, at the annual boat race festival in Luang Prabang in August 1973. One of my favourite shots. Note the puff of smoke from Souvanna Phouma's cigar. The king and the crown prince died of disease and malnutrition in a jungle labour camp several years after the communist takeover.*

20. *An unexploded 250-pound cluster bomb unit dropped by US planes on northern Laos, much of which was littered with unexploded ordnance.*

21. *My first meeting with the Dalai Lama, at Dharamsala in northern India, July 1972.*

22. *The wilderness years. Leaders of the Labour left assemble in my garden at Brixton Road three days after the June 1983 election. Tony Benn had just lost his seat after more than thirty years in parliament. Also present* Ken Livingstone (below left), *leader of the Greater London Council, and* Jeremy Corbyn (below right), *newly elected MP for Islington North.*

25. The Tribune Rally, Brighton, 1983. I am in the process of being denounced by Neil Kinnock, who had been elected Labour leader three days earlier. Others on the platform include David Blunkett (then leader of Sheffield City Council), the Nicaraguan ambassador and MPs Jo Richardson, Judith Hart, Ian Mikardo and Michael Meacher.

26. John Silkin, Russell Kerr and Lord Donald Bruce arriving at Tribune's Grays Inn Road offices in an attempt to take control of the paper.

27. *Alongside Tony Benn at the Durham miners' gala, after being chosen as the Labour candidate for Sunderland South. Bob Clay, MP for Sunderland North is on the right.*

28. Ho Chi Minh City, April 1987: my wedding day.

29. Ngoc's father, Nguyen Tang Minh, on his coffee plantation in the central highlands.

30. Ngoc (back row second from right) and her many siblings.

31. On the film set of A Very British Coup *in December 1987. Left to right: Alan Plater, who wrote the screenplay; CM, author of the novel; Ray McAnally, who played prime minister Harry Perkins; and director, Mick Jackson.*

32. Twenty five years later: on the set of Secret State. Left to right: Robert Jones, screenplay, CM, Gabriel Byrne, who played the lead, Johann Knobel, producer, and director, Ed Fraiman. CM and Byrne are holding the earlier photo.

33. With the Birmingham Six outside the Old Bailey minutes after their release, 14 March, 1991.

34. Actor John Hurt (left), *playing CM in the Granada Television docu-drama,* Who Bombed Birmingham?

35. The Sun's version of events.

Menu mission: Sir Ivan Lawrence, Mrs Barbara Roche and Mr Chris Mullin head for lunch at MI5 yesterday

The four men and one woman tried to look inconspicuous ... They were on their way to lunch with a woman so mysterious that only one blurred photograph of her exists

By Robert Shrimsley and Robert Hardman

Secrets: Stella Rimington

THE four men and one woman huddled together near the Members' Entrance of the House of Commons trying to look inconspicuous.

Their leader was wearing a heavy sand-coloured raincoat of the type favoured by American secret agents.

To his left stood a balding, middle-aged man wearing a thick blue overcoat and scarf. Opposite was a small grey-haired woman in a skirt suit and two taller men in grey suits.

The five, all members of the Commons select committee on home affairs, were waiting for two Ford Granadas which were to shuttle them to a secret location for an unprece-

dented lunch with the head of MI5, a woman so mysterious that only one blurred photograph exists of her.

Mrs Stella Rimington was receiving the Tories Sir Ivan Lawrence, Mr John Greenway and Dame Jill Knight (who joined them at the secret location) and three Labour MPs, Mrs Barbara Roche, Mr Mike O'Brien and one of the country's leading conspiracy theorists, Mr Chris Mullin.

The meeting was granted by Mr Clarke, Home Secretary, after he had refused to let Mrs Rimington give evidence before the committee. Sir Ivan, committee chairman, said it was a "getting to

know you lunch". If Mrs Rimington's reputation is to be believed she probably knows them very well already.

To add spice to the lunch, which consisted of smoked salmon, lamb cutlets reform with duchesse potatoes and tossed salad, and soufflé Monte Christo, the five had not been told where the meeting would take place — though it was widely expected to be held in a private dining room at MI5's headquarters in Gower Street.

At 12.18pm, three minutes later than expected, security personnel ushered the five into the Granadas (one blue, taking the Labour members,

Continued on P3

36. Front page news: With colleagues of the Home Affairs Select Committee, departing for the first ever meeting between backbench MPs and the head of M15, Daily Telegraph *19 January 1993.*

37. In Ho Chi Minh City with Ngoc's large family, summer 1991. Ngoc and Sarah (right); *CM at the back.*

38. With my family on the Border Ridge near our home in the north of Northumberland. (l to r) *CM, Sarah, Ngoc, Emma.*

beginning to bloom. Which had implications both for the future of George Strauss and for the Labour Party as a whole.

Even though Vauxhall was separated from Westminster only by the width of the Thames, George's appearances in his constituency were becoming increasingly rare. By the time I joined, the best hope of catching a glimpse of him was attendance at the monthly meeting of the party's management committee, an amusing little ritual. George would totter in a few minutes late, nodding vaguely in the direction of people he dimly recognised. He would go into a huddle with the chairman, who would then announce that George had urgent business to attend to back at the House and would we mind bringing his report forward so that he could get away? Whereupon members would shrug wearily, George would deliver a surreal account of what he thought was going on in the world, the chairman would ask for questions, members would again shrug wearily and he would wander off, still nodding at people whose faces were vaguely familiar. Obviously, this could not go on. George Strauss had been a big figure in his day (a founder of the left-wing journal *Tribune* and a minister in the Attlee government), but his day was long gone. No one wanted a bust-up. However, the news that he was contemplating contesting the 1979 election was a provocation too far. Four of the five ward branches passed resolutions calling on him to stand down. For a while he considered declaring a Trotskyite conspiracy (a favourite tactic of old-guard MPs under pressure), but it eventually dawned on him that, after fifty-five years as the candidate and Member of Parliament, even the *Daily Express* would have trouble swallowing that. So, reluctantly he agreed to go.

Despite the thirst for change, Vauxhall Labour Party was by no means a left-wing stronghold. Indeed, for some months before George Strauss announced his retirement it was apparent that the constituency was in the process of being quietly taken over. A host of new trade union 'delegates' appeared, most of whom no one had ever seen before, and, come the annual meeting, they swept the board. One man in particular stood out. Charles Williams, the newly appointed trade union liaison officer, who appeared to be orchestrating the takeover. He gave his home address as 66 South Island Place, a street of late-Victorian houses close to the Oval. A member of the General and

Municipal Workers Union, on his membership application he described himself as 'a bank employee'. No sooner had Williams and his friends taken control of the party than they moved that we proceed at once to select a successor to George Strauss. Considering there had not been an open parliamentary selection in Vauxhall since 1924, this seemed indecent haste. Alarm bells began to ring.

One evening, shortly after the takeover, Bill Hall, an elderly councillor who had recently been replaced as secretary, remarked that he did not believe that Charles Williams lived at South Island Place and offered to buy me a pint (itself an extraordinary development), if I could find out his real address. A little detective work soon produced the answer: Williams lived at a somewhat grander address in Kensington. His claim to be a bank employee was, in a manner of speaking, accurate. He was a managing director of the City merchant bank Barings. In a blinding flash, all became clear. Lambeth Vauxhall was a plum seat. The Labour government of the day was urgently in need of strengthening its economic know-how. A man with Williams's credentials would swiftly have found himself on the front bench and might well have ended up a Treasury minister.

At this point, he made his first mistake. A woman moved into the constituency who worked at the headquarters of the National Union of Mineworkers on Euston Road. She soon received a visit from Williams asking if she wanted to join the General and Municipal Workers Union, but declined on the grounds that she was already a member of another union. That, she thought, was the end of the matter, but a few days later through her letterbox came a card showing that she was now a fully paid-up member of the Camberwell Branch of the General and Municipal Workers' Union. It was accompanied by a letter from Williams saying that, 'as usually only eight people out of a membership of 2,000 turn up at branch meetings, you needn't worry about going'. He added that he was 'making arrangements' for her to be appointed a delegate to the management committee of Vauxhall Labour Party. At this point she spilled the beans and the plot began to unravel.

The showdown took place in the Durning Library at Kennington Cross in the spring of 1976. Jock Macpherson Quinn, a technician with a local television company, led for the prosecution with all the skill of an experienced Queen's Counsel. Taking care to conceal that he had in his possession damning documentary evidence, he gently inquired how it came to pass that the woman in question had been wafted on to the management committee as a representative of a union which she had not applied to join and without paying a membership fee. Jock Quinn waited until Williams's not-very-convincing explanation was on record and then read out a letter from the woman concerned comprehensively rebutting it. Game, set and match. Williams's downfall was written up in the national press, which did not go down well with his colleagues at Barings. Fate was kind, however. Not long after his foray into Lambeth he was appointed chairman of the Price Commission and later elevated to the House of Lords. A former county cricketer, he went on to write some well-received books on the game as well as biographies of De Gaulle and Pétain.

What I witnessed in Vauxhall prompted me to join the Campaign for Labour Party Democracy which, in due course, became one of the most successful pressure groups in the history of the party. The campaign was initially organised around one simple demand: that any sitting Labour MP who wished to contest a subsequent election should be obliged to reapply for the nomination, subject only to a guarantee that the sitting member would automatically qualify for a place on the shortlist. In other words, no more safe seats for life. The enemies of accountability would later represent this as a left-wing conspiracy to purge the parliamentary Labour party, and there may have been some who saw it this way, but so far as I and most CLPD members were concerned it was merely a long overdue attempt to make members of the parliamentary party accountable to the wider membership. Needless to say, that is not how it was seen by the party Establishment. On the contrary, the very notion of accountability struck fear into the hearts of many sitting Labour MPs, especially the lazier ones. Although the campaign was widely portrayed as some sort of Trotskyite conspiracy it was in reality a popular uprising, a reaction to the disappointments of Labour governments in the 1960s and 70s.

The campaign was run from a cluttered house in north London, the home of Vladimir Derer, a naturalised Czech émigré, and his wife Vera. A softly spoken, self-effacing man, Derer was for several years one of the least known and most influential figures in the Labour

Party. I was not a founder member, but I signed up early and before long I was on the executive. As it gained in popularity, more prominent people began to climb on the bandwagon. Gradually constituency Labour parties, some of which already had a turbulent relationship with their MP, began affiliating. Prompted by CLPD, they began sending resolutions to annual conference, calling for mandatory reselection. In the early days these were easily seen off by the party leadership, with the help of the trade union block vote. Later, however, the campaign began organising within the unions and gradually the hitherto monolithic block vote began to crumble. Gradually, too, the balance of power on the party's national executive committee began to shift as a new generation of MPs – Neil Kinnock, Joan Maynard, Dennis Skinner and Jo Richardson – were elected to the executive and began to speak up in favour of the proposed rule change. So, too, to the fury of many of his colleagues, did Tony Benn, a senior member of the government. Before long it was clear that mandatory reselection enjoyed overwhelming support among active members and the struggle became increasingly bitter.

The party Establishment tried every trick in the book to suppress the uprising. An obscure regulation known as the three-year rule was deployed to prevent the subject being debated at the annual conference. This decreed that once a subject had been debated it could not be discussed again for another three years. Fair enough, but what the three-year rule did not entitle the organisers to do was to then quietly 'lose' the resolutions excluded on this basis. In 1976 there was outrage when it emerged that reselection was the subject that had attracted by far the largest number of resolutions and yet they had all quietly been junked. The following year even more resolutions flowed in and the national executive came under pressure – to which it succumbed – to allow the subject on to the agenda. Attention also began to focus on the role of the Conference Arrangements Committee, a hitherto obscure body entirely controlled by the unions which, it later emerged, had for long been massaging the conference agenda. Some years later an academic sifting through the papers of an American diplomat, formerly based in London, came across letters from Derek Gladwin, the trade union baron who chaired the committee, boasting of the lengths to which he had gone to manipulate the agenda.

In 1975 an event occurred which changed everything. Newham North East Labour Party voted to deselect their MP, Reg Prentice. Prentice was an undistinguished, middle-of-the-road MP, a minister in both the Wilson and Callaghan governments who in the ballot for membership of the Shadow Cabinet in the early 1970s had somehow contrived to attract the support of both the pro- and anti-marketeers, thereby topping the poll. Naturally, he ascribed the rebellion in his constituency party to Trotskyite infiltration, but the truth was more complicated. To be sure, his management committee did contain a handful of active Trotskyites, including a leading member of the so-called Militant Tendency, but as was often the case with long-serving MPs, Prentice had neglected his constituency with the result that he had lost the sympathy of most members of his local party, who did not take kindly to being denounced as extremists. The Prentice affair became a cause célèbre. The Labour Establishment immediately swung behind him. A letter signed by Prime Minister Jim Callaghan, half the Cabinet and more than half the parliamentary Labour party was sent to the Newham North East party singing the praises of Prentice and appealing to them not to deselect him. A number of leading Labour politicians, including the former Chancellor and Home Secretary Roy Jenkins and Education Secretary Shirley Williams, two of the so-called 'Gang of Four' who would later defect from Labour and found their own party, travelled to Newham and staged a tumultuous rally in support of Prentice. The story led the bulletins. Meanwhile, the right-wing press ran lurid stories about 'bedsit infiltrators' – left-wing activists moving into Newham for the sole purpose of deselecting the MP.

In the middle of all this two young Oxford graduates, Julian Lewis and Paul McCormick, appeared out of the blue. Lewis moved into the constituency, joined the local Labour Party and, advised by McCormick, commenced a series of legal actions against the Labour Party both locally and nationally. Initially they were very successful, tying the Labour Party in knots and causing it to incur huge legal bills. At one point they were threatening legal action against half a dozen other constituency Labour parties and, as one commentator remarked, appeared to have devised a formula for disrupting any Labour Party in the country. As to their source of funding and their motives, the media – so interested in left-wing infiltration – proved remarkably uninquiring. During one of the hearings, a High Court judge tried to prise out of Lewis and McCormick where their money was coming from. He, too, was unsuccessful. I teamed up with Greg Dyke, later to become director general of the BBC, but then a young reporter for London Weekend Television, and we eventually discovered that Lewis and McCormick were being funded by the Freedom Association, a right-wing pressure group. They eventually lost their legal action and disappeared from Newham as quickly as they had arrived. Eventually, they fell out and, true to form, one started suing the other. Some years later I received an anonymous telephone call saying that, if I were to go to the High Court and request certain documents for which I was provided with reference numbers, I would learn something of interest. Sure enough the documents, disclosed as part of a legal dispute between Lewis and his erstwhile co-conspirator, set out precise details of the generous funding accorded by the Freedom Association for their Newham escapade. The story was splashed across the front page of *Tribune*, but most of our free press was entirely uninterested. Julian Lewis later became a Conservative MP. The Prentice affair raged for two years until one morning Prentice got up and announced, to the dismay of his supporters, that he was defecting to the Conservative Party. In a gratuitous blow to those who had loyally supported him he added not only that he was a Conservative, but also that he had been one for the previous four years. He later became a minister in Mrs Thatcher's government. As for the letter signed by all those MPs and ministers, it disappeared quicker than you could say 'extremist'. I have, however, retained a copy for the historical record.

Once reselection was on the party statute book, it was desirable that it be used – and in a responsible manner. I, therefore, wrote a pamphlet which explained the mechanics of reselection and the philosophy behind it. My pamphlet contained an appendix, reprinting the relevant section of the party rules governing parliamentary selections. Hitherto this information had been available only to party officials, and they were anxious to keep it that way in order that they might remain the sole interpreters of the rulebook, a responsibility some party apparatchiks had grievously abused. My pamphlet aroused great interest, not least because it was denounced by those whose interests were threatened. It sold well and was swiftly reprinted.

Although widely interpreted as a guide on how to get rid of your MP, the emphasis was actually on changing the relationship between Labour MPs and their constituency parties. And although, thirty-five years later, I would not defend every word, it has by and large stood the test of time.

After Prentice, the tide in favour of mandatory reselection became unstoppable. At subsequent Labour Party conferences the Campaign for Labour Party Democracy swept all before it. Besides reselection the CLPD had two other demands, both of which came to pass. First, that the party's national executive committee and not the Cabinet or Shadow Cabinet should have the final say over the contents of the party's election manifesto. This we achieved, and the result was the controversial 1983 manifesto, not such a triumph. Second, it was proposed that responsibility for choosing the party leader, until then solely the remit of the parliamentary party, should in future be passed to an electoral college in which MPs, trade unions and party members should have a say. To the dismay of the party Establishment, this motion was passed at a tumultuous Labour Party conference in September 1980. It was agreed that a further conference would be convened in January 1981 to decide the precise make-up of the college. Within days the Labour leader James Callaghan resigned, in an attempt to pre-empt the new arrangements. As a result, the election for his successor had to be held under the old rules by which MPs alone decided the outcome. The choice was between that old flame-thrower and former Chancellor Denis Healey and Michael Foot, an elderly, much loved left-winger who had long since drifted towards the centre. A majority would undoubtedly have preferred Healey, but in a desperate effort to protect themselves from the wrath of party members a number of those on the right took the hitherto unthinkable step of voting for Foot, who narrowly defeated Healey. The result was the worst of all possible worlds. Foot, a decent man entirely out of his depth, became a prisoner of the right. He was to prove a hopeless leader.

In January 1981, in a special conference at Wembley, the Labour Party voted to establish an electoral college in which 40 per cent of the votes went to the trade unions and the remaining 60 per cent was divided equally between the parliamentary Labour party and the wider membership. The die was cast. The following day Jenkins and Williams, along with two other former Labour ministers David Owen and Bill Rodgers, announced that they were leaving Labour and setting up the Social Democratic Party. With the support of a compliant media, the SDP briefly enjoyed a surge in the polls. For a time there was wild talk that they might even form a government. The principal impact, however, was to split the anti-Tory vote almost directly down the middle. Labour embarked on a decade of introspection. The rise of the SDP, combined with a surge of jingoism following the Falklands war, ensured that Margaret Thatcher and the Conservative Party would reign supreme for years to come, although even at the height of her ascendancy Mrs Thatcher never attracted more than 44 per cent of the popular vote. The SDP was eventually wound up after a by-election in which their candidate came fourth behind the Monster Raving Loony Party. The survivors were assimilated into the Liberal Party. By then, however, the damage was done. It was eighteen years before the Labour Party saw office again, and by then it was a very different animal.

It is sometimes alleged that Tony Benn was single-handedly responsible for rendering Labour unelectable in the 1980s. It is true that he was, for a period, the single most influential figure in the campaign to democratise the party and that his attempt in 1981 to unseat Denis Healey as deputy leader was hugely divisive, but it is a wild exaggeration to suggest that he was either the sole or even principal cause of Labour's misfortunes. It overlooks the part played by the Callaghan government's surrender to the IMF in 1976,* which resulted in an attempt to impose unrealistic limits on wage rises which resulted in the so-called Winter of Discontent. This, combined with Jim Callaghan's last-minute decision not to hold an election in the autumn of 1978, but instead to wait until the spring of 1979, was the key reason

---

*We had to wait until the then Chancellor, Denis Healey, published his memoirs thirteen years later to discover that this may not have been necessary. In a single sentence, buried on page 381, Healey wrote, 'If I had been given accurate forecasts in 1986, I would never have needed to go to the IMF at all' (*The Time of My Life*, Michael Joseph, 1989).

for Labour's defeat. Mrs Thatcher's victory in the Falklands, the foundation of the SDP combined with weak Labour leadership and a preoccupation with internal affairs ensured defeat in the two subsequent elections. Other commentators, some of whom played a part in the events they describe, have suggested that left-wing intolerance was a major cause of the decline in the party's fortunes, but one has only to note the virulent and public denunciations of their colleagues by many on the Labour right to see that intolerance was by no means the exclusive preserve of the left.*

Do I regret what happened? Yes. Do I think it was all the fault of one side or the other? No. Labour in opposition has always been prone to civil wars in which neither side has a monopoly of virtue, though by and large the left has behaved better than the right who, in 1955, came within a single vote of expelling Nye Bevan from the Labour Party. Until the uprising of the mid-1970s the Labour Party was machine controlled. The grossly undemocratic trade union block vote was used ruthlessly to suppress dissent. The Labour right were always content to shelter behind the block vote until they briefly lost control of it in the late 1970s. Only then did they begin to notice how undemocratic it was. Mandatory reselection was never the threat to the established order that it was made out to be. There may have been some who saw it as an excuse for a wholesale purge of the parliamentary Labour party, but for most of us involved it was about curbing the arrogance of the party Establishment by making MPs more accountable to their constituency parties and more sensitive to the interests of party members. Witness the fact that, once implemented, few MPs lost their seats, and with a handful of exceptions, those who did so were deselected for reasons of idleness, longevity or drunkenness, rather than ideology.† In addition, a handful of others, who might

---

*Denis Healey, never a man to mince his words, spoke of 'Trotskyist space invaders', Roy Hattersley publicly denounced Benn as 'an ambitious lunatic', John Silkin falsely alleged that Benn was using his personal wealth to buy votes and the leader of the engineering workers' union described the Labour Party as 'a sewer with all kinds of rubbish floating in'. With friends like these the Labour Party didn't need enemies.

†Frank Hooley in Sheffield and Reg Freeson in the London Borough of Brent were two notable exceptions.

otherwise have remained beyond their sell-by dates, now retire voluntarily before each election. The overall result, however, is that Labour MPs are nowadays far more attentive to the opinions of their constituency parties and the needs of their constituents than they ever used to be.

With the passing of years some myths about the struggles of the 1970s and early 80s have only become more deeply engrained. Every so often I run into an old colleague who was active on the other side. 'Of course,' he says, 'you wrote that pamphlet, didn't you?'

'Yes,' I reply. 'What do you think it was called?'

At this point hesitation, for occasionally it dawns that this is a trick question. Usually, however, they blurt out, 'How to De-select Your MP'.

'No,' I say, 'It was called How to Select or Reselect Your MP, and written in generally responsible terms. Safe seats for life was Old Labour. A contract renewable every four or five years, is New Labour.'

In a nutshell, I was New Labour ahead of my time.

CHAPTER ELEVEN

A Little Local Difficulty

Nobody in their right mind would have wanted to become editor of *Tribune* in May 1982. No rent or rates had been paid since the beginning of the year. There was an outstanding debt to the printers of £25,000, tax and national insurance contributions of several thousand pounds were owing for 1980 and 1981 and there was an outstanding libel bill. Sales of the paper had been in continuous decline for the previous twenty years and in the previous two years had started to haemorrhage.

Although not all of this was known to those of us on the staff at the time, we knew enough to realise there would not be a long queue of talented and ambitious applicants for the post of editor – at a salary of just £6,000 a year. I had other reasons for not applying. I had just completed my first novel and was anxious to write another. Above all, I realised that if I were to become editor and the paper were to go down the plughole – as seemed likely at the time – there would be a chorus of 'this is what happens when the extremists take over'. So when the job was advertised I did not apply. Only after being approached by several colleagues, hours before the deadline, did I allow my name to go forward.

Although by the time I came on the scene it had fallen on hard times, *Tribune* had an illustrious history. Founded in 1937 by two wealthy left-wing MPs, Stafford Cripps and George Strauss, former editors included such Labour luminaries as Nye Bevan and Michael Foot; George Orwell had once been the paper's literary editor and many other leading lights on the Labour left had been regular contributors. The annual *Tribune* rally was one of the highlights of the Labour Party conference. Although always loyal to the party, it had been a thorn in the side of successive Labour leaders. Even at the best of times its reputation had exceeded its circulation and, if truth be told, the paper had always been dependent on subsidy from wealthy supporters and sympathetic trade unions. Nevertheless, within the Labour movement it was a force to be reckoned with. I had been writing for it occasionally since the early 1970s and a part-time member of the editorial staff since leaving the BBC World Service in 1978.

The board of directors was responsible for appointing the editor. It consisted of six outsiders and four members of staff plus the outgoing editor, Richard Clements. The outsiders were two senior trade unionists, an academic and three Labour MPs – John Garrett, Neil Kinnock and Michael Meacher. I won seven of the eleven votes on the first ballot. Of the other three candidates, none received more than two votes. Clements made no attempt to conceal his disappointment at the outcome. Although we didn't always see eye to eye, in many ways I admired him for his unfailing good humour and unstinting efforts to keep the paper afloat during his twenty-one years as editor. Although from the start I considered the paper to be grievously mismanaged, it was not until the election of former editor Michael Foot as party leader that serious differences between us began to emerge. These came to a head during the bitter contest for the Labour deputy leadership in the summer and autumn of 1981, during the course of which the paper remained neutral regarding Denis Healey and Tony Benn. It was then that the steady decline in the paper's readership turned into a haemorrhage.

I took over as editor on 3 May 1982, as the Falklands war was getting under way. My first task was to detach the paper from the ridiculous stance then being taken by the Labour leadership – supporting the sending of the fleet, but not its use. We looked back through our archives to the Suez crisis in August 1956, when Foot had been editor. Sure enough, we found that *Tribune* then had been forthright in its opposition to the British fleet being sent to Suez. The parallel was not precise, but close enough. We reproduced *Tribune*'s front page of August 1956 and called for the task force to be brought home.

Later we published an article strongly critical of Foot's handling of the Falklands. This provoked strongly worded replies from Neil Kinnock and Michael Foot. Foot wrote: 'I fear for *Tribune* … Never for long has *Tribune* been afflicted by infantile leftism. I hope it survives the present bout.'

My second issue carried an editorial setting out the policy the paper would follow: 'This paper is not the property of any sect, tendency or personality … To have a say in *Tribune* it will not be necessary to agree with the editorial line of the paper. We will provide a forum, not only for our friends, but for our opponents. Informed controversy is healthy and we shall encourage it.' I went on to pledge the paper's 'relentless' opposition to the fudging of party policy, 'unequivocal' support for Labour Party and trade union democracy and 'unbending' resistance to those who wanted a purge of dissidents. Not everyone was happy with this approach. Joe Haines of the *Daily Mirror* told a mutual friend that the *Mirror*'s advertising would cease. It did, though not immediately. At the TUC Congress in September the *Mirror* placed a full-page advert denouncing Tony Benn and at the Labour Party conference a month later, in a parting shot, the *Mirror* took another full page to denounce *Tribune*. Then the adverts ceased.

Almost immediately Clive Jenkins, general secretary of the white-collar union, ASTMS, withdrew his union's weekly advertisement. He was ordered by his executive to put it back in, but a few weeks later it was withdrawn as part of an 'economy drive'. From every corner word reached us of trade union leaders planning to cut off or reduce their unions' advertising and much of my time was spent trying to reassure them or frantically lobbying our friends in an effort to limit the damage.

Meanwhile, it soon became evident that the financial situation of the paper was a great deal worse than we had been led to believe. The printers were pressing for payment of their outstanding bills. A summons arrived from Camden Magistrates Court inviting me to appear and explain why no rates had been paid. The worst shock came in July – a bill from our landlords, the Transport and General Workers' Union, demanding seven months' unpaid rent. A month before his departure Richard Clements had told the board that he was negotiating with the deputy general secretary of the TGWU an arrangement under which *Tribune* would be given a one-year rent holiday. This was, he said, a confidential arrangement and should not be minuted. The subject had come up at more than one board meeting and Clements had been closely questioned about it. Suppose, he was asked, that after he had departed, the union denied all knowledge. Don't worry, he said, just call me and I will sort it out. When the rent demand arrived we sent him a copy and asked for his comments. He did not respond.

Subsequently we obtained a copy of an internal union memorandum dated 27 September 1982 setting out Alex Kitson's version of events. Kitson, the TGWU deputy general secretary, wrote, 'Dick Clements came to see me to tell me of [*Tribune*'s] financial difficulties and asked to be spared payment of rent for one year. I said I couldn't take a decision on this and it should be referred to the TGWU ...' In his next sentence Kitson said that, when Clements had resigned as editor, 'he told me to forget the request'. He went on, 'I have now spoken to Dick Clements on the phone, who confirms the position outlined above, that no such arrangement was ever entered into.'

The amount of rent outstanding by September was £7,000. We also owed £5,000 in rates and £3,600 in unpaid tax and insurance, in addition to the unpaid libel damages and costs. The printers' bill stood at around £22,000. Just how serious the situation was became apparent only after the paper's business manager, Carl James, left in July. He had been the candidate for my job favoured by Richard Clements. He did not work enthusiastically under my editorship and his letter of resignation was greeted with general relief. On the day of his departure he told me that we would be through the bottom of the overdraft by the end of the following week. An examination of the books showed that for some time James had been making little or no effort to collect money owing to us from advertising revenue. Some of the sums owed to us were considerable and would have gone a long way to meeting our debts. To avert disaster Sheila Noble and Sheila Marsh, two long-serving members of staff, set to work chasing up our largest debtors. Each week they managed to collect just enough money to keep us solvent. That was how we lived all summer.

On 25 August, three weeks after Carl James left, we received a letter from a former *Tribune* director, Lord Bruce of Donington. 'I am increasingly perturbed,' he wrote, 'about the paper's future within the perspective established originally by Aneurin Bevan and continued by his successors until comparatively recently.' Lord Bruce went on to allege irregularities in the way the company was run. He pointed out – correctly – that no annual returns had been made to Companies House since 1979. He suggested – incorrectly – that the company was trading while insolvent and went on to call for a shareholders' meeting to be convened 'so that the development and present state of affairs of the company may be fully disclosed to the shareholders, employees, creditors and readers'. What Lord Bruce omitted to mention, however, was that most of the irregularities of which he complained had originated during his period as company secretary between 1973 and 1981. Despite his expression of concern for the health of the paper, he had attended only one board meeting in the final two years of his tenure. Twice he had been asked to stand down if he was unable to attend the monthly meetings. He had finally resigned in March 1981.

We realised at once that we were facing an attempted coup. At about this time we learned that a proposal was circulating in the House of Commons outlining a plan for taking over the paper and running it along lines more acceptable to the Labour Party and trade union leadership. The plan had been drafted by our erstwhile business manager, Carl James, and another former member of staff. We also learned that Richard Clements – who was by now a political adviser to Michael Foot – had given Foot a copy and tried to persuade him to back a takeover bid. In September the chairman of the company, Michael Meacher, went to see Foot and asked if the takeover would have his blessing. Foot said it would not and promised to make this clear to Lord Bruce. A little later Foot telephoned Meacher and said that he had seen Lord Bruce and we had nothing to fear. Relieved, we went ahead and fixed a shareholders' meeting for 9 December.

Meanwhile, there had been a new outbreak of civil war in the Labour Party and *Tribune* was in the front line. At the end of May 1982 we had published a front-page article by Tony Benn warning that the Labour leadership had plans for watering down the party's election manifesto. Then we learned that the party's national executive committee was drawing up plans for a list of non-affiliated organisations in what was clearly a thinly disguised preparation for a purge of the left. The history of such purges is that they rapidly get out of hand. Last time around, in the mid-1950s, a purge which had started with the expulsion of a few Trotskyites ended up coming within a whisker of expelling Nye Bevan. 'If there is one cast iron way of Labour losing the next election,' we said in a leading article on 25 June, 'it is by reopening the civil war which has engulfed the party for the last three years.' The editorial went on: 'Labour Party members around the country must be in despair that, even at this late hour, the parliamentary leadership is unable to fight Margaret Thatcher and the Social Democrats with a fraction of the enthusiasm they are able to muster for fighting members of their own party.'

The next week the Tribune Group of MPs voted narrowly to support the proposed register and, by implication, the coming purge. That week, in an editorial headed 'The Death of the Tribune Group?', we called on the left in Parliament to regroup and in the next few months more than thirty MPs abandoned the Tribune Group to set up a rival organisation, the Campaign Group. A few weeks later the annual conference endorsed the proposed register of non-affiliated organisations. That week *Tribune*'s leading article was headed, 'You Cannot Have Unity and a Purge'. It was illustrated by a reproduction of a *Tribune* front page from August 1954 headed, I CALL THIS BAN AN OUTRAGE, over an article that denounced the purge as 'stupid, cowardly and totalitarian'. The author had been *Tribune*'s then editor, Michael Foot.

By November there were indications that Labour's policy on nuclear weapons was undergoing a subtle shift. While Michael Foot was prevaricating over Labour's commitment to remove nuclear weapons from American bases, Denis Healey was being commendably frank. He said he would not serve in a government committed to getting rid of nuclear weapons. As for Labour's defence spokesman, John Silkin, I had been trying to interview him on the subject for more than a year. When he declined I offered him space to write an article setting our readers' minds at rest on Labour's nuclear policy. When he did not respond, *Tribune* published a front-page leading article headed 'When Will John Silkin Speak Out?' The answer came sooner than we expected.

Despite Michael Foot's assurance that we had nothing to fear, the staff viewed the approach of the shareholders' meeting with apprehension. We were well aware that *Tribune*'s moribund shareholding structure left the paper vulnerable to takeover. The company had been set up in 1937 on an authorised share capital of 1,000 £1 shares. Of these only 423 had ever been allocated. There were twenty-seven original share-holders of whom eighteen or nineteen were dead. Among the living, Michael Foot held sixty shares, as did Jennie Lee (the widow of Aneurin Bevan). Another sixty were held by Lord Bruce, our former accountant. Of the remaining shares the Labour MP Russell Kerr and the former general secretary of the Transport and General Workers' Union, Jack Jones, each had ten; so did John Platts-Mills QC, while a former editor, Jon Kimche, had five. So far as we could determine, the rest were held by the executors of shareholders long dead. No shareholder had been seen at *Tribune* since their last recorded meeting in 1972, and they had played no active part in the paper's policy for as long as anyone could remember. Yet, in the event of a takeover bid, the only shares we could count on were the twenty held by Jack Jones and John Platts-Mills.

A month after I became editor, the paper's board, in an effort to address this antiquated ownership structure, decided to turn the company into a friendly society in which readers would be invited to buy shares. The society would be controlled by a committee of man-agement drawn from staff (who already had four seats on the existing board), representatives of reader-shareholders and a small number of distinguished outsiders. Besides placing the ownership of the paper on a sound footing the scheme would have had the additional advan-tage of raising some badly needed investment capital and of bringing readers closer to the paper. Precise details were still being worked out with the Registrar of Friendly Societies. Once we had the registrar's approval we needed to seek the consent of the surviving shareholders. In the meantime, capital raised by the sale of shares in the friendly society was to be paid into the bank account of our solicitors. Fund-raising began in June 1982. One hundred thousand leaflets were dis-tributed and the response was encouraging. By mid-1983, when we were finally forced to call a halt, about 750 readers had purchased more than £8,500 worth of shares. Shareholders included the new Labour leader Neil Kinnock.

'When Will John Silkin Speak Out?' appeared on 26 November. We did not have long to wait. That very afternoon a messenger arrived bearing an envelope from the offices of Lewis Silkin and Partners, the Silkin family firm of lawyers. The envelope contained a statement signed by Jennie Lee appointing John Silkin as her proxy at the forthcoming meeting of shareholders. It also contained a letter from Russell Kerr MP nominating John Silkin and Lord Bruce to the board along with three other existing directors. He did not nominate the editor or the other three worker-directors. Between them Messrs Silkin, Kerr and Lord Bruce had 130 shares. We were clearly in trouble. Over the weekend I took soundings from such good friends of *Tribune* as Tony Benn, Ian Mikardo and Jo Richardson. Their advice was unanimous: go public immediately. I then rang the chairman of the Tribune Group and asked to address their meeting scheduled for the following Monday.

I was not popular with many Tribune Group MPs. Although as editor of *Tribune* I had a standing invitation to attend its weekly meetings, I had only made the occasional appearance. Partly because the timing of the meetings – four o'clock on Monday afternoons – did not fit with the paper's tight production schedule and partly because I was anxious to play down the cosy relationship that had developed under the previous editor between *Tribune* and the parliamentary Labour party. Nevertheless, I was given a fairly sympathetic hearing at a well-attended meeting. By the time I emerged everyone knew what was happening because I had left an embargoed statement with the parliamentary press gallery. Since the staff lacked the shares to win a vote at the shareholders' meeting our only hope was to arouse sufficient indignation within the Labour movement to dissuade Silkin from taking over. Messages of support began to flood in, many from people who did not agree with the paper's editorial line. The publicity also had the effect of forcing Silkin and his colleagues to come clean about their plans. Lord Bruce told the *Guardian* it was 'possible' they would be appointing a new editor. He said, 'The paper's never fallen into the hands of any ruddy sect. I think it has gone too far in that direction.' In a BBC interview Russell Kerr said, 'We think a major sectarian element has entered the paper … it is now a Trotskyist publication.' Our editorial on the day of the shareholders' meeting, signed by every member of staff, was headed, 'We Shall Not Be Moved'.

The meeting itself was an ill-tempered affair. Silkin demanded an apology for the editorial in that day's issue in which he was described as 'a rich and ambitious lawyer'. When none was forthcoming he hinted darkly at a libel suit. More light relief was provided by Russell Kerr, who fell asleep during the meeting and woke up to find himself voting for me by mistake. Silkin and Bruce had initially planned to remove me and the three worker-directors from the board until Jack Jones pointed out that it would not look good if a member of Parliament sponsored by the Transport and General Workers' Union were seen to be turfing worker-directors off the board. At this point Silkin, Bruce and Kerr went into a huddle and announced that they were prepared to accept two worker-directors. Sheila Noble and Sheila Marsh, the two longest serving members of staff, were then re-elected Advertising manager; George Hopkins, and I were then replaced by Silkin and Bruce. The four outside directors were re-elected.

My removal from the board was widely interpreted as meaning that I was no longer in charge of *Tribune*'s editorial policy, but I remained editor and Silkin's supporters were still a minority in the boardroom. It was, however, open to them at any time to call another shareholders' meeting and conduct a clean sweep. We realised this was what would happen if we tried to transfer the business to the proposed friendly society. We consulted lawyers and were advised that, under the terms of the 1980 Finance Act, it was possible for the board to establish an employee shareholding scheme. We were also advised that, since only 423 of the original 1,000 shares had so far been allocated, there was nothing to stop the board distributing the remainder among the staff.

The staff representatives, therefore, summoned a special shareholders' meeting for the morning of 23 December. The meeting was attended by the two staff representatives, the chairman Michael Meacher, and our solicitors, Michael Seifert and Sarah Burton. Of the other directors one could not attend, but gave his consent to the proposed employee shareholding scheme by telephone during the meeting. Another came in later that day and signified his consent by signing the share certificates. Silkin and Bruce gave their apologies.

The board went on to award me a three-year contract and approved applications from nine of the ten staff members for fifty shares each. The staff now had 450 shares between them, against the 130 that Silkin and Bruce could muster. We issued a press statement announcing the changes and went home for Christmas and to await Silkin's reaction.

A fortnight later each member of staff received by special delivery a letter from Silkin and Bruce denouncing the employee shareholding scheme as invalid and threatening legal action. At the next board meeting on 13 January they attempted to cancel both the scheme and my contract, but were defeated by three votes to two. Silkin and Bruce then proposed that Michael Meacher and I meet with them to see if a compromise could be found. If no agreement was reached within seven days, said Silkin, he would sue.

Negotiations took place in Silkin's room in the House of Commons. At first they were amicable. It was agreed that my contract be reduced to one year (I had no intention of staying much longer anyway). Silkin and Bruce offered to accept employee shareholders if the staff promised not to use their shares for a period of one year. The staff agreed, provided that Silkin and Bruce gave a similar undertaking. They declined and the talks broke down. A few days later writs were served on the company, on Michael Meacher as chairman and on each of the nine new shareholders seeking damages on the grounds that (a) two of the directors should have been disqualified from taking part in the meeting that allocated shares, since as workers they stood to benefit; and (b) that our motives in setting up the scheme were self-serving. As the 1980 Finance Act is silent on the subject of motivation, the outcome of any legal action would depend on a judge's interpretation of what was reasonable. Apart from which the spectacle of a Labour MP petitioning the courts to disqualify worker-directors from taking part in board decisions on the grounds that, as workers, they stood to benefit, is one that all connoisseurs of Labour movement intrigue will savour. As a member of the Shadow Cabinet Silkin had helped compile Labour's draft manifesto, which promised 'we will bring in legislation to provide, where employees choose, for parity representation between workers and representatives of shareholders on the main policy board'.

Immediately we set about raising the money to repel the invaders. A Friends of *Tribune* fund was launched by three sympathetic

Labour MPs, Ian Mikardo, Judith Hart and Jo Richardson. This quickly raised £7,500. In January Silkin and I addressed the Tribune Group MPs, after which a resolution was carried calling on him to drop the action. One MP told him, 'If you sink *Tribune*, you'll never be forgiven.' Newspaper coverage was sympathetic (the fight with Silkin was one of the few campaigns with which I have ever been involved that, from the outset, enjoyed a sympathetic press). The *Observer* published a leading article roundly condemning Silkin. It said, 'The next time he or any of his colleagues chooses to summon up the bogey of the capitalist press, the only proper response will be a loud and resounding chorus of jeers.'

We began to receive telephone calls from members of John Silkin's constituency party in Deptford asking what they could do to help. 'Invite me to your branch meeting,' I replied. To my astonishment I received invitations to seven of the eight branches and each in due course passed a resolution calling on him either to drop the writs or stand down as an MP. I was then invited – along with Silkin – to address the Deptford Labour Party management committee. He spoke, I spoke, and then the resolution was put to the vote. By forty-three votes to nine the committee ordered that he should drop the writs or step down. Five days later a general election was announced. Silkin was safe for the time being, but his reputation was in tatters.

In contrast to the support we received elsewhere there was an eerie silence from trade union leaders. When the *Tribune* staff wrote to Moss Evans, general secretary of the Transport and General Workers' Union – of which Silkin was a member – they received no reply. When I raised the matter with his deputy, Alex Kitson, he informed me that he was neutral. The Campaign for Press Freedom, which was heavily dependent on trade union funding, confined itself to anodyne pronouncements urging conciliation on all sides, until its annual meeting seven months later voted for a resolution critical of Silkin. There was an eerie silence, too, from former *Tribune* editor and Labour leader Michael Foot. Had he chosen to speak out, he could at any time have stopped what was happening.

The dispute dragged on for another two years. It soon became apparent that, while Silkin and Bruce were not keen to see the legal action reach court, they were not prepared to drop it. Two further attempts were made to achieve a negotiated settlement, one presided over by Ian Mikardo and one by John Jennings of the Campaign for Press Freedom. Both attempts broke down when it became clear that Silkin and Bruce were not prepared to accept any formula which did not leave them in control. They continued to suffer from the delusion that they were the only rightful owners of the paper's tradition and remained on the board throughout most of the following year, but made no further attempt to interfere in the running of the paper. In November 1983 they turned up to a board meeting and unleashed a torrent of abuse, mostly directed against me. They then announced they were resigning and stormed out. I held the door open for them.

Although we succeeded in preserving *Tribune*'s independence, it would be wrong to pretend that Silkin and Bruce inflicted anything other than great damage on the paper's fragile economy. We had to abandon plans for a friendly society and consequently for the relaunch. The money we had raised remained in the bank account of our solicitors until August 1984, when we were obliged to offer it back to those who had subscribed. Happily, most of them returned it to us as a donation. Although we stopped the spiral of decline into which *Tribune* was locked at the time I became editor, we did not succeed in reversing it. We did, however, produce a substantially better product than had been seen for some years, an improvement that even our severest critics acknowledged. We did so with an editorial staff which at no time consisted of more than four people. Anyone falling ill stretched the system to breaking point. In my first two years as editor I had just six days' holiday.

However rough the going got we continued to uphold the *Tribune* tradition – providing a platform for all shades of opinion within the Labour movement, including some of our bitterest critics. Michael Foot, Neil Kinnock and Roy Hattersley were among those who wrote for the paper during my time as editor. Even John Silkin was eventually persuaded to set out his version of events in our pages. Anyone who felt they had been maligned or misrepresented was given space to reply. When we made mistakes we owned up forthwith. We were, in short, the kind of newspaper to which many trade union and

Labour leaders pay lip service. Yet my experience at *Tribune* taught me that many of those same leaders would have about as much difficulty in coming to terms with a free press as, say, Rupert Murdoch.

CHAPTER TWELVE

Deep North Two

In the summer of 1987, within a month of being elected, I purchased a large, early-Victorian terraced house in St Bede's Terrace, a short tree-lined street close to the centre of Sunderland. Further south such a house would have been well beyond my means, but in the north-east it was easily affordable. A glance at the Victorian street directory shows that in 1851, when the house was built, St Bede's Terrace was rather grander than it is today. There were gates at each end and, as late as the 1930s, older residents could recall a night-watchman. Most of the nineteenth-century residents were shipowners, although another MP once lived at number 4. Shipowners usually had shares in several different vessels, rather than owning one outright, in order to avoid losing everything if the vessel went down. The Victorian resident of our house, number 7, was John Doxford, a cousin of Sir William Doxford, one of the town's biggest shipbuilders and latterly the town's Member of Parliament. Initially John Doxford was listed as the owner of an upmarket high-street grocery, but by the late 1860s he seems to have had a stake in at least two ships, the *John George* (named after his only child) and the *Mary*. By the time he was in his fifties he appears to have been a gentleman of leisure, apart from a bit of Methodist lay preaching. He married twice. Both his wives were called Mary. The first died in 1859; the second outlived him. According to the census returns, they had two servants. John Doxford died in 1899 and Mary the Second in 1912. In due course I found their graves in Monkwearmouth cemetery. Between them, they lived at 7 St Bede's Terrace for sixty-one years.

Anyone who lived in my house for more than sixty years deserved to have their photograph hanging in the hall, I thought. Finding one, however, proved easier said than done. At first, I reckoned it would simply be a question of tracking down the current generation of Doxfords (they were, after all, a prominent family), and that sooner or later I would come across the family photo album. John and the first Mary had only one child – John George. John George had four daughters, born in the late 1880s and 90s. At which point the trail went cold. Not one of the daughters had married, probably because they all came of age around the time of the First World War and there were not enough men left. One day Douglas Smith, a local antiquarian, mentioned that he had a box of glass plates from the nineteenth-century photographer's shop in the High Street. He looked through them and found one labelled 'John Doxford'. I had it developed and out of the darkness into which he had receded in 1899 emerged a stern, bewhiskered figure in a stiff collar. At which point I wrote an article in the *Daily Telegraph* recounting my search for the Doxfords and illustrating it with the recently acquired photograph. This prompted a letter from a woman in Kent who said that, when she was a child, she had lived next door to a woman, known to her as 'Doxy', who had given her several studio photographs of her Victorian forebears: a man, his wife and three of his four granddaughters. Looking at the picture which illustrated my article, she could see that the man was John Doxford. She was kind enough to send them to me, and the Doxford photos were given pride of place on the wall of our hallway. We left them there for the new owners when we eventually sold the house in 2014.

Although a huge divide separated the fortunate from the less fortunate, Sunderland at the turn of the century was relatively prosperous, boasting of being the largest shipbuilding town in the world. Tens of thousands of men once worked in the shipyards lining both sides of the River Wear which runs through a deep gorge in the city centre. As late as the 1950s near the town centre, it is said that you could hear the sound of hammers on rivets. Thousands more worked at Monkwearmouth colliery on the north side of the Wear. The miners and the shipyard workers lived in terraced cottages that stretched in rows down to the water. From these terraces, before dawn each morning, a great river of cloth-capped men would emerge, streaming towards the yards and the pithead. The distinctive Sunderland cottages are famous. Although some were tied, owned by the coal companies, there was a remarkably high rate of owner occupation (27 per cent in the 1890s, compared with just 3 per cent in Birmingham). Nowadays many remain owner-occupied and they make comfortable homes.

To the south of Sunderland were two former pit villages, Ryhope and Silksworth. The decision by the Boundary Commissioners in the 1970s to include them in the Sunderland South constituency turned it from a marginal to a safe Labour seat. The local pits had once been the property of the Lords Londonderry, a family of mine-owners famed for their ruthlessness. The sixth marquess is still remembered for ordering the eviction of striking miners from their pit cottages in Silksworth in the winter of 1891. Hundreds of miners, their families and their possessions were bundled into the streets and spent weeks in the freezing cold, camped in church halls and churchyards.

Most of the little towns along the Durham coast started life as pit villages. The pits came first and the people followed. Which is why, when the Tories closed the mines in the 1980s and early 1990s, the impact was so devastating. For generations it had been taken for granted that young men would follow their fathers down the local pit and when the pits went there was nothing left. My former colleague John Cummings, who represented Easington – one of Labour's safest seats – and who was elected to Parliament on the same night as I, was a fifth-generation miner, his family having worked in the pits continuously since the 1840s. John himself worked at Murton Colliery for nearly thirty years before becoming an MP. Seaham, a few miles south of Sunderland, was also a colliery town with a pit owned by the Londonderrys. Indeed, they owned much of the town. The harbour was built by the third marquess following a dispute with the port of Sunderland over tariffs. The Londonderrys were masters of all they surveyed. Their Seaham residence, a grand white mansion, now a five-star hotel, overlooked the town and the North Sea. Grand though it is, Seaham Hall was by no means their principal residence. That was twenty miles away at Wynyard Park, a vast palace set in thousands of acres, now owned by another great and ruthless businessman Sir John

Hall, erstwhile owner of Newcastle Football club, who made his fortune building the Gateshead Metro Centre.

In Victorian times the owners of the mines, shipyards and mills tended to live in close proximity to their employees and the best ones took a paternal interest in their welfare, building not only homes, but also schools and social facilities. Because they lived so close to those they employed there was a chance they could be influenced. Later, as they became richer and as the cities expanded, the employers sold up and moved away to grand country residences. Today, in this era of takeover and globalisation, the owners of an industrial plant in Sunderland or elsewhere may live on a different continent and decisions affecting the lives of thousands are taken by people who never have to look them in the eyes.

Relics of that apparently golden age when Sunderland hummed with life are all around us. The Victorians thought big. The public buildings they constructed exuded confidence. They were intended to last and, by and large, they did, until destroyed by either German bombers or the 1960s planners. In Sunderland, to the consternation of many, the planners demolished the old town hall, the Grand Hotel and the shopping arcade which ran between St Thomas Street and High Street West. A German bomb took out one end of the railway station and the planners destroyed the other. The magnificent Winter Gardens, attached to the back of the museum, were seriously damaged by a parachute bomb in 1941 and eventually demolished in the 1960s. The same bomb also took out the Victoria Hall, scene of a great tragedy at Christmas 1883 when, at the end of a children's concert, a stampede for presents resulted in 183 deaths. It was the Aberfan* of its day. The doors opened inwards and the little bodies piled up behind them. One small girl was found several streets away, carrying home the body of her dead sister. A statue of a weeping mother clutching her dead child stands, encased in glass, in Mowbray Park, a few yards from the scene of the tragedy.

The mansions of the newly rich were to be found mainly in the

---

*Aberfan was a south Wales pit village where, in October 1966, an avalanche of colliery waste engulfed the local primary school, killing 116 children and 28 adults.

south of the city. Many have now been demolished, but some remain. Langham Tower, a splendid Gothic mansion built for William Adamson, a trader in ships' stores, still stands intact on the corner of Mowbray and Ryhope Road. A later owner is said to have moved away after Ryhope Road was widened in the 1920s, leaving him with a grand entrance, but without a carriage drive up to it. The house was one of a number of Victorian mansions taken over by the polytechnic, an institution in the habit of scientifically stripping of original features any venerable old house that came into its possession. Mercifully, Langham Tower avoided this fate, perhaps because it contained the office of the Principal, who had the use of an apartment in the building. On the other side of the road is a much renovated nineteenth-century mansion, now divided into apartments, once the home of the Backhouses, a family of bankers. The Backhouse bank was one of several that merged to form Barclays. One of the early Backhouses was an astronomer and the house still has the turret from which he observed the stars and which, with the aid of a lever, can still be revolved. The Backhouses moved away in the 1930s leaving their park to the local authority along with a smaller mansion built for another Backhouse. The house, occupying a commanding position above the valley which forms the park, is undistinguished, but attached to it was a magnificent Victorian winter garden which, in keeping with the spirit of the age, was destroyed in the 1960s and replaced with a brutalist monstrosity. The house became the School of Art, though I never saw anything resembling art on display there. Behind Backhouse Park is the mansion built for Hiram Craven, a rope maker. To judge by the size of the Craven mansion, there was money to be made out of rope in the old days.

The Victorian terraces stretch into the city centre, many now shops or offices. Some are sadly vacant as the centre drifts westward. They would still make fine houses or apartments, if only a way could be devised of making the streets around them habitable again. Unfortunately, in Sunderland as elsewhere, the impact of post-war planning policy, with its focus on concreting over green fields, has been to hollow out city centres in Sunderland and elsewhere. Lately, thanks to the heroic efforts of the local social housing company, an effort has been made to rehabilitate some of the old terraces with a view to restoring life to the inner city, but despite considerable public invest-ment, there is as yet little sign of private sector interest.

When I first came to Sunderland, St Bede's Terrace and the two neigh-bouring streets were home to several people who had lived at the same address for more than eighty years. Mr Munro, at 10 Park Place East; Mr and Mrs Painter at number 13, a double-fronted house with lovely gardens – all clocked up more than eighty years apiece. Andy Bigham and his sister, Violet, who lived nearby, stayed more than ninety years in the same house. In 1918 they had moved in with an uncle who had been there since 1895. Much of the furniture was original. At Christmas, when my daughters were small, I used to take them to sing carols for the Bighams. Almost to the end of his life, Andy would put up the same home-made decorations he had been using for decades. Just inside the front door there was a cardboard model of a little church, inside which he had fitted a light bulb and stained-glass windows made from coloured sweet papers. If you stood in the hall and closed your eyes, all you could hear was the ticking of grandfather clocks.

Before the Second World War the poor of Sunderland were crammed into the East End, only a short walk, but a world away, from the mansions and villas of the rich. While the boys went into the mines and the shipyards, the girls went to be servants in the big houses. And not just in the mansions. A glance at the census returns shows that middle-class terraces like St Bede's averaged two servants apiece. Later, the working classes spilled out of the East End and into the great post-war housing estates – Grindon, Farringdon, Pennywell, Plains Farm, Thorney Close. This was the golden age of public housing. An era when, unlike today, Labour and the Tories competed to see which party could build more homes.

The result was streets and streets of neat, two- and three-bedroom brick houses with gardens front and back. While full employment prevailed, these were good places to live. Some remain so to this day. Come the Thatcher decade, however, and the return of mass unem-ployment, civilised life in some areas broke down. A generation of young people grew up who had no prospect of work and many began to behave badly. 'A few years ago,' a policeman remarked to me not

long after I was first elected, 'most of these youths would have followed their fathers into the shipyards and the mines where they
would mix with adults and adjust their behaviour accordingly. Now
they loiter at the schools gates setting a bad example to those who
come afterwards. School is the last institution with which they will
have contact, unless they fall foul of the criminal justice system,
which all too many of them will.' The collapse of work led to an epi-
demic of anti-social behaviour. In some areas civilised life broke down
to such an extent that entire neighbourhoods had to be abandoned.
In the early years, my weekly surgeries were a parade of desperate
people begging to be evacuated from the worst-hit areas. The tragedy
was that one usually ended up evacuating the victims rather than the
villains, with the result that the situation continued to deteriorate.

Pennywell, a vast post-war housing estate on the western edge of
the city, was one of the worst affected. The contrast was striking.
Within a few streets one could go from neat houses with well-kept
gardens to utter devastation. And once the rot set in it spread with
terrifying speed. A large part of the Pennywell estate, consisting of
otherwise habitable houses, was abandoned and eventually demolished. For years entire streets of derelict and often burned-out houses
stood as a grim testament to the scale of the social collapse that was
under way. Trapped in the middle, desperately trying to keep up
appearances, were decent, law-abiding citizens who had made the
mistake of buying their council houses and whom the local authority
therefore had no obligation to rehouse. These were often people on
small occupational pensions who had used redundancy money to buy
their homes, calculating that they would never have to pay rent again.
Often they had added a porch or an extension. Their homes were
their only asset and now they were worthless. It was heartbreaking. I
was once called upon to rescue an elderly man who had bought his
council house and was trapped amid the dereliction. Five houses on
either side and all ten along the back were boarded and abandoned.
Some had been firebombed. Over his greenhouse he had stretched a
net to catch incoming missiles. When his wife had died the previous
year, the vehicles carrying the funeral party had come under attack
from stone-throwing youths.

For years the centre of Pennywell was dominated by a derelict shopping centre. By the end only one little business, a Chinese chippie, remained. The rest had fled. Above the shops there had been four storeys of flats; these too were abandoned. We once had a visit from the Secretary of State for Employment, Gillian Shephard, a decent woman who represented a leafy part of Norfolk and was perhaps unacquainted with the harsh realities of life in constituencies such as mine. I took her on a brief diversion through Pennywell and pointed out the derelict shopping centre. 'Ooh look,' she said, 'there's someone on the roof.' We looked up and, sure enough, there was a juvenile delinquent lobbing tiles into neighbouring gardens.

Where were the police while all this was going on? All too often they were nowhere to be seen. Until the 1970s and 80s many police officers lived among the communities they served. Every estate had a handful of police houses. Later, a series of large pay rises, combined with lucrative overtime during the miners' strike, enabled most of them to move to the better part of town where they gradually lost contact with the communities they served. I was once visited by a police inspector's wife who remarked that there were thirteen officers living in the short street in which she lived. By contrast, I doubt whether, by 1990, there were any police officers still living on the vast public housing estates that surrounded Sunderland. If the police visited at all, it was in large raiding parties where they glared at the locals from transit vans with reinforced windscreens, protected by wire mesh. Gradually they retreated into fortified police stations, emerging only in vehicles with flashing lights and bristling with the latest technology.

Under the leadership of Sir Stanley Bailey, a copper of the old school, many of the most senior officers in Northumbria retreated into the force headquarters at Ponteland, a leafy village north of Newcastle. Prising them out proved difficult. If you visited Ponteland your coat was liable to be taken by a chief superintendent and, grateful though you might be, you couldn't help wondering whether he might be better employed elsewhere. I was once interviewed by a television crew who had just come from the airport where they had been filming the arrival of a minor royal. The cameraman remarked that he had counted fourteen carloads of Northumbria Police top brass on hand to greet the visitor. I later made inquiries. He had counted correctly.

It was not until John Stevens, later the Metropolitan Commissioner, became chief constable that the culture of policing began to change, but it was a long, slow process. The police helicopter was forever hovering over the more difficult parts of Sunderland, but with a handful of exceptions, getting the policemen on to bicycles proved nigh-on impossible.

In the midst of the mayhem there were rays of light. The Pennywell Youth Centre was one. In the early 1990s some enlightened person worked out that for the cost of locking up one delinquent youth for a year, it would be possible to provide constructive activity for several hundred youngsters during school holidays. A scheme called 'Breakout' was devised, initially run to a large extent by parents and local citizens, which provided a range of activities – football, bicycle repair, vegetable growing, trips to the seaside and further afield – for teenagers who might otherwise be roaming the streets getting into trouble. Later, the centre benefited from an injection of government regeneration funding and built itself a smart new headquarters in the centre of the estate, run by full-time youth workers. Over the following decade Pennywell was transformed. The derelict shopping centre was demolished and replaced with sheltered housing. A new shopping centre, incorporating crèche facilities and a doctor's surgery (until then no doctor had ever been based on the estate) was built nearby. The housing association demolished the acres of derelict properties and began building new, high-quality homes. A smart new academy replaced the failing comprehensive school in the centre of the estate and, above all, the rule of law was restored by police officers based there.

Today Pennywell, though still not without its problems, is light years away from where it was. Crime and antisocial behaviour have reduced dramatically. The dereliction has gone (much of it replaced by large open spaces) and school exam results are improving, albeit from a low base. There are clouds on the horizon, however. The regeneration money that helped to fund the youth centre long ago ran out and, with the recession, grants from other sources also dried up. At the time of my retirement the saintly man who ran the youth centre was tearing his hair out with frustration as the hard work of years was threatened by lack of funding. No longer able to afford to employ a cleaner, he was coming in early to sweep the floor and clean the toilets. Today, with the disappearance of local authority and other funding, the centre is a shadow of what it once was. The recent award of a lottery grant has enabled it to resume some of its activities, but unless a stable source of funding can be found, the long-term prospects are bleak, as they are for all future youth provision. Those who do not learn from history are destined to repeat it. If we are not careful, the whole wretched cycle of neglect, endemic criminality, dereliction and ruined lives could begin again.

By the early 1990s the worst affected areas were into second-generation unemployment. Young people were growing up who would not have been capable of work even if, by some miracle, it became available the next morning. Although not often remarked upon, benefit culture is one of Margaret Thatcher's most enduring legacies. Low wages – a pound an hour was not uncommon as late as the mid-1990s – eroded the gap between the world of work and the world of benefit, to the point where work simply didn't pay. Also, the world of poorly paid, part-time work was notoriously insecure and, once off benefit, it was often difficult to get back on, with the result that you risked going into debt. Asking someone to give up benefit in return for work that might last only a few weeks was inviting them to take a big risk. A bigger risk than most middle-class people would dare take. I came across a number of people who had done exactly what was asked of them – come off benefit, taken a job which disappeared after a few weeks and who, as a result, ended up deeply in debt. The logical option, therefore, was to remain on benefit and perhaps earn a few quid doing odd jobs on the side. The result was an underclass trapped in a vast benefit culture from which they had little hope of escape. The problem was compounded in the late 1980s, as unemployment soared, when the government instructed local benefit offices to sign claimants on as disabled rather than jobless in an unsuccessful effort to prevent the number of unemployed passing three million. I didn't believe this at first, until I met one of the civil servants involved, who confirmed that it was so. A detail to bear in mind when one hears Conservative MPs, egged on by their friends in the tabloid media, demanding action on 'welfare scroungers'.

The Thatcher decade spawned a vast yob culture. There was more work available for women than for men and as a result, women not only kept home, but were often breadwinners as well. The collapse of work for the unskilled or semi-skilled male led to the rise of a new phenomenon – the useless male: no use as a provider; not much use around the house. Teenage pregnancies soared. Many of the births were to young women incapable of managing their own lives, let alone bringing up a child. They often ended up being housed in the sink estates, only adding to the social breakdown. Before long there were areas where yob culture was the norm. A head teacher in one of the worst affected areas in my constituency (83 per cent of the children at her school qualified for free meals and half were classified as special needs) told me that some children arrived barely able to speak, unable to hold a knife and fork never having sat at a table to eat a meal. It was not just poverty that was the problem, but a collapse of the human spirit. Those who talk about 'benefit culture' are not wrong, though they are sometimes in denial about what caused it.

In fairness, Margaret Thatcher and her ideology are not solely to blame for the mayhem that coincided with her tenure. The disappearance of so much manufacturing industry afflicted the entire developed world. The invention of wondrous new technology has meant that industry requires less human input to make the wheels turn and corporations are increasingly ruthless about disposing of those who are surplus to requirements. Globalisation has inevitably meant that much of the West's industrial capacity has disappeared in the general direction of eastern China. This process was under way before Mrs Thatcher came to power and it continued long after she left office. The thousand or more textile workers in my constituency who in 1997 were still producing suits, shirts and underwear for Marks & Spencer (which used to pride itself on selling British-made goods) are long gone. One by one Marks & Spencer's competitors started buying their clothing from countries where wages were a fraction of those in Britain and in the end they had no choice but to follow. A race to the bottom has begun and it is by no means over.

The Tories can also reasonably point out that it was on their watch that in Sunderland the Japanese automobile manufacturer Nissan opened one of the most successful motor manufacturing plants in the world. True, though but for the efforts of the city's

Labour council the company could easily have chosen a different location. The success of Nissan, by the way, gives the lie to the old myth that the indolence of the British worker was responsible for the decline of British manufacturing. Hard evidence that, given good management, a willingness to invest and responsible trade unionism, the British worker is as good as any.

What can be said about the Thatcher decade is that it exacerbated a process that was already under way and that she and many of her supporters were oblivious to the social consequences. Indeed, as one of her henchmen is alleged to have remarked, unemployment was 'a price worth paying'. Margaret Thatcher was in many ways a courageous politician. On some important issues (trade union reform, for example) she was right, but she was also lucky. If just one more British warship had been hit by an Exocet missile, the outcome of the Falklands war could have been very different. Her government, more than any other, had the benefit of North Sea oil (and squandered much of the proceeds on tax cuts for the already prosperous and a hugely increased bill for unemployment). She was blessed with an Opposition split down the middle and presided over an era in which a culture of greed was positively encouraged (to this day the Tory Party is to a large extent funded by Mrs Thatcher's billionaires). The 1980s was the era in which the chief executives of FTSE 100 companies began stuffing their wallets and they have been at it ever since. The sale of public assets at knockdown prices enabled her to purchase the undying loyalty of the meaner elements of Middle England and thereby to mobilise the fortunate against the less fortunate with unprecedented ruthlessness. The bills for the Thatcher decade are still coming in. The so-called Big Bang of 1986, which allowed American banks with their culture of bonuses and dodgy lending practices to set up in the City, sowed the seeds of the 2008 banking crisis. The sale of council houses in areas of shortage, especially in London and the south-east, sowed the seeds of a housing crisis with which we are still grappling. The most devastating critique of the Thatcher decade is to be found, not in the writings of her political opponents, but in a book by a former member of her Cabinet, the late Sir Ian Gilmour, a Tory gent of the old school. Sir Ian wrote:

> Many people did well out of Thatcherism, and in consequence still support it ... Because of the coarsening of society and the bombast of Thatcherite propaganda, the beneficiaries of Thatcherism believe that some benign process was at work. They did not realise – and apparently still do not – that what happened was a large redistribution of wealth from the poor to the rich.*

Nowhere was the impact greater than in Sunderland. The New Labour leadership, to be fair, understood what the problem was and, to a large extent, grasped the nettle. It is fashionable in some quarters (not only on the right) to allege that the thirteen years of Labour government were largely wasted. This is nonsense. There was a huge effort, probably the greatest that will ever be made in my lifetime, to stem and then to reverse the social breakdown that had engulfed some less prosperous areas of the country. One of Gordon Brown's first acts as Chancellor was to impose a £5 billion windfall tax on what were widely considered to be the excessive profits of the privatised utilities. The proceeds were used mainly to fund a programme of job training for the young long-term unemployed and, by and large, it worked, helped no doubt by the fact that the economy was on an upturn. A national minimum wage and tax credits were used to open up a gap between the world of work and the world of benefit. After a slow start, substantial sums were invested in other social programmes. Sure Start was set up to help young mothers cope with bringing up children and getting them into education and work. Huge resources were invested in primary and secondary education. Teachers' salaries were significantly increased. Most of the schools in the poorer parts of my constituency were entirely rebuilt with state-of-the-art facilities and dynamic new head teachers with results that were often impressive. To take but one example: in the mid-1990s less than 10 per cent of children leaving Sandhill View, a 1960s secondary school, achieved the so-called bog-standard five A to Cs at GCSE. *Less than 10 per cent.* Today, the school has been entirely rebuilt. Its library and sports facilities are open to the entire local population, and getting on for 80 per cent of pupils, from exactly the same catchment

---

Dancing with Dogma (Simon and Schuster, 1992), p. 278.

area, now leave with five A to Cs. If that ain't a change for the better, I don't know what is.

I am conscious on rereading this chapter, focussing as it does on much that went wrong in the 1980s, that the casual reader might conclude that Sunderland was not a good place to live. On the contrary, my family and I lived there happily for twenty-five years. We made many friends. Sunderland people are, for the most part, warm, generous and resilient, qualities much remarked upon by visitors. They are also fiercely loyal to their city and in particular (despite many disappointments) to their football team. Although a work in progress, the transformation that has occurred since the dark days of the Thatcher decade is remarkable. A magnificent stadium now occupies the site of the old Wearmouth pit. The dereliction along the river has been replaced by new businesses and a fine new university campus with state-of-the-art facilities. With help from the Heritage Lottery Fund the city's historic parks and other landmarks have been restored to their former glory. One of my favourite walks, especially when entertaining visitors from elsewhere, was to go out of my front gate, through Mowbray Park, along the cobbled Victorian streets around Sunniside, across the bridge and down to the river; past the university and the marina to the sea front and along the two miles of sandy beach to Whitburn, a Georgian village, just over the frontier in North Tyneside. There we would treat ourselves to a cup of tea and a cake in the local cafe before catching the bus back to the city centre. A five-mile walk through four entirely different landscapes and all without having to get in the car.

In a park near the centre of my constituency there is a statue of John Candlish, one of my Victorian parliamentary predecessors, paid for by public subscription. Happily, the days when people built statues of their MPs are long gone and I do not regret their passing. Quite apart from which my paltry achievements pale when compared with those of Candlish, a local self-made businessman who employed 600 people in his bottle-making factories and who was renowned for the care he took of his employees, building social housing, a school and a library, services that these days are, rightly, expected of the state. I can only claim to have been a small cog in a very big wheel. What I can say, however, hand on heart, is that during the thirteen years of Labour government the lives of many of my poorest constituents improved immeasurably for the better. And I do not believe that such changes were confined to Sunderland. Whether or not they will be sustained, given the determination of New Labour's successors to denigrate and dismantle much of what was achieved, I cannot say. But for all the disappointments of the New Labour era – and there were many – I am proud to have played a small part in a government that, when the chips were down, did its best to protect the less fortunate from the tyranny of the fortunate.

CHAPTER THIRTEEN

Loony MP Backs Bomb Gang*

My friend Peter Chippindale was the first person to alert me to the possibility that there was something wrong with the conviction of six men for the Birmingham pub bombings, at that time the biggest murder in British history. He also remarked that he thought the wrong people had been convicted of the Guildford and Woolwich pub bombings. Chippindale, a journalist on the *Guardian*, had reached that conclusion mainly through his attendance at the trial of the men who later became known as the Birmingham Six, and the appeal of the three men and one woman who would become known as the Guildford Four – and from talking to relatives of the convicted. That was in 1975, the year after the bombings. My interest was aroused from that time onwards, but it was some years before I was able to do much about it.

Not long after the Birmingham Six had been put away, two Northern Irish Catholic priests, Father Denis Faul and Father Raymond Murray, published a pamphlet setting out for the first time the defendants' version of events, but it attracted little attention outside the Irish community. Later Paddy Hill, the most vociferous of the six, wrote me a long letter describing what had happened to him and his friends in police custody and forcefully asserting their innocence. I was in no position to verify his claims, but it was a story that deserved to be told and I arranged for Hill's letter to be published in the form of an article in *Tribune*. Again, it attracted little attention.

---

*Front page headline in the *Sun*, 29 January 1988.

From the outset it was clear that any serious investigation would require resources I didn't have, so I attempted to interest Ray Fitzwalter, editor of ITV's premier documentary series, *World in Action*, to take a look at the case. Initially, I was unsuccessful. In the mid-1980s Carmen Callil at Chatto and Windus agreed to commission a book on the case but the advance was modest and would not begin to finance the necessary research, so I again approached Fitzwalter and this time he agreed to take me on. By now I had left *Tribune*, but there was a lot going on in my life. In June 1985 I had been selected as the Labour candidate for Sunderland South, which, although a safe seat, was one that required a lot of nursing. My second novel was published and I had started work on a third. The pub bombings investigation involved a great deal of travelling, searching out witnesses including police officers long since retired and former IRA men, many of whom were not in the least keen to be interviewed. On top of which I was hoping to marry someone on the other side of the world. The logistics were complicated.

Ian McBride, a *World in Action* producer, and Charles Tremayne, a researcher, were assigned to work with me.* There were two main planks of the case against the men who came to be known as the Birmingham Six. First, uncorroborated confessions signed by four of them and repudiated as soon as they left police custody. Second, forensic tests that were said to have proved positive against two of the men. We began by tracking down serving or retired police officers who had been involved in the case to see if any of them would tell a different story from the one they had told at the time. We started in Lancashire, where five of the men had been held after their arrest at the Heysham ferry terminal, on their way to Belfast a few hours after the bombings. We reasoned that since no allegations of violence had been made against Lancashire Police they would be more likely to talk to us. Initially, however, we made little progress. Although one or two of the former Lancashire officers hinted that everything was not quite as it seemed, none was willing to go on record.

In Birmingham we searched for anyone who had been in Queens

---

*For a detailed account see my book *Error of Judgement: The Truth About the Birmingham Bombings* (Chatto and Windus, 1986; Poolbeg, 1997).

Road police station during the two nights and days that the men had been held there. It was here that three of the four confessions had been extracted amid accusations of threats and violence, including mock executions and the use of dogs and shotguns in the cells. Here, too, we got nowhere. At this point we turned our attention to the other main plank of the case against the six men – the forensic evidence.

The key forensic witness was Dr Frank Skuse, who had been called to Morecambe police station to test the five men arrested at Heysham for traces of explosive. Dr Skuse had relied on a simple formula known as the Griess test which involved swabbing the suspects' hands with ether. Greiss was only to be a screening test and a positive result was not conclusive. If he got a positive, Skuse was supposed to take the sample back to his laboratory and subject it to tests more sensitive than Greiss. Only then could he be certain that a suspect had recently handled explosives. Skuse, however, did not do this. Having obtained a positive result from the hands of two of the suspects, Billy Power and Paddy Hill, and a faint positive for nitrate and ammonium from the hands of Johnny Walker, he informed the waiting police officers that he had a result. From that moment onwards the fate of the suspects was sealed.

Almost from the outset it had been asserted that there was a range of innocent substances (anything containing nitrocellulose) that could produce a positive Greiss test. In particular anything containing varnish or polish. Even packs of playing cards used to be coated with nitrocellulose and several of the men had been playing cards on that fateful train journey from Birmingham to Heysham. At the trial in the summer of 1975, the defence employed a former Home Office Chief Inspector of Explosives, Dr Hugh Black, to rebut the evidence of Dr Skuse, who had told the court that, on the basis of his positive Griess tests, he was '99 per cent certain' that two of the men had recently handled explosives. Dr Black, however, was adamant that a positive Greiss test was no basis for asserting that the accused had handled explosives. The problem was that he had not done the experiments necessary to support his evidence. He had apparently offered to, but had been told by defence barristers that it would not be necessary since the court would be bound to take seriously a scientist of his distinction. Regrettably, this was not the case. Dr Skuse, whatever his faults, was a good witness and his confident assertion that a positive Greiss test was evidence of guilt was found credible by the court. In his summing up the judge, Lord Bridge, who throughout the trial made no attempt to conceal his views from the jury, destroyed the unfortunate Dr Black, who would in due course, though not before many years had passed, be vindicated.

At *World in Action* we decided to test the scientific evidence. Two independent forensic scientists were commissioned to carry out, independently, Greiss tests on household substances with which the men might reasonably have come into contact. Sure enough, they quickly established that a range of innocuous substances would give a positive Greiss test. Among them were furniture varnish, lacquer, a cigarette packet, a picture postcard and, most interesting of all, packs of old playing cards. Ian McBride, the *World in Action* producer, was then asked to shuffle the cards and his hands, too, tested positive. Or as Dr Skuse might have said, there was a 99 per cent chance that McBride had recently handled explosives. With that, the evidence of Dr Skuse collapsed. In October 1985 *World in Action* broadcast the first of four documentaries and immediately there were calls for the case to be reopened. Two former Home Secretaries, Roy Jenkins and Merlyn Rees, were among those who spoke up. Three days after the first programme was broadcast Dr Skuse, at the grand old age of fifty, took early retirement from the Home Office Forensic Science Service. It was to be another fourteen months before MPs managed to prise out of the Home Office an admission that Dr Skuse had been retired on the grounds of 'limited efficiency' and, even then, ministers continued to deny that his limited efficiency compromised his testimony in the Birmingham bombings case.

At this point I wrote a letter to the *Birmingham Post*, saying that there were many people in Birmingham who knew what had happened to the men in Queens Road police station on the nights of 22 and 23 November 1974. Until then, I wrote, they might have kept quiet because they believed that, however the confessions had been obtained, the forensic evidence was conclusive. The forensic evidence had now collapsed and this was the moment to come forward. Almost immediately I was contacted by a retired police officer, Tom Clarke.

Mr Clarke, a policeman for twenty-three years, had been on duty at Queens Road on both nights that five of the six convicted men had been detained there. He had been one of the officers in charge of the cell block and he had seen and heard a great deal of what went on there and he was willing to talk. At which point we made a further documentary: 'A Surprise Witness'. It was broadcast on 1 December 1986, with the result that pressure for the case to be reopened intensified.

Meanwhile I was pursuing a third line of inquiry, one in which my Granada TV colleagues were not immediately interested. From the outset it had seemed to me that you could go on knocking down the case against the six men until the cows came home, but that would not prove that they were innocent, only that the case against them was weak. The only way to prove innocence was to track down the people who were genuinely responsible and persuade them to own up in sufficient detail that it was not possible to go on pretending that the right people had been convicted.

I began with a visit to Sinn Féin leader Gerry Adams in Belfast in July 1985. I put it to him that the time had come to resolve this case. I did not expect him to deliver up to me the real bombers; indeed, that would only lead to charges that I was a stooge of the IRA. What I wanted was for him to indicate that they had no objection to my talking to certain individuals whose names I would put to them. In particular, I wanted to talk to Michael Murray, a former Birmingham resident who was widely rumoured to have been involved in the bombings. Murray was a former workmate of Johnny Walker and Richard McIlkenny. He had been arrested a few days after the bombings and placed on trial alongside the other six. His presence in the dock was deeply damaging to the other defendants. He clearly knew several of them. He made no secret of his IRA membership and, like a true IRA man, refused to recognise a British court and sat in silence throughout the trial. Indeed, by the end, it became apparent that the judge, Lord Bridge, had developed a sneaking regard for Murray. 'You may think,' he told the jury, 'that Murray's conduct in this trial has shown a certain measure of dignity which is totally absent from the conduct of some of his co-defendants. You may find difficulty in withholding a certain grudging measure of respect.' Richly ironic, in view of the fact that Murray was the only person present in court who had anything to do with the bombings. He subsequently served twelve years in a British jail, having been convicted at an earlier trial of other offences. By the time I went looking for him, he was living in Dublin.

Murray was not at all keen to meet me, but agreed to do so after the intervention of intermediaries. We met one Saturday morning in July 1985 at a flat on a housing estate close to the centre of Dublin. There was a fifteen-minute delay while the occupant was turfed out of bed and told to make himself scarce. The basis of the interview was that I would not disclose his identity (he has since died, so I am free to do so now) and that, when we came to a question he did not wish to answer, he would say so, but would not mislead me. We had two further meetings, in November 1985 and April 1986. At our second meeting he said, 'I don't like you very much, Mr Mullin. I think you're only doing this for yourself. You're a member of the British Labour Party, the Establishment as far as I'm concerned.' The first interview lasted three hours. Despite his reluctance, he provided a detailed account of what happened on the night of the bombings. Two men had planted both bombs in both pubs. The targets had not been the pubs but the buildings they were part of – one of the pubs was in the Rotunda, a local landmark, and the other was below the New Street office of the Inland Revenue. At our first meeting he had refused to discuss his own role, but on the second occasion he was frank. He was one of two men who made the bombs and it was he who made the botched warning phone call.

I soon realised that it would not be enough to say that I had met the man who made the bombs. The police had never claimed to have caught the organisers; indeed, they never offered any explanation as to where the bombs came from. They did, however, claim to have caught the men who planted the bombs. In fact six is far too many. Any more would be a serious embarrassment. It followed, therefore, that if I was to convince anyone that the men inside were innocent, I would have to find one or both of the planters and persuade them to describe what they had done in such detail that it would be impossible to go on pretending the right people were in prison. I began with some basic detective work of the sort one might have commended to the West Midlands Police had they been interested in this line of inquiry. I drew up a list of all those known to have been involved in planting bombs in and around Birmingham – there had been about fifty explosions, culminating in the pub bombings in November 1974. Tracking them down wasn't difficult, since many had been convicted and served long terms in prison. One by one I traced and interviewed them. Most co-operated to a greater or lesser extent. I started with those in prison at the time of the pub bombings and who, therefore, could not have been involved. They didn't necessarily know the identity of the pub bombers, but they did know who had been left outside and any member of the Birmingham IRA still at liberty on the night of 21 November 1974 was a potential suspect. On one point they agreed: none of the six convicted men had been members of the IRA.

I then began to track down, one by one, those still at liberty on the night of the pub bombings, knowing that sooner or later I would come to the bombers. Where possible, I gave no notice of my appearance on their doorstep so it could not later be alleged that I had been misled. I travelled to some fairly dark places: You are several floors up in a bleak Dublin council estate. All you can see around you is concrete. You ring the doorbell and say, 'Hello, I've come to talk about your role in the Birmingham bombings.' You cannot always be sure of the reception you will receive.

There were some poignant moments. In Birmingham I found the elderly father of a man who had not been seen since shortly after the bombings. He wouldn't give me contact details for his son, but did agree to pass on a letter. Then one day, out of the blue, came a phone call from the suspect's wife. 'My husband doesn't know I am calling you,' she said. We arranged to meet. The woman was distressed. 'For eleven years,' she said, 'I have been living with the possibility that my husband is one of the Birmingham bombers. All I know is that we had to leave England very suddenly and that he can never go back. I want you to find out for me.' We agreed that I would call unannounced later that evening. 'I will let you in and then it's up to you.' I did as she suggested. The man agreed to talk and I was later able to cross-check his version of events with others. He was not one of the pub bombers, but one of three men who planted the bomb which did not explode at an office block at Hagley Road on the same night. Having identified and eliminated the three men who planted the Hagley Road bomb, the field narrowed.

Gradually I reduced the list of suspects to a handful and when I had been given the same name from three separate and widely dispersed sources, I moved in on him. The man I went to see lived on a bleak public housing estate. At the time of our meeting he was aged around thirty and would, therefore, have been in his late teens in 1974. He had joined the IRA in the summer of 1973 and remained a member throughout the entire West Midlands campaign. He had been involved in seven or eight bombings, including one of the two Conservative clubs bombed shortly before the city-centre pubs. He began by giving me a sanitised version of his career. As we approached the night of 21 November 1974, his voice began to tremble and at times almost faded. At first, he did not tell the truth, saying he had been warned to stay at home that night because something big was going to happen. Once we were past 21 November his voice grew stronger. When he had finished I said quietly, 'I think you were in the pubs.'

There was a long silence. We were sitting on the floor. He stared straight ahead, smoking. Then it all came out. This is his story:

> On the evening of the bombings a person came to see me and said, 'You're needed for an operation.' I went with him to a house. We went by car. The bombs were in the parlour, behind the sofa. One was in a duffle bag and the other was in a small brown luggage case. I was given the duffle bag and a pistol. I put the gun in my coat pocket. The other man carried the case.
>
> We walked into town. It was a good mile. The other fellow told me the targets about ten minutes before we arrived. He said, 'The one in the Tavern is for the tax office and the one in the Mulberry Bush is for the Rotunda.' He added, 'There'll be plenty of warning.' Believe it or not, I accepted it. I didn't want a stigma of cowardice attached to me. He kept saying, 'Don't worry, those people will be well out of there.' I kept on about it and he repeated there would be substantial warning.
>
> We approached down Digbeth. Just before we arrived we stopped in the entrance to a row of shops. The other guy opened the case and was fiddling with something. Then he reached inside

> my duffle bag. That's when the bombs were primed. We crossed the road without using the underpass, because the police were sometimes down there. There was hardly any traffic.
>
> We did the Tavern first. Up New Street, past the Mulberry Bush. The other fellow went to the bar and ordered two drinks. I took both bags and found a seat. I was shitting myself. The other person came back with the drinks. We took a sip and then got up leaving the duffle bag under a seat.

I drew a crude diagram in my notebook and asked him to mark the spot where the bomb had been left. Without hesitation he drew a seat which, he said, ran along the wall abutting New Street to the right of the stairs. In front of that he drew a table at which he had sat. The bomb, he said was left under the seat near the table. Only two categories of people could have indicated the site of the bomb with such accuracy. Either someone with access to the trial transcript containing the evidence of the forensic scientist, Donald Lidstone, or someone who was present when the bomb was planted.

At the Mulberry Bush the procedure was the same. The other man was carrying the case: 'This time I ordered the drinks. The other person found a table at the back. The bomb was left by a telephone.'

Again, I drew a rough sketch of the pub and asked him to mark the site of the bomb. Again, without hesitation, he marked a spot at the rear. For good measure he also drew in the rear exit, which I had omitted. He continued:

> We went outside. The other fellow took the gun off me. He told me to go home and keep my head down. Nobody would be hurt. I last saw him walking off down Digbeth. I don't know whether it was his intention to kill people. If they'd have said, 'We're going to kill people,' there is no way I would have gone. They just needed a carrier and I was available. I am not blaming anyone or making excuses. What's done is done.
>
> I walked home. Took about an hour. Didn't hear the bang. Then all those people got killed. Jesus, I can't make excuses …

We talked for nearly four hours. I pressed him repeatedly for the name of the other man. He refused. He did, however, reveal from where the bombs had been collected. It was the same house in

Bordesley Green from which a week earlier James McDade, an IRA man who had blown himself up while trying to bomb the Coventry telephone exchange, had collected the bomb that killed him. As I left he said, 'No offence, Mr Mullin, but I don't ever want to see you again.' But, as we shall see, we were destined to meet again.

Subsequently, I tracked down and interviewed the owner of the house in Bordesley Green, who was almost certainly the other bomber. He owned up to his involvement from the beginning in the IRA's West Midlands campaign, but flatly denied involvement in the pub bombings. Instead he stuck doggedly to the remarkable view that the bombings may have been the work of British agents bent on discrediting the IRA – something which even the IRA has never alleged. Apparently this was the line he and other IRA men who fled Birmingham in the months after the pub bombings had spun to the organisation's internal inquiry into what had happened. I later interviewed an IRA veteran who had sat on the inquiry. He said

> A lot of lies were told. The people who had come out of England all said it wasn't them. At the time I firmly believed them. Eighteen months later I was sitting in the house of one of the people who had been active in Birmingham. People had had a few drinks and they started talking. It became clear that we [the IRA] had done it. A second inquiry was held. It concluded that we had been lied to and that the people who had done it were walking around free.

When *Error of Judgement* was published in the summer of 1986, it caused only a mild flurry. 'A book that could put him in prison ... Mr Mullin ... is either a liar or a hypocrite,' shouted the *Sunday Express*. An interview arranged with Radio Four's *Today* programme was cancelled at the last moment. At the time I was told I had been displaced by a more urgent story about the South African athlete Zola Budd. Later, however, I heard that I was considered too insubstantial a person (I had yet to be elected to Parliament) to be permitted to claim that I had traced and interviewed the real bombers. Later, after protests, the producers changed their minds and a brief interview was broadcast. The reaction of the media in Birmingham was interesting. On the local ITV channel, Central TV, the story led the news bulletins, but from the BBC's *Midlands Today* silence. 'We haven't got space to review all new books published,' sniffed a woman on the news desk when I rang to inquire what their plans were. A BBC insider later told me that the problem was that the local management were too well in with the police. Librarians at Birmingham public library initially declined to stock *Error of Judgement*, but changed their minds after protests. In a prominent Birmingham bookshop I found a handful of copies on a shelf labelled 'Irish interest', as though the issue was of no interest to citizens of Birmingham. There were honourable exceptions – a local commercial radio channel, BRMB, and Ed Doolan on BBC West Midlands radio. Both showed an interest from the start. Gerry Hunt, an assiduous reporter on the *Birmingham Post*, was eventually allowed by his masters to write up the story, but only on condition he did it in his own time. Much of Birmingham, it seems, was in denial. As for publishers, all the main British publishing houses declined the paperback version of *Error of Judgement*. In the end, it went to Poolbeg, a tiny but energetic Northern Irish imprint, where it ran to four editions, selling over 60,000 copies.

From the Home Office, too, there was silence. Sir John Farr, a Tory MP who took an interest in the case, attempted to arrange a meeting with a minister for us both, but at the last minute he received a message from the minister's office: 'Come alone. Don't bring Mullin.' In the early hours of one morning in July 1986 a group of Labour MPs organised a debate on the case. I sat in a little gallery at the rear of the chamber. When the debate ended, the minister David Mellor, approached and invited me to come and see him. Later, he asked Assistant Chief Constable Tom Meffen of the West Midlands Police to question me. Mr Meffen was not keen. His opening words were, 'We've been dragged here by the scruff of the neck by the Home Office.' From the beginning I made clear that I was not willing to disclose my sources, but I was prepared to be cross-examined to enable the authorities to test (a) whether I was telling the truth and (b) whether I was the victim of an IRA deception. Mr Meffen was affable, but sceptical. I have no idea what conclusion he reached since the Home Office has to this day stoutly refused to publish his report, but if I were asked to guess, he probably concluded that, okay, I may have tracked down one or two others who had been involved in the bombings, but they were additional to, and not replacements for, those who had already been convicted. The problem with this line of argument is that, although it is true that the police never claimed to have caught all those responsible, they did claim to have caught the planters. In due course, there would be several more police inquiries, one of which turned out to be a great deal more rigorous than the others.

By now pressure to reopen the case was irresistible. On 20 January 1987 the Home Secretary, Douglas Hurd, announced that he was referring the case to the Court of Appeal. The appeal opened, in a blaze of publicity, at the Old Bailey the following November. The Lord Chief Justice, Lord Lane, presided. A brilliant barrister, Igor Judge (who would later become Lord Chief Justice) led for the Crown. Michael Mansfield and Lord Gifford represented the appellants. Distinguished observers – among them the Irish Cardinal, the Irish ambassador, a former Irish foreign minister and that veteran of earlier miscarriage of justice campaigns, Ludovic Kennedy – came from far and wide. The jury box was set aside to accommodate them. I was there, too. My claim to have traced and interviewed several of those who had carried out the bombings was hearsay and, therefore, of no relevance to the appeal (although copies of the book could be glimpsed around the court nestling discreetly among the mountains of paperwork). Instead the appeal focussed on the new forensic evidence and the validity of the confessions. By now another witness, a former police officer, had come forward to testify to the abuses she had witnessed while the men were being interrogated. In addition, there was evidence from the cleaner who claimed to have found blood on one of the cell walls at Morecambe, and from solicitors who had originally acted for the men who claimed to have seen their injuries. The judges sat stony-faced throughout. Nothing in their demeanour indicated the slightest evidence of open minds and no one was surprised when, at the end, they unanimously dismissed the appeal, Lord Lane adding gratuitously, 'The longer this hearing has gone on the more convinced this court has become that the verdict of the jury was correct.' Words he would come to regret.

'A black day for British justice,' I remarked in a statement immediately after the verdict, which brought down the wrath of the *Sun* upon my head. 'Loony MP Backs Bomb Gang' screamed its front-page headline the next day. An editorial on an inside page said, 'If the *Sun* had its way, we would have been tempted to string 'em up years ago.'

I was on the receiving end of considerable hate mail which continued to arrive long after the Six had been exonerated and released. Much of it bore West Midlands postmarks. For years to come, one individual would send me a seaside postcard addressed simply to 'Chris Mullin, IRA, Sunderland', which always found its way to me. Most of my hate mail was anonymous and consisted of foul abuse, but every so often there was a gem. My favourite was the following from Mr R. C. Sindle of Glamorgan, South Wales:

> Watching you on *Newsnight* ... you certainly came across as a smug, sanctimonious git, if ever I saw one. Lord Lane has done more for his country than all the muck-raking scum of the Labour Party put together. And, if the name of Mullins [sic] implies what I think it does, then why are you not peddling your crusade for human rights in Ireland? God almighty! What country needs it more?
>
> Mind you Mullins, they are probably silly questions, aren't they? Crusaders among the bigots of Ireland, are just as likely to get the shit shot out of them, and we couldn't have that happen to you, could we? But then again, why not?

By now, however, it was becoming apparent that the lid could not be kept on much longer. The appeal judgment was so over the top that it produced widespread criticism, even in parts of the Establishment. 'Three unwise judges', was the heading over a leading article in *The Times* shortly afterwards. Campaigners for the release of the Six refused to lie down and they were beginning to attract some powerful allies, both at home and abroad. But it was a breakthrough in another case that tipped the balance. Under public pressure – notably from a heavyweight delegation comprising Cardinal Basil Hume, former Home Secretaries Roy Jenkins and Merlyn Rees and retired law lords Patrick Devlin and Leslie Scarman – the Home Secretary had asked the Avon and Somerset Police to re-examine the evidence against the four people convicted of the Guildford and Woolwich bombings.

This was in many ways a greater scandal. Much more so than Birmingham. In the Birmingham case it was apparent that all concerned believed from the outset – and many still do to this day – in the guilt of the defendants. In the Guildford case there is evidence to suggest that some of those involved knew almost from the outset that they had the wrong people. The campaign to prove their innocence had been kept alive over the years by Alastair Logan, a tenacious Surrey solicitor. I had originally intended to investigate the convictions of both the Guildford and Birmingham defendants, but it rapidly became clear that this was much too big a task for one individual. Instead, the cause was taken up by the journalist Robert Kee and later by Ros Franey and Grant McKee of Yorkshire Television, who wrote an excellent exposé.*

Paddy Armstrong, whom I interviewed in prison, said that, after he had been interrogated in Guildford police station, where he was grievously mistreated, he was taken for a drive around town so that he could show detectives the route he had taken to plant the bombs. By this time, after nights without sleep and all manner of threats and violence, he was signing whatever they put in front of him and desperate to help the police, if only to get them off his back. Like the others, he naively thought, the confessions could be repudiated once he was out of police custody. The problem was he had never before set foot in Guildford. He was soon directing the detectives the wrong way down one-way streets and along the High Street which was closed to traffic on Saturdays (the bombing had been on a Saturday). Fed up, they took him back to the police station and threw him back into a cell. A little later a face appeared at the flap in the cell door and a voice said, 'That confession you've given us. A load of fairy tales, innit?'

'Yes.'

'You didn't do it, did you?'

'No.'

'We know that, but we need bodies, so we are going to do you.'

In the end the Guildford and Woolwich convictions were the first to collapse and the end, when it came, was sensational. The Avon and Somerset investigating officers went back to the original paperwork and quickly stumbled across what appeared to be edited drafts of interviews with Armstrong suggesting that, contrary to the sworn

---

* *Trial and Error* (Hamish Hamilton, 1986) and *Timebomb* (Bloomsbury, 1988), respectively.

testimony of a succession of Surrey Police officers, their notes were far from contemporaneous and that the supposed confessions had been fabricated. They also found a bundle of alibi statements for another of the four, Gerry Conlon, to which the prosecutors had attached a handwritten note reading, 'Not to be given to the defence.' In addition, custody records were shown to have been fabricated.* Since the entire case had been based on confession evidence, there was nothing left. This time there was no prevarication. The Director of Public Prosecutions immediately came out with his hands up and the case was referred back to the Court of Appeal. It all happened with astonishing speed. I was present in the Old Bailey on 19 October 1989, when the Lord Chief Justice, Lord Lane, through gritted teeth, quashed the convictions. Within hours Gerry Conlon was propelled through the front entrance of the Old Bailey. Almost the first words he uttered in public were, 'Let's hope the Birmingham Six are soon freed.'

Immediately, however, the Establishment closed ranks. Within hours Douglas Hurd was on his feet in the House of Commons indignantly denying that the release of the Guildford Four had any implications for the six men convicted of the Birmingham bombings, but the similarities between the two cases were all too obvious. First, they were both heavily dependent on confessions extracted in police custody and repudiated as soon as the defendants were out of the clutches of the police. Second, both sets of arrests and convictions took place around the same time and in the same climate of hysteria induced by a succession of IRA atrocities. Finally, and above all, the decision of the DPP to call a halt was a momentous admission. For the first time the British political and legal Establishments were obliged to concede that police officers – to say nothing of other people in high places – were capable of organising fraud and perjury on the scale necessary to obtain and sustain convictions for some of the most high-profile murders in recent history. A huge psychological barrier had been breached. If it could happen once, it could happen twice.

---

*Later scientific tests on police notebooks showed that notes of interviews with all four defendants appeared to have been fabricated.

Even before the Guildford Four were released, there were signs that something was about to give. Two months earlier, on 14 August 1989, the Chief Constable of the West Midlands, Geoffrey Dear, had announced the disbanding of the notoriously corrupt West Midlands Serious Crime Squad. It was, he said, the blackest day of his career. The disbanding of the Serious Crime Squad and the release of the Guildford Four led to renewed pressure on the Home Secretary. By now the case was attracting worldwide attention. Supporters abroad were organising vigils outside British embassies around the globe. Amnesty International had expressed concern. Even the Kremlin, weary of being lectured on human rights by successive British governments, started taking an interest.

Two months after the release of the Guildford Four, Gareth Peirce, solicitor for five of the Birmingham Six, wrote a nineteen-page letter to the Home Secretary setting out new evidence which might form the basis of a further reference to the Court of Appeal. After due consideration the Home Secretary announced that he had asked the Devon and Cornwall Police to conduct a second inquiry, their first having proved woefully inadequate. This time the chief constable himself took charge and their second inquiry proved to be a great deal more rigorous than their first.

But first a diversion. Unknown to me, my former colleagues at *World in Action* had established contact with the self-confessed bomber I had traced. He had agreed to be interviewed on the strict understanding that his identity would not be disclosed. He also set one other condition: that I conduct the interview.

It was all very hush, hush. Not even the camera crew knew what we were up to. Ian McBride and I flew to Dublin in a chartered plane. We put up at the Shelbourne Hotel, where that evening we were contacted by a man who told us that we should proceed to Sligo on the west coast. There, at 11 a.m. on the day after tomorrow, we should wait in the car park of a local motel where someone would contact us and tell us what would happen next. In Sligo we were told to proceed to a remote corner of the Donegal National Park. We raced up the coast and skidded into the car park in Donegal. It was a damp day, and there was only one other vehicle. In it were two men wearing check

cloth caps, which, as I was coming to realise from previous encoun-
ters, were an important part of the IRA dress code. They ordered us to
transfer ourselves and our equipment to their vehicle. We then set off
into the wilderness, along an unpaved track. After a mile or so, in the
middle of nowhere, we came across a car with its bonnet up and a
man in a peaked cap pretending to fiddle with the engine. As we
passed, he acknowledged us with a slight movement of his right hand.
We came down to a stone bridge over a little river by which stood a
lone fisherman. He, too, was wearing a cloth cap and he, too, acknowledged our passing. We came to a remote house, in a high place with
spectacular views across a loch. And there, heavily disguised and very
nervous, was the man we had come to see. Slowly, quietly, in a voice
that sometimes trembled, he retold, this time in front of a television
camera, the story he had first related to me four years earlier.

Interview over, there was suddenly a great panic. It seems the
house had been borrowed without the knowledge of most of the
family that lived there, who were away on a shopping trip. Now word
reached our minders that they were on their way home, and we were
bundled out of the back door more or less as they entered through the
front, speeding away down the track that led to the river, past the
cloth-capped fisherman and the still-stranded motorist. Thirty
minutes later we found ourselves back in the deserted car park of the
Donegal National Park. The interview with the bomber was broadcast
on 23 July 1990. The West Midlands Police responded by demanding
that Granada Television make available 'all material and documents,
transmitted and untransmitted'. A letter from the deputy chief constable indicated how they proposed to cope with this new development: 'If, as your programme suggests, another person was *also* [my
italics] involved in those murders, then it is incumbent on me to
investigate those claims.'

By now, however, the game was almost up. A month later the
Devon and Cornwall Police reported to the Home Secretary that
scientific examination of the West Midlands Police notebooks
appeared to indicate that some or all of the interview notes had been
fabricated. Indeed, it later became apparent that some officers had
been rewriting their notebooks months after the event. Each page was
supposed to be date-stamped to demonstrate that the notes were

contemporaneous. Anyone rewriting his notebook would, therefore, have to rewind the date stamp. On examination of the notebooks it became apparent that officers had been winding back the day and the month, but they had omitted to change the year. There was no conceivable innocent explanation for this. Within days of receiving the report the Home Secretary announced that he was again referring the case to the Court of Appeal. Although the Crown Prosecution Service fought a bitter rearguard action, the outcome was a foregone conclusion. On 14 March 1991, amid much official wailing and gnashing of teeth, the convictions were finally quashed. The Birmingham Six emerged triumphant from the front entrance of the Old Bailey to face a wall of cameras. News of the event spread around the world. Even my wife's family in Vietnam saw it. One of the planet's most arrogant legal systems had been humbled. As the author Robert Harris wrote, 'Whoever planted the bombs in Birmingham … also planted a bomb under the British legal Establishment.'

For me, too, it was a big moment. Years of painstaking research had finally paid off. I had coped with years of abuse. My constituents had been told repeatedly that their MP was a supporter of IRA terrorists and now, in the most public way possible, I was vindicated.

Astonishing though it may seem, in a country that not infrequently used to boast of having one of the best criminal justice systems in the world, the wrong people – a total of eighteen in all – were put away for *all* the major IRA bombings of the mid-1970s. Of those, ten would have hanged, had the death penalty still been in force. In addition, following the disbanding of the West Midlands Serious Crime Squad, more than thirty other convictions were quashed.

Could disasters on this scale happen again? At the risk of sounding complacent, I believe it is unlikely. False confessions lie at the root of most major miscarriages of justice. Incredible though it now seems, until relatively recently British courts were imprisoning people for life (and on occasion sending them to the gallows) on the basis of unrecorded, uncorroborated confessions. The discovery of DNA and the advance of digital technology makes possible a standard of evidence far more rigorous than that available in the past. And where mistakes do occur, the Criminal Cases Review Commission, established in the wake of the Birmingham Six case, provides an (albeit imperfect) mechanism for correcting them. In addition, there is now a greater willingness among both the public and a new generation of judges to accept that the system over which they preside is not infallible.

But never say never. A terrorist outrage followed by a bout of tabloid hysteria leading to the rounding up of usual suspects is all it takes to start the ball rolling. And, as we have seen, an error of judgement once made can be extraordinarily difficult to reverse. We can never be too vigilant.

CHAPTER FOURTEEN

The Path to Respectability

Upon election to Parliament in June 1987 I did not expect to be carried shoulder high into the tea room, and I was not disappointed.

At the first parliamentary party meeting of the new session there was a post mortem on the election result. Since we had just lost three elections in succession it seemed a good idea to see what lessons could be learned. I got up and made a conciliatory little speech, the gist of which was that we must all turn our guns outward and shoot at our political enemies instead of at each other. I had, however, overestimated the wisdom of our leadership. Up spake Neil Kinnock. 'That comes all very well,' he said, 'from the author of a slim little volume entitled "How to Deselect Your MP".' Before I could protest that actually it was called 'How to Select or Reselect Your MP', Roy Hattersley was on his feet. 'What Chris ought to know,' he said, 'is that we are not taking any prisoners.'

.   They were as good as their word. Soon after my arrival, I put my name down for a place on the Home Affairs Select Committee. Without result, which was not unreasonable since places on the main select committees were heavily oversubscribed. Thereafter, each time a vacancy arose, I put my name down. Always without result. Eventually, I went to see the chief whip, Derek Foster, to ask what the problem was. 'Talk to Roy,' he advised. Besides being deputy leader, Roy Hattersley was also Shadow Home Secretary.

I went to see Roy, who stood with his hands in his pockets looking at the floor and said ambiguously, 'I'll see what can be done.' I know exactly what was done because Derek Foster told me afterwards. A message came from Neil Kinnock's office saying that the Leader understood there was a vacancy on the Home Affairs Committee and he had one or two names in mind for who might fill it. Would the chief whip please call on him to discuss the matter? When Derek got there he discovered that the Leader had no names in mind for who might fill the vacancy, but one name in mind for who should not.

No matter. I was undaunted. Life was good. *A Very British Coup* had just been made into a successful television series and I was heavily involved in the campaign to rescue the innocent people convicted of various IRA atrocities in the mid-1970s. So I set up my own department, a little Ministry of Justice. Every month I drafted questions to the Home Secretary and the Attorney General designed to keep miscarriages of justice in the public eye. It did not make me popular with either front bench. Roy Hattersley was a Birmingham MP and, like most people in the West Midlands, he was firmly of the view that the right people had been put away for the pub bombings, whatever the irregularities in the case against them. Oral questions to ministers are allocated by ballot. Each member is allowed only one. I would draft twenty or so questions and distribute them among well-disposed colleagues and, if their names came high in the ballot, I provided them with supplementaries. Fortune frequently smiled upon us. On occasion, as many as half a dozen of my questions would be reached with the result that the Labour front bench had no choice but to join in, however reluctantly. Ingenuity was sometimes called for. So, if, for example, someone was complaining about the burgeoning prison population, I would get up and remark that one way of reducing the pressure on the prison population was to release the innocent.

Gradually one or two Tories began to take part. This was particularly helpful since in order to keep the ball in play it was necessary to generate interest from both sides of the chamber. At first the Tory interventions would consist of someone from the West Midlands, perhaps Jill Knight or Anthony Beaumont-Dark, getting up and inviting the Home Secretary to agree how scandalous it was that the Hon Member for Sunderland should be questioning the integrity of the West Midlands Police who, as everyone knew, were a fine, upright body of men, etc., etc. I was even accused of giving succour to terrorists. The junior Home Office ministers would usually concur with enthusiasm, but the Home Secretary, Douglas Hurd, a thoughtful man, was more circumspect. Many years later Hurd wrote: 'A minister answering parliamentary questions learns which backbenchers to fear ... real danger comes from the quiet questioner who knows his subject. Such a one was Chris Mullin. I learned to respect him when he was on his feet.'

Within hours of the release of the Birmingham Six, amid much official breast beating, the Home Secretary announced the setting up of a Royal Commission. Suddenly, overnight, via this improbable cause, I was respectable. Law lords, cardinals, Tory Home Secretaries – even the odd Labour frontbencher – were happy to be seen in my company. I could no longer be denied the place I coveted on the Home Affairs Select Committee. And, five years later, scarcely an eyebrow was raised when I was appointed chairman. Actually, there was one eyebrow raised. That of the Speaker's secretary, Nicholas Bevan. After I had been chairman for a few weeks I noticed that I was not accorded the same degree of precedence in the chamber as my Conservative predecessor, Sir Ivan Lawrence. One day, I came across Mr Bevan in the library and asked why this was so. 'I think we are having difficulty adjusting to your new status,' he replied. To which I responded, 'Well, I'm not.' After that everything was normal.

Select committees are one of the success stories of the modern Parliament. The humbling of the great oligarch Rupert Murdoch before a House of Commons select committee in July 2011 was a good moment for Parliament. Likewise, appearances by senior bankers before the Treasury committee have given us a glimpse of people who would not otherwise be seen in the light of day. At a time when it is fashionable to lament the decline of Parliament, select committees have grown in strength and self-confidence to the point where they now offer an alternative career path for a young upwardly mobile politician who does not fancy the vagaries of life on the ministerial ladder. Unlike the chamber, where the best that can be hoped for is an exchange of sound-bites, select committees provide an opportunity for sustained questioning of ministers and officials and for in-depth inquiry into issues of public importance with a possibility, if used sensibly, of making an impact on government policy. This presumes, of course, that members take them seriously, which is not always so. The concentration span of the average MP is notoriously short and made worse with the coming of pagers, Blackberries, iPhones and other tools supposedly essential for a modern politician. My rules for successful select committee membership were simple: (1) read the brief; (2) keep your backside in the seat throughout the session; and (3) ask concise, relevant questions. (I'd be happy to arrange short courses for the last if necessary; it never ceases to amaze me how apparently intelligent people often have such difficulty framing clear, simple questions.) The other great advantage of select committees is that they provide an opportunity to reach conclusions on the basis of evidence rather than engaging in destructive and unproductive tribal warfare. A unanimous report requires compromise. Reports that are unanimous, or more or less so, are likely to be taken more seriously by government and the outside world than those which divide along tribal lines, although there are – as we shall see – occasional exceptions.

Appointments to select committees were, for many years, the subject of gross abuse by the party machines. Members, particularly those of the governing party, were often chosen for their willingness to toe the party line rather than from any burning desire to hold the executive to account. Patronage was in the hands of the whips, usually in consultation with the very ministers whose departments were supposed to be the subject of scrutiny. When I eventually became chairman of the Home Affairs committee, I suggested to the chief whip that he appoint the newly elected Bob Marshall-Andrews, an able (but from New Labour's point of view not entirely reliable) lawyer, to the committee only to be told that he had been vetoed 'at the highest level'. In other words the prime minister himself had found time to vet the list of proposed committee members. An early example of the control freakery which would rebound on New Labour in the years ahead.

Happily, that has since changed. At least in relation to select committees, prime ministers and chief whips no longer enjoy the powers of patronage they once had. Today select committee chairmen are elected by a vote of the whole house, and members by backbenchers on each side. Which is as it should be. How can it be right in a democracy for the executive to decide who shall scrutinise it? Also, these days chairmen are paid, which means they are less likely to be tempted away by office or the prospect of office.

Sir Ivan Lawrence was chairman when I first joined the Home Affairs Select Committee. Bright, good humoured and a talented pianist, he was generally on the right of the Tory Party and saw it as his job to keep the committee out of mischief, with the result that we wasted many hours on pointless inquiries into subjects on which we had little useful to say, some of which were no more than excuses for foreign travel. Sir Ivan, a man of prodigious energy, was also a practising barrister, which meant that the committee couldn't meet until after chucking-out time at the Old Bailey, as a result of which its deliberations received very little media coverage since most journalists had filed their stories by early evening.

I was determined to change this way of working. My first act on becoming chairman was to decree that in future the committee would meet at 10.30 a.m. instead of 4.30 p.m. I was also determined to take the committee into previously unexplored territory. Indeed, I had a little list. This included the accountability of the security service (although this was not, strictly speaking, within the committee's remit), funding of political parties, appointment of judges and (since I'd noticed that a number of the police officers involved in controversial cases appeared to be Masons) the role of Freemasons in the criminal justice system. My fellow Labour members of the committee were by and large up for this, but in 1992 the majority of committee members were Tories and most were not keen to venture far from the beaten track. The trick, therefore, was to divide and rule. One way or another, and despite a great deal of huffing and puffing in certain quarters, we managed to get all of these issues on to our agenda.

I had long taken an interest in the work of the security services – MI5, and the Secret Intelligence Service, MI6. One has to pinch oneself today to recall how little was known about them until the controversies of the 1980s. A great deal of unnecessary cloak-and-daggery surrounded their activities. Even the identities of the directors general were a state secret. In theory, the service heads were accountable only to the prime minister, though in practice they were often a law unto themselves. Ever since the Zinoviev letter which helped to bring down the first Labour government in 1924* there had been suspicion that some at least of the supposed guardians of all we hold dear were more inclined to serve the Tory Party than the elected government.

From time to time incidents have occurred that seemed to confirm this suspicion. Harold Wilson, prime minister in the 1960s and 70s, was convinced that he was being spied upon by MI5 and this was later confirmed by the disclosure that an MI5 file on him, under the name Henry Worthington, was kept in a safe in the Director General's office. In the 1970s a person or persons unknown went to the trouble of setting up Swiss bank accounts for Labour's deputy leader, Ted Short. An attempt was also made to smear Merlyn Rees, the Northern Ireland Secretary. In 1975 Colin Wallace, a former SAS officer based in Northern Ireland, resigned from the civil service, alleging that he had been part of an operation codenamed Clockwork Orange, one of the purposes of which had been to discredit members of the elected government. Despite initial denials, ministers were eventually forced to confirm the existence of such an operation.[†] In 1985 Cathy Massiter, an MI5 officer, resigned, protesting that much of the organisation's resources were targeted not against enemies of the State, but against legitimate sources of dissent such as the Campaign for Nuclear Disarmament and various trade unions. The role of MI5 in the miners' strike of 1984–5 has never been satisfactorily explained.

Some years ago, at a book signing, I was approached by a retired BT engineer who in the 1980s had worked at the telephone exchange in Gray's Inn Road, opposite the offices of *Tribune* and close to the headquarters of a number of trade unions. He told me that a large number of the telephone lines which went through that exchange had taps on. All this was given great impetus in 1987 when Peter Wright, a

---

*A letter addressed to the British Communist Party purporting to come from the head of the Comintern which called on communists to mobilise 'sympathetic forces' in the Labour Party and organise 'agitation-propaganda' in the armed forces. Four days before the election it was leaked to the *Daily Mail*, which ran the story under the banner headline: 'Civil War Plot By Socialists' Masters'. An investigation by the chief historian of the Foreign Office in 1999 concluded that it had been forged by an MI6 source and leaked by either MI6 or MI5 to the Conservative Party.
† 'See Paul Foot, *Who Framed Colin Wallace?* (Pan Books, 1990).

former senior officer of MI5, published *Spycatcher*, a memoir in which he talked of 'bugging and burgling our way across London'. He also owned up to being part of a small cabal of officers who believed that Harold Wilson and Sir Roger Hollis, director general of MI5 between 1956 and 1965, were Soviet agents. By now it was apparent that the service had lost its way and was riven with paranoia and incompetence. 'We've cleared out a lot of deadwood,' Tory Home Secretary Kenneth Baker whispered to me after the shake-up that followed the Peter Wright revelations. 'There was a lot of drinking and laziness,' Sir Stephen Lander, director general 1996–2002, remarked when members of the Home Affairs Select Committee visited him some years later.

Soon after I was first elected I had a little run-in with the Speaker, Jack Weatherill, over the presence of MI5 officers in the Commons. I noticed that a number of shadowy figures appeared every time we debated the Intelligence Services Bill and persuaded one of the door-keepers to give me the names of those in the officials' gallery. I then went to the library and matched them against the Civil Service List and, sure enough, two names did not appear. I then went to the Table Office and put down a question to the Home Secretary – 'if he would list the responsibilities of Messrs so-and-so'. The next day I was summoned by the chief clerk. 'The Speaker would prefer that these questions did not appear on the Order Paper,' he said.

To which I replied, 'I would prefer that they did.'

'In that case the Speaker will want to talk to you.'

The next summons came not from the Speaker but from Derek Foster, the Labour chief whip. 'Jack Weatherill has had a word with me,' he said, 'and he has assured himself that the security of these individuals would be at risk were their names to appear on the Order Paper.'

'Fine,' I said. 'All he has to do is satisfy me and there won't be a problem.'

The next call was from the Speaker's office, inviting me to discuss the matter. Jack Weatherill was a kindly, avuncular man, a former master tailor, who saw himself as the headmaster of a well-run public school, determined that the rules should be obeyed, but at the same time anxious to avoid unpleasantness. He appealed to me 'as a citizen and a patriot' to withdraw the question.

I replied that, sadly, not everyone these days believed that the security services were the protectors of all we hold dear. 'In any case,' I said, 'I don't understand why you are seeking to persuade me to withdraw since you are not going to allow these questions on to the Order Paper whatever I say, are you?'

He confirmed that this was so, quietly conceding that the reason for this interview was that he wished to maintain the fiction that he never censored the Order Paper.

We agreed that I would consider and drop him a note. A day or two later I wrote to him saying that, on reflection, I proposed to ask a point of order inquiring why my questions had disappeared.

Quick as a flash I received a message saying that I was to do no such thing and summoning me to discuss the matter once more. This time the Speaker was accompanied by his private secretary, Sir Peter Kitcatt, who, I later learned (not entirely to my surprise), was a former intelligence officer. I was left in no doubt as to Mr Speaker Weatherill's displeasure. He presented me with the form of words I was to use in raising my point of order. There followed a few minutes' negotiation over the precise wording and off I went. That afternoon I duly raised my point of order and was given short shrift. From that moment on my card was marked. As in the best gentleman's clubs, I had been blackballed. It would be well over a year before I caught his eye at random again in the chamber, in either questions or debates. In December 1989 we debated UK relations with Vietnam. At that time I was one of the very few members who had any first-hand experience of the country and so, on paper at least, I ought to have been an obvious choice. The presiding Deputy Speaker, Sir Paul Dean, studiously ignored me. After three hours it came down to a choice between myself and Tommy Graham, an incomprehensible Glaswegian who could barely pronounce the word 'Vietnam', let alone have anything useful to say on the subject. To general astonishment, Sir Paul chose Tommy. Afterwards I approached the chair and asked why I had been overlooked, adding, 'I have been travelling in Vietnam for twenty years, I am chairman of the Britain Vietnam Association, secretary of the All-Party Vietnam Group, my wife is Vietnamese and most of her family still live there.'

Without batting an eyelid Sir Paul replied, 'Anyone could make those points.'

Something similar happened when we debated Cambodia, again a country with which I was familiar, having been there both during and after the war. Again, it came down to a choice between me and one other colleague, Pat Wall. By this time it was clear to everyone what was going on and when the time came to call the final speaker, Pat Wall bless him, remained in his seat, leaving the deputy speaker with no choice but to call me. That was the only occasion I slipped under the wire in more than a year.

In January 1991 Jack Weatherill wrote an article in *The House* magazine in which he explained how he bent over backwards to be fair to everybody. A backbencher, he said, could expect to be called to speak in a mainstream debate no more than three or four times a year. I tore out the article, highlighted the paragraph setting out the criteria and attached a note pointing out that, with one trivial exception, I had not been called in a major debate since 28 November 1988.

Someone present at the Speaker's conference next morning later remarked that my note had caused a stir. Weatherill, not a man to bear grudges, had long ago forgotten the reasons for my disfavour, but the shadowy Sir Peter Kitcatt had not. But for my note, who knows how long the boycott would have lasted? Overnight, however, my fortunes were transformed. A few days later I found myself called at random during prime minister's questions and shortly afterwards I was called, amid the privy councillors, in the early stages of the Maastricht Treaty debate. After that, life returned to normal.

Soon after I joined the Home Affairs Select Committee we had a visit from the Home Secretary, Kenneth Clarke. Could we, I asked, meet with Stella Rimington, who had recently been appointed head of MI5?

The answer was a firm 'no'. I suspected, however, that in private she was briefing national newspaper editors. I rang a couple who confirmed that this was so. Next time Ken Clarke appeared I inquired how it was that she was permitted to meet the unelected, but not the elected. He went away saying he would think about it and a little later, on 18 January 1993, five of us were invited to lunch with Mrs Rimington at MI5 headquarters in Gower Street. It was to be her first encounter with backbench MPs.

Much excitement surrounded the event. MI5 sent cars to collect us from the members' entrance. The details were supposed to be private, but word inevitably leaked and a posse of photographers with long lenses assembled by the gate to record our departure. They then mounted motorcycles and chased us across London. Every time we stopped at traffic lights camera lenses would appear at the windows. Several papers reported the outing as though it were something out of a John le Carré novel. The next day's *Daily Telegraph* carried a front-page photograph of us getting into the car. It was headed: 'The four men and one woman tried to look inconspicuous ... They were on their way to lunch with a woman so mysterious that only one blurred photograph of her exists.'

Our visit also features in Stella Rimington's memoirs. In particular an exchange she and I had regarding a framed quotation from Edmund Burke which hung on the wall behind her desk. Apparently it had been left there by one of her predecessors. It read:

> Those who would carry on great public schemes must be proof against the most fatiguing delays, the most mortifying disappointments, the most shocking insults and most of all the presumptuous judgement of the ignorant upon their designs.

Mrs Rimington wrote, 'I was rather embarrassed about this and hoped no one would notice it, but as luck would have it Chris Mullin did, and later sent a message asking about the wording. I did not give it to him, as I suspected it would only turn up later in some sardonic article. Instead I removed it.' Actually, she sent word that it had been lost when the organisation's HQ was relocated from Gower Street to Thames House in Millbank. As clear an example as one could wish for of a politician being given the runaround by the security services.

Years later, when we both served as judges of the Man Booker Prize, I got to know Stella Rimington and found her to be excellent company – gratifyingly normal and down to earth. In short, not at all the upper-class stereotype that we had come to expect of the mandarins who ruled the secret world. Her appointment must have been a breath of fresh air in what had become an insular, stuffy world peopled by ex-colonial types of limited competence and a fondness for long, boozy lunches.

Little by little the door to the secret world was prised open. What tipped the scales was not so much pressure from Parliament, but the fact that Britain was the only member of the European Union whose intelligence services had no legal basis. The government, fearing that they were vulnerable to a challenge in the courts, decided the time had come to place them on a statutory footing. The result was the Intelligence Services Act which not only legalised MI5, MI6 and GCHQ, but also provided for some limited form of accountability. A committee of senior parliamentarians was established to whom the intelligence services were supposed to account. The committee met in a secure room in the Cabinet Office, but its powers were limited. It reported not to Parliament, but to the prime minister and was heavily dependent on the goodwill of the very services whose work it was supposed to be overseeing.

From time to time there was a suspicion that the committee was having the wool pulled over its eyes. When, for example, following 9/11, it emerged that the United States government was in the habit of kidnapping suspected terrorists and franchising their interrogation to foreign torturers, the question arose: what part, if any, did our security services play – and, even if not directly involved, to what extent were they aware of what was happening? The Intelligence and Security Committee, despite several attempts, failed to get to the bottom of this. Following the fall of the Libyan tyrant, Muammar Gaddafi, however, a remarkable document emerged which showed that, despite repeated protestations to the contrary, British hands were far from clean. A fax from a senior MI6 official, Sir Mark Allen, to the head of Gaddafi's intelligence service, Musa Kusa, showed that Britain had played a key role in the kidnapping and rendition to Libya of one of Gaddafi's opponents, Abdel Hakim Belhaj, and his pregnant wife. Mr Belhaj was handed over to Libyan torturers, but following the fall of Gaddafi he became a senior official in the new Libyan regime and attempted to sue the British government over what had happened to him. Instead of owning up and apologising, the government moved heaven and earth to prevent the truth coming out and the taxpayer ended up paying £2.2 million to Mr Belhaj in order to dissuade him from continuing the case.

In opposition, Labour was in favour of making the Intelligence and Security Committee accountable to Parliament, but once in government Tony Blair was swiftly persuaded to stick with the status quo. I pressed both Blair and his Home Secretary, Jack Straw, on the issue. Straw was sympathetic, but the PM (no doubt on the advice of the services themselves) refused to budge. He did, however, concede that Parliament should be allowed to debate the committee's heavily censored annual report and, after I became chairman, the Home Affairs Select Committee was granted occasional briefings from the head of MI5, always on the understanding that they were informal rather than a right. It wasn't ideal, but it was progress of a sort.

We made better progress on party funding. Until the late 1990s, the funding of the Tory Party was one of the great mysteries of British politics. Most Tories didn't have a clue where their party's money came from. Even members of the Conservative Party's board of finance could not find out. By contrast, there was no secret about Labour Party funding. It mostly came from party membership fees and the thirty or forty pence a year given by the four or five million trade unionists who paid the political levy – payments that were recorded in both the party's and the unions' published accounts. The Liberal Democrats relied heavily on their members and a small number of private donors, but attracted only a fraction of the funding of the other two parties. The Tories, however, were immensely wealthy. At general elections they massively outspent their rivals, but the source of their funds was concealed behind a web of front organisations such as British United Industrialists and a number of 'river companies' (so-called because they were all named after British rivers). Donors would pour money into BUI, from where it would flow via a river company straight into Conservative Party coffers.

The accounts of public companies occasionally provided a clue, but by the 1990s many of the Thatcher decade's nouveau riche preferred to express their gratitude via private companies whose accounts were not published. Every so often a scandal would lift the carpet by an inch or two – receivers who moved in on the fugitive businessman Asil Nadir, for example, discovered evidence of large cheques made out to the Conservative Party. There was also a remarkable correlation between the award of peerages and donations to the ruling party (an abuse not confined to the Tories). A number of foreign billionaires – the Greek shipping magnate John Latsis and the Hong Kong business-man Li Ka-shing to name but two – also chipped in. Later, it emerged that the Tories were using public facilities such as the House of Commons dining rooms and even 10 Downing Street for fund-raising activity. Such abuses were by no means unique to the Tories, but since they alone were so tenacious in defence of the existing arrangements, it was not unreasonable to assume that they had rather more to hide.

The first time I raised the subject at the select committee, Con-servative members fell over themselves to say how boring and point-less an inquiry would be. No one, they asserted, would ever take us seriously again if we were to waste our time on this issue. After they had gone on in this vein for twenty minutes or so, it became clear that, far from being bored by the subject, they were riveted by it. Since they were in a majority, there was no reason provided that they stuck together, why they should not veto an inquiry. There was, however, one dissident Tory – David Ashby – who was a good deal more open-minded than most of his colleagues. With his support, we had a majority. Thus a day came when we had before us the treasurer of the Tory Party,* a television camera was switched on, we asked him where the Tories' money came from and he flatly refused to say. Among other witnesses was Eric Chalker, an elected member of the Conserva-tive Board of Finance, who complained that he, too, had been unable to discover the source of much of his party's funds. He told the com-mittee, 'In 1991, press reports started to appear of some very specific, very large donations, including some from abroad; this caused me grave concern and, as a consequence, I asked the then chairman of the board for information that I believed would reassure me and the constituency associations that I represented ... No answers were forthcoming.'

This was one of those rare occasions where there was no prospect of a meeting of minds and no suggestion of compromise. One was either in favour of transparency or one was opposed. Predictably, the

---

*Tim Smith, an accountant, who soon afterwards was obliged to resign from the government following allegations that he had been in receipt of cash in brown envelopes from Mohammed Al-Fayed.

committee split precisely along party lines. The Tories (David Ashby was back on board by this time) produced a majority report concluding that little or no change was required. To which I drafted a lengthy amendment which became the minority report. I knew that in the end we would be vindicated. And so we were when, six years later, by which time government was under different management, Parliament passed the Political Parties, Elections and Referendums Act which, among other things, banned foreign donations and required all parties to state clearly where their money was coming from. Interestingly, the Bill had the support of the Tories, a reversal of their previous position, anxious no doubt to distance themselves from the allegations of sleaze that had helped to bring about their landslide defeat in the election of 1997. Accompanying my advance copy of the White Paper announcing his intention to legislate was a letter from Home Secretary, Jack Straw, which read as follows: 'While the immediate impetus for the draft Bill is the Neill committee report, its provisions are also a tribute to your own advocacy of the need for openness and transparency in the funding of political parties in your minority report following the select committee inquiry ...'

And so to the judges. One fact of life I have learned over the years is that it is possible to be very clever and stupid at the same time. Take, for example, the notorious miscarriages of justice that unravelled in the 1980s and early 1990s. Many people of average intelligence managed to work out that there was something wrong with the convictions in the Birmingham, Guildford and other celebrated miscarriages of justice, long before word reached those at the top. Having spent many hours at the Old Bailey observing the Appeal Court in action, I had the opportunity of studying at close quarters some of the most senior judges in the land. They were undoubtedly bright. They grasped every detail of the complex forensic evidence and understood every point put to them over a period of many weeks – but they entirely missed the big picture: namely, that they had the wrong people in front of them. What's more, they were prepared to engage in the most extraordinary intellectual gymnastics in order to sustain the shakiest of convictions. The judges who refused the initial appeal by the men wrongly convicted of the murder of the West Midlands newspaper boy Carl Bridgewater actually said in their judgment, 'We accept that the witness Mervyn Ritter is a pathological liar, but on this occasion we believe he can be relied upon as a witness of truth.' It is difficult to respond rationally to stupidity on this scale.

One reason for the extraordinary degree of ignorance and complacency (for purposes of argument, I will not allege mendacity) exhibited by many of our finest legal minds is that they come from a remarkably narrow background. Until fairly recently, 80 per cent of our senior judges were educated at the same handful of public schools and universities. For years no women ever penetrated the high legal echelons. Not until 1988 was Elizabeth Butler-Sloss appointed as the first female Appeal Court judge. Of course, she was eminently qualified, but she also happened to be the daughter of a High Court judge and the sister of the Lord Chancellor. It was some time before any less well-connected woman was admitted to the inner sanctum. Another limiting factor was the fact that, until relatively recently, only barristers were allowed rights of audience before the higher courts, which severely limited the pool from which the judiciary could be drawn.

The key issue, however, was the appointments system. Until 2006 there was no formal method of appointment. Instead judges were chosen by a system of informal 'soundings', rather in the same way as leaders of the Conservative Party used to 'emerge'. The soundings were conducted by officials in the Lord Chancellor's department who simply canvassed senior lawyers, many of whom would have been familiar with the candidate since school days. The result was a self-perpetuating clique of elderly gents of broadly similar background, outlook and astounding complacency. Collectively they tended to believe that the British legal system was the best in the world and incapable of any more than the most trivial error. When it came to police evidence they were particularly gullible. Sir James Miskin, the Recorder of London, once remarked that in his entire career he had not come across a police officer in the witness box who had lied or exaggerated in the slightest degree. The idea that fraud and perjury had occurred on the scale alleged in the more serious miscarriages of justice that came to light in the mid-1980s and early 1990s was simply beyond the ken of most senior judges. Indeed, many of the old school, to this day, believe that just about all those whose convictions were reluctantly quashed were in fact guilty. I have lost count of the number of times someone has whispered in my ear, 'I had dinner with Lord Justice so-and-so last night and you should hear what he was saying about the Birmingham Six.' There were, of course, honourable exceptions such as Lords Scarman and Devlin, but they stood out precisely because they defied the stereotype. Lord Justice Lawton, who had a hand in a number of celebrated miscarriages of justice, had been a member of the British Union of Fascists before the war, yet when he died the Lord Chief Justice, Geoffrey Lane, wrote: 'If Fred Lawton ever made a mistake, I cannot think of it.' I leave aside the inconvenient fact of Lawton's role in jailing the innocent, but presumably even Lord Lane would agree that Lawton's flirtation with fascism was a mistake.

In 1995 the committee, at my suggestion, took a look at judicial appointments. One commentator subsequently described the inquiry as 'a welcome progression from the dark ages of almost total lack of information and accountability'. Many of those who gave evidence, noting the almost complete absence of women and non-whites from the upper reaches of the judiciary, called for the creation of a judicial appointments commission, but the judicial Establishment in the shape of the Lord Chancellor and Lord Chief Justice made clear that they were implacably opposed to the advertising of vacancies. So, too, was our chairman, Sir Ivan Lawrence QC. Indeed, I had to explain to him the concept of advertising: circulation of vacancies, job description, written applications, a selection panel etc. He just didn't see the need. Inevitably, the majority report, while recommending several minor changes, concluded with a whimper – 'We have not found the need for fundamental change.' An amendment, which I tabled, calling for a judicial appointments commission was voted down. Soon after I became chairman we returned to the subject in evidence sessions with the Lord Chief Justice, Tom Bingham, and new Lord Chancellor, Derry Irvine, and at last there were signs of movement. The 1997 Labour manifesto had included a commitment to establish an appointments commission, but in the face of continued judicial resistance this was quietly shelved and it was not until 2006 that the stranglehold of the legal Establishment was finally broken and an appointments commission finally established. The result has been a considerable improvement in the range and quality of the judiciary, although there is still some way to go.

Probably the most controversial area into which the committee strayed on my watch was our inquiry into the role of Freemasonry in the criminal justice system. There is a great deal of unjustified paranoia about Freemasonry, and I have no wish to add to it, but the Masons with their cult of secrecy and their strange oaths are their own worst enemies. They vehemently deny that they are a secret society. Their position is that they are a society with secrets, a distinction lost on most people who are not Masons. One of my former colleagues in Parliament once related that when her father died she and her mother went to view his body in the funeral parlour and were astounded to find him dressed in full Masonic regalia – he had managed to keep the fact that he was a Mason secret even from his wife and daughter.

Masons generally insist that their principal purposes are social and charitable, but one can't help noticing that they tend to graduate towards positions of power or influence. They seemed to be particularly thick on the ground in professions that involved the wearing of uniforms – police, armed forces, ambulance service. In my early years in Sunderland the command structure of the Northumbria Ambulance Service was almost wholly Masonic. I know because I was contacted by refugees from the service who, despite being Masons themselves, described to me what went on there. On local authorities they seemed to graduate towards planning committees. In 1995 the chairman of the now defunct Medina Borough Council on the Isle of Wight resigned from both the council and the Conservative Party, saying he could no longer cope with pressure from the Masonic cabal on the council. He alleged that twelve of the eighteen Tory councillors were Masons. In 2000 a BBC Television documentary revealed that, of sixteen known Masons on Dorset County Council, thirteen were members of the planning committees and that there had been repeated failures by Masonic councillors to declare their interest when dealing with applications from local Masonic builders.

In the police, Masons tended to favour the elite squads and I began to wonder whether the wall of silence that usually greeted inquiries, official and unofficial, into alleged police misbehaviour had anything to do with the high incidence of Masons in certain forces. Sir Robert Mark, the Metropolitan Police commissioner in the 1970s (who famously remarked that he wanted to catch more criminals than he employed), certainly thought so. On his watch about 500 officers, many of them Masons, were sacked or forced to retire; several were jailed for corruption. His successor, Sir Kenneth Newman, published a code of ethics which included the following: 'The discerning officer will probably consider it wise to forgo the prospect of pleasure and social advantage in Freemasonry so as to enjoy the unreserved regard of those around him.' Far from complying, the reaction of the Masons in the Met was to go out and set up a Scotland Yard Lodge, the Manor of St James, which, if nothing else, suggested a certain self-confidence. Years later I was sent, anonymously, a colour photo of Manor of St James members in full regalia. I showed it to the then Metropolitan commissioner, Sir John Stevens, remarking, 'Here is your alternative command structure.' In fairness, as he pointed out, most of those in the picture had retired by this time, but it was an impressive sight. So far as I am aware, the Manor of St James is still active.

Sir Gerald Vaughan, the most senior Mason in the House of Commons, once remarked to me, 'If I have any criticism of Free-masonry, [and he didn't have many] it is very difficult to leave once you have joined.' And that, of course, is the point. You can be called upon to assist a brother in trouble at any time. You can lapse, but you can't resign. A number of lapsed Masons have said to me over the years that they only joined because they were told it would improve their career prospects. Some, in the private sector, were under the impression that it helped them win contracts. A surprising number of magistrates and some judges are Masons. The clerk of a magistrates' court in the south of England once told me that, on discovering that more than a third of his bench were Masons, he had raised the matter with the local lodge officials and they agreed a moratorium on the recruitment of any more Masonic magistrates. Later, he discovered that instead of recruiting Masons, they had simply waited until non-Masonic magistrates had been recruited and attempted to sign them up afterwards.

Since membership of the Freemasons is difficult to prove, it is rare for Masons to be caught out in skulduggery, but it does happen. Martin Short's classic *Inside the Brotherhood* (HarperCollins, 2009) contains many examples. On a couple of occasions the local government ombudsman has upheld complaints of undue Masonic influence on planning decisions.

One of my favourite Masonic tales involves two businessmen from Leicester who, in April 1988, were staying at the Queen's Moat Hotel in Blackburn, the constituency of Jack Straw. Arriving late, they gatecrashed a private function in search of drink only to be ordered to leave by a number of burly men in dinner jackets. An incident occurred and the two were arrested and charged with assault. While they were in custody their car had been vandalised, apparently by someone who had access both to hotel records and to the car keys which had been left in their room. It turned out that they had stumbled into a 'Ladies Night' organised by the Victory Masonic lodge, whose members included a number of serving and former policemen as well as the manager of the hotel. The police officer later called upon to investigate the incident also turned out to be a Mason. Among those present were a local solicitor and former police prosecutor who later acted for several of those involved. When the case came to trial, among the questions the judge invited the jury to consider was 'whether the closeness of Masonic membership of some of the prosecution witnesses has affected their willingness to tell the truth'. The jury concluded that it had. The two were unanimously acquitted. The judge ordered that their costs be paid from the public purse.

They then took out a civil action for damages claiming assault, wrongful arrest and malicious prosecution. During the course of the action the offices of their solicitor were allegedly burgled and papers relating to the case stolen. The civil case was settled out of court seven years later with damages paid to the plaintiffs of £85,000 (£70,000 of which was paid by the Lancashire Police Authority) along with further substantial sums in costs. An internal investigation supervised by the Police Complaints Authority led to disciplinary charges against two police officers and lesser measures being taken against a number of others. This was, remarked Martin Short in evidence to the committee, 'a quintessential Masonic scandal'.

My interest in Freemasonry was prompted by the activities of the West Midlands Serious Crime Squad. Like many such elites, members

of the squad had developed a culture of their own. They called themselves 'The Serious' and appeared to model themselves on the television series *The Sweeney*. Their modus operandi was to take over a
police station and order the local coppers to make themselves scarce
while they went about their business. The squad was well in with the
local Establishment, even organising an annual dinner to which
favoured crime reporters, lawyers, prosecutors and members of the
local judiciary were invited. I am pleased to report that the dinner due
to be held in the Albany Hotel, Birmingham, soon after the release of
the Birmingham Six, had to be cancelled at the last minute. The
remarkable thing about all this is that there were never any consequences. On the contrary, in 1988 one of the longest-serving members
of the squad, who had the distinction of being probably the most
complained about officer in the most complained about police force
in the country, was awarded the Queen's Police Medal. The citation
described him as, 'A superb police officer' who 'imparts invaluable
experience to junior detective colleagues who benefit greatly from the
excellent example of professionalism which he sets'. Someone up
there has a sense of humour.

Needless to say, my suggestion that we should have an inquiry
into the role of Freemasonry in the criminal justice system met with
considerable resistance from the Tories on the committee, two of
whom, it emerged, were Masons. The chairman, Ivan Lawrence, who
was not a Mason, made it clear that he, too, was wholly opposed.
Nevertheless, with the assistance of David Ashby, the same renegade
Tory who had helped us achieve an inquiry into party funding, an
inquiry was agreed. It was not a very satisfactory affair. A succession
of witnesses suggested there was not a problem that needed to be
solved. My suggestion that Grand Lodge be invited to tell us how
many of the policemen involved in the Birmingham pub bombings
case and in the Stalker inquiry* were Masons did not find favour with

---

*In 1983 John Stalker, a deputy chief constable of Manchester Police, was
appointed to inquire into allegations that the Royal Ulster Constabulary had
engaged in a policy of shooting to kill suspected members of the IRA. He soon
found himself to be the subject of a barrage of allegations, none of which was
proved, which led to his removal from the inquiry.

the committee and the result was an anodyne report which, but for a change of government, might have led nowhere.

The committee returned to the subject shortly after I became chairman. This time there was no difficulty in getting approval either for an inquiry or for the questions I had earlier been prevented from asking. The highlight was a televised exchange with the secretary of Grand Lodge, Commander Michael Higham. In private Commander Higham had agreed to provide the details requested, but he later backtracked. Refusing to co-operate with a select committee is a contempt of Parliament. We, therefore, summoned Commander Higham to a showdown. The Speaker, Betty Boothroyd, later told me that she was in a quandary as to what to do had he continued to defy the committee. There were no recent precedents and the penalties available to the House were uncertain. Our bluff was in danger of being called. Fortunately, the Masons blinked first. In due course Commander Higham reluctantly provided us with the names of a handful of members of the West Midlands Serious Crime Squad who he said were Masons. Quite how reliable his information was is unclear, since it took Commander Higham several attempts to come up with what he claimed was a definitive list, and even then he omitted the name of an officer who had admitted on television that he was a Mason. Nevertheless, on the evidence available it would have been difficult to argue that Freemasonry was a significant factor in the culture of impunity that surrounded the activities of the squad. The Stalker inquiry was more interesting. It transpired that several of those prominently involved were Masons.

Following the change of government, the Lord Chancellor's department distributed a survey to all judges, magistrates and Crown prosecutors inviting them to declare voluntarily membership of any secret society. Of the judges, 263, or 5 per cent of the total, admitted to being Freemasons while another 5 per cent refused to answer or did not reply. The figures were roughly similar for magistrates, although, of course, since many magistrates are female, this suggested that anywhere up to about 20 per cent of male magistrates were Masons. Only a handful of Crown prosecutors admitted to being Freemasons, although a large number either refused to respond or did not reply. Little or no progress was made obtaining information from other parts of the criminal justice system.

The conclusions of our second inquiry were rather more robust than the earlier one. We recommended that police officers and members of the judiciary should be obliged to declare membership of a secret society. The Home Secretary, Jack Straw, was sympathetic. The Lord Chancellor, Derry Irvine, less so. After some debate, however, the government agreed to require that new applicants for either the police or the judiciary should be obliged to declare membership of a secret society. Police authorities and the Lord Chancellor's department were also asked to keep a record of existing members of secret societies, not for publication, but merely as a point of referral in the event of future controversy. There was a great deal of official foot-dragging. Much talk of how impractical it all was. It is unclear to what extent the policy was implemented, or if it was implemented at all. The Masons fought back, even threatening to take their case to the European Court of Human Rights. In 2010, just before Labour left office, I received a note from Jack Straw (by this time Justice Secretary) saying that he had been advised that he would lose and that he was going to back down. A victory for the proponents of secrecy.

Was it all a waste of time? No. The overall effect of the row over transparency was to make Freemasonry a little less fashionable than it had once been. Like most organised activity in these days of solitary, sedentary pursuits, Freemasonry is in steep decline. The headquarters of the County Durham Masons was just round the corner from my home in Sunderland and it was evident from the parade of ageing men with their distinctive regalia cases who trooped in and out that it was a dying cult. Of late the Durham Masons have had to lease half their premises to a gym club which attracts a wholly different clientele.

One might have expected that my campaign for transparency would have made me unpopular in those professions where Freemasonry is rife. On the contrary, however, it won friends. On one occasion I was queuing at the classical music counter in the Oxford Street branch of Virgin Records when a man behind me remarked, 'Mr Mullin, you've got a lot of support in the Metropolitan Police.' This came as news to me, but, as he explained, police officers who are non-Masons deeply resent the stain on their reputation brought about by the various Masonic police scandals, to say nothing of the suggestion that the promotion system is sometimes manipulated in favour of Masons.

There are some who see Masonic conspiracies in everything that goes wrong with their lives. I am not one of these. Much as I like a good conspiracy, I have come to realise that cock-up rather than connivance is the explanation for most of life's little mysteries. I do, however, believe that in certain professions Freemasonry has proved an obstacle to the advance of women and people of ethnic minority origin, and that occasionally it has been a source of corruption. If grown men wish to indulge in bizarre rituals and swear strange oaths to each other, that is a matter for them. My only point is that it cannot be right for some public servants (or businessmen vying for public sector contracts) to be members of a secretive cult one of the aims of which is mutual self-advancement. The solution is not bans or proscriptions, but transparency, after which the problem will melt away. Until they grasp this nettle, Masons have only themselves to blame for the suspicion and resentment which their activities generate.

Guns were another issue on which the committee split along party lines. The massacre of sixteen primary school pupils and their teacher in Dunblane sparked public outrage and demands for a ban on the use of handguns and a tightening of restrictions on other weapons. We duly set up an inquiry and were surprised to discover the quantity of weapons legally in circulation. No less than 1.9 million handguns, rifles and shotguns, not to mention several million air weapons for which no licence was required, even though they were responsible for a great deal of low-level mayhem and a number of fatalities. We were also surprised to learn that gun licences were issued to just about anybody – less than 1 per cent of first time applications and no fewer than 0.2 per cent of applications for renewal were refused. Finally, there was no escape from the central fact that the weapons used by Thomas Hamilton at Dunblane had all been legally held. So were the weapons used by Michael Ryan in an earlier massacre at Hungerford. No amount of bluster about the use by criminals of black-market weapons could get round this inconvenient truth.

The key question, in the light of Dunblane, was whether private citizens should be allowed to possess handguns. Most of our witnesses, not to say public opinion, were unequivocally against. This, for example, was the Police Federation view: 'No amount of further amendments to firearms legislation, short of an outright ban on handguns, will ... ensure that all steps have been taken to prevent another atrocity.' The Tories and the gun lobby, however, mounted stiff resistance. My amendment, calling for a ban on handguns, an end to shotgun licences in urban areas and for airguns to be brought within the licensing system was defeated six votes to five, a straight Tory/Labour split. No doubt our chairman, Ivan Lawrence, thought he was doing Home Secretary Michael Howard a favour by concluding that nothing could be done but, not long afterwards, fearing public wrath, Howard was obliged to backpedal. A Bill was swiftly introduced banning the private ownership of handguns, leaving Sir Ivan and his colleagues gently swinging in the wind.

After seven years on the Home Affairs Select Committee, including two as chairman, I was becoming curious to see the inside of government. The call came in July 1999. How would I like to be the lowest form of life in John Prescott's vast Department of Environment, Transport and the Regions? Actually there was nothing I would like less. 'I'll sink without trace,' I said. 'Don't worry,' the prime minister replied cheerfully, 'I'll keep track of you.' After thinking about it overnight, I rang Number 10 and declined. Only for The Man to ring back. 'Come off it, Chris,' he said. 'It's only for a few months and then I'll find you something more up your street in the Home Office or the Foreign Office.' I am afraid I fell for that and, with a heavy heart, off I went.

CHAPTER FIFTEEN

A Little Light Governing

'The prime minister has a high regard for Chris Mullin,' the Labour chief whip, Derek Foster, remarked to Peter Mandelson.

To which The Great Ingratiator responded in that patrician drawl of his, 'Yaaas. Extraordinary, isn't it?'

The feeling was mutual. These days it is unfashionable to admit it (actually it wasn't all that fashionable at any time among some of my colleagues), but I had a sneaking regard for Tony Blair from the moment I first became aware of him. He was bright, personable and capable of thinking outside the box. This was first brought home to me when as Opposition spokesman on energy, faced with a massive Bill designed to privatise the electricity industry, he opted out of the traditional trench warfare with its weeks of time-wasting filibuster and all-night sittings, which in those days was a substitute for adequate scrutiny. Instead he offered to let the Bill through committee in reasonable time in exchange for the government permitting debate on three or four key issues at a time of day when the outside world was awake. No doubt the fact that he had young children and a home to go to (living as he did in Islington) was the key to this unusually rational approach, but it made sense from every point of view. The result was general happiness: the Opposition because it managed to get its arguments on record at a time when someone was listening; the government because it got the Bill through without undue delay, and everyone else, because they could get a good night's sleep. There is – or was – a school of thought that regards this approach as treasonous. Time is the Opposition's only weapon, they argue, and it is their job to make the government's life as difficult as possible. I beg to differ. In my experience nothing turns off the great British public so much as pointless ya-boo politics. A government with a reasonable majority is always going to get its legislation through. The best an opposition can hope for is to persuade the government to make some sensible amendments, and that is more likely to be achieved by rational argument than playground tantrums. The only time when there is a case for obstruction is when a government with a small majority is up to something particularly diabolical.

Tony Blair again caught my attention when, as Shadow Home Secretary, he managed to make law and order a Labour issue rather than a Tory one. This he achieved with the aid of a brilliant sound-bite, endlessly repeated until it caught on in the world outside Parliament, that a Labour government would be 'tough on crime and tough on the causes of crime'. It had long struck me as amazing that we had allowed the Tories to get away with pretending that law and order was their issue and that Labour was somehow soft on criminals. All the more astonishing considering that the Thatcher decade, involving as it did mass unemployment, was accompanied by a tidal wave of crime and antisocial behaviour which disproportionately affected Labour voters who tend to live in the less leafy areas. How had we let them get away with it for so long? Anyway, Blair nailed them. I was duly impressed and, when I finally managed to get a long sought-after place on the Home Affairs Select Committee, I went out of my way to strike up a working relationship with him. It worked both ways. At the time I was seeking to set up an independent review body to examine alleged miscarriages of justice and he threw the Opposition's weight behind my amendment to the 1994 Criminal Justice Bill. The Tories were not the least bit keen, but they gave in eventually.

So when, following the unexpected death of John Smith, there was suddenly a vacancy for the Labour leadership, it seemed to me obvious that Blair was one of the most attractive contenders. Had Robin Cook stood I would probably have supported him, but for all his intellectual brilliance Robin had never made much attempt to cultivate a base in Parliament and he was never likely to be elected, which is no doubt why he did not stand. That left just three candidates: Margaret Beckett, John Prescott and Tony Blair. Prescott, I knew, was not leadership material. I suspect he knew it, too. To be sure, he had a certain appeal to the northern working-class male, but it was not the votes of the northern working-class male that we needed to win general elections. Had we chosen Prescott, we'd be looking at a fifth Tory government. He did, however, prove to be an inspired choice for deputy leader, since – at his best – he could reach parts of both the party and the electorate that Blair couldn't. Beckett I could easily have supported. With hindsight, knowing what we now do about the catastrophe of Iraq and all that flowed from it, perhaps I should have done. In years to come Beckett would prove to be an outstandingly capable minister, rarely putting a foot wrong, but was she in the same league as Blair when it came to striking behind enemy lines? Blair in contrast to the other candidates, was a star. He soared above the rest of us. Young, fluent, able, he was not from the traditional, machine-controlled right. What's more, the public liked him. All the polls suggested that most open-minded people were desperate to see a credible Opposition, but, still not quite trusting Labour, were practically shouting at us to give them Blair.

One shouldn't be too starry-eyed. Some shortcomings were obvious from the outset and became more so as time went on. Blair's apparent dependence on the dark arts of Peter Mandelson, for one, and the fact that he seemed more at home in the company of glitterati than stalwarts of the dear old Labour Party to which he owed everything, for another. Also, his habit of telling people what they want to hear. As Jack Straw put it to me years later, 'Tony is like a man who goes around saying I love you to seven, eight, nine different women and they all go away feeling happy until they start to compare notes.'

From the outset it seemed to me obvious that Blair was the one. In May 1994 we didn't know that three years later Labour was going to win the election by a landslide. Yes, we were ahead in the polls, but we had been ahead many times before only to be disappointed come the election. My feeling was that, having lost four elections in succession, we couldn't afford even the slightest gamble on the outcome of the fifth, but my support for Blair was not unconditional. The minimum wage was my bottom line. I wanted to hear from his own lips that, contrary to rumour, Labour's commitment to a minimum wage would not be abandoned. I also wanted to hear his views on coping with the power structure – the concentration of media owner-ship, reform of party funding, accountability of the intelligence and security services and so on. I went to see him and we discussed all these issues. On the minimum wage he was sound (and in due course it proved to be one of New Labour's most popular social policies). Likewise on the reform of party funding (a Bill requiring all parties to disclose their source of funds became law in 2000). On media owner-ship he was non-committal, though he did say that if, during the election campaign, the press started to behave as they had done at previous elections, he would call a halt to our campaign and spend a couple of days talking about who owned them and why they behaved as they did. Satisfied, I made up my mind to support him and wrote an article for *Tribune* setting out why. I was duly denounced for my pains by my old friend Hugh MacPherson, a respected *Tribune* col-umnist. I later heard that my endorsement was received with rapture at the Blair campaign headquarters, not because it influenced the outcome – by this stage Blair was on course to win anyway – but because it was the first evidence of support by someone he regarded as a member of 'the sensible left' (which, incidentally, came to include Dennis Skinner, whose judgement Blair also respected). 'Tony owes you,' Jack Straw remarked to me some time later. I never saw it that way. Indeed, although I voted for him, I didn't nominate him pre-cisely because I was keen to distinguish myself from those who were flocking to his banner merely because he was a winner.

It was some time before I had any further contact with Blair. Then, in November 1994, he invited me to his office and asked if I would be willing to go on the front bench. This was not the first time I had been asked (I was by now very respectable). As long ago as 1992 John Smith had asked me to be housing spokesman and I had declined in favour of remaining on the Home Affairs Select Committee. Blair talked of 'pepping up' the front bench and giving it a radical edge. 'So many of the left are ...'

'Impossibilists,' I said.

'I was going to say "conservative". Their idea of being radical is to defend the status quo.' An astute observation and one that was hard to deny. The Labour left at this time had few new ideas beyond repealing the Tory trade union laws (some of which were sensible and popular) and reversing all changes in the management of the NHS, regardless of whether or not they made sense. I replied that I had no objection in principle to going on the front bench, but my immediate ambition was to become chairman of the Home Affairs committee. No doubt he was bewildered by this. Select committees played little part in his thinking. Faced with a choice between Parliament and government he was a government man every time. 'My absolute priority is to win,' he said. 'I know that sounds unprincipled, but I just see that as my role in life.'

We discussed a number of possibilities – Home Office, Foreign Office, Heritage ('if we are intending to do anything about media ownership') and there we left it. I heard no more until October 1996, when Blair's parliamentary private secretary, Bruce Grocott, asked if I had received a call. I hadn't, as it happened. He said they had talked about giving me international development instead of Clare Short. I am glad they didn't. Clare proved to be an outstanding success as International Development Secretary. She presided, not without difficulty (the Foreign Office mounted a fierce rearguard action), over the creation of a separate department and a revolution in the way British development assistance was delivered. What's more she was left in post long enough – six years – to make a difference, and she did. By the time she departed, Britain's overseas aid programme was respected around the world and much of that was down to her.

Come the election, it was taken for granted that I would chair the Home Affairs committee. In those days the choice of committee chairmen was dependent on the patronage of the party leadership and I had two powerful patrons: Jack Straw and the prime minister. I was also elected to the parliamentary committee, an obscure but influential body which comes into its own when Labour is in government. Membership consists of the prime minister, the deputy prime minister, the chief whips from the Lords and the Commons, a couple of cabinet ministers, a backbench peer and six elected backbenchers from the Commons, of which I was one. The committee, which is intended to act as a liaison between the foot soldiers and the government, met weekly, usually in the prime minister's room at the House of Commons and occasionally in the Cabinet room at 10 Downing

Street. Blair did not take it seriously at first, often absenting himself, but as times got harder he soon learned to appreciate the value of dialogue with the poor bloody infantry. In both capacities (chairmanship of the Home Affairs committee and membership of the parliamentary committee) I enjoyed far more influence than I ever would as a junior minister. This being so, I was in no hurry to join the government, though from time to time hints were dropped that there was a job for me if I wanted it.

The only possible excuse for trading the chairmanship of a major committee for a junior job in government was the possibility that it might lead to something better. One or two of my more discerning friends remarked that I had sold myself cheap, and so I had. The job was fine for an ambitious thirty-something, but not for someone who had been around for as long as I had. Still, it was a way to satisfy my curiosity to learn how government worked from the inside, and with hindsight I don't regret it, but that is not how it seemed at the time. Adjusting to being the lowest form of ministerial life in John Prescott's vast department – Environment, Transport and the Regions – was not easy and involved frequent humiliation. Invitations that would start out with the secretary of state would be passed down until they arrived in the in-tray of the humble parliamentary under secretary. Often, usually at short notice, I would be required to address conferences of experts on subjects such as coastal erosion or sustainable drainage. I would be handed a jargon-ridden, undeliverable speech which I would be expected to go off and deliver in front of assembled experts and then the terrifying moment would come when the chairman would say, 'the minister has time to answer a few questions'. Once I was dispatched, in lieu of the local government minister, to a posh hotel in Mayfair to address a conference of 300 local authority bigwigs on the virtues of 'best value', then only a gleam in New Labour's eye. The speech I was given, which appeared to be written by someone on work experience, repeated the key phrase 'Best Value' forty-three times, but nowhere defined it. I was expected to stand there and chant it like a Maoist slogan. Hitherto the little bit of esteem I had accumulated arose from opening my mouth only on subjects I knew about. Now I was expected to opine daily on things about which I knew nothing.

Despite working in the same building, a glitzy, glassy modern block near Victoria Station, we junior ministers saw little of our secretary of state, universally referred to as JP. His responsibilities were vast and the management of human beings was not his forte. At first, I saw more of him on TV than I did in the flesh. Later there were fortnightly meetings of ministers in his vast top-floor office. These consisted mainly of him slumped in an armchair, tie askew, one leg over the arm of the chair, giving vent to a long stream of consciousness about whatever had hit him on his way into work that morning. Our role was to provide sycophantic laughter at appropriate intervals. My colleague Keith Hill and I took to timing these diatribes. The longest lasted twenty-nine minutes, broken only when the fire alarm went off inadvertently and he paused to abuse the anonymous voice coming from the ceiling.

JP had his faults – he could be insecure, bad-tempered, foul-mouthed, constantly interfering in matters best left to underlings – but he had strengths, too, which only gradually became apparent. He had excellent political antennae (one reason Blair valued him), he was loyal to colleagues, surprisingly tolerant and could hold his own in the company of colleagues far cleverer and more sophisticated than himself. He started his working life as a steward on the *Queen Mary* and ended as deputy prime minister for ten years – longer than anyone else – and by the end he had some solid achievements to his name, including reforms to the tax regime for merchant shipping which led to a substantial reduction in the use of flags of convenience. He also helped bring about better working conditions for merchant seamen and workers in the offshore industry and made a considerable impact at the climate-change negotiations in Japan which led to the Kyoto agreement. Above all, he was critical in helping John Smith and Tony Blair drive through the internal reforms which helped make Labour electable again.

Question time was a white-knuckle ride. Because I was responsible for everything and yet nothing, there were few limits to what I could be asked about – environment, local government, housing, aviation. Rarely was I questioned concerning issues that came within my brief. I lived in terror of the unexpected supplementary. Short questions are the most dangerous. On one memorable occasion I was dealing with a question about pollution when up got Desmond Swayne, a Tory troublemaker. 'What about particulates?' he asked. That was all he said and then sat down. I hadn't a clue what he was talking about. My mouth opened, but no words emerged. A deathly hush descended. The Tories began poking fun. 'Help,' someone called. JP, whose interventions were not usually helpful, muttered something about 'difficulties with Europe'. I duly repeated this with as much authority as I could muster, adding, 'The honourable member can rest assured that our finest minds are working on it.' The House erupted. The Speaker Betty Boothroyd beamed. Everyone was suddenly on my side. With one bound I was free, but it was a close-run thing. The line between triumph and humiliation is wafer thin.

Besides answering questions and addressing conferences, my duties consisted primarily of signing letters to colleagues, replying to adjournment debates and helping to shepherd Bills through committee. The letters came in by the hundred. Frequently we were on the receiving end of letter writing or postcard campaigns by environmental pressure groups such as Greenpeace or Friends of the Earth. Many MPs, instead of constructing their own reply based on our widely circulated briefing notes, would simply forward these to the hapless minister and demand a reply, personally referring to the constituent concerned, who had often done no more than put their signature to a postcard. The letters and postcards would disappear into a vast departmental letter-writing machine and reappear some weeks later in an orange folder for the minister to sign. Some colleagues would send as many as ten identical postcards and expect individual replies to each one. After a while, I refused to sign multiple copies and dropped the worst offenders a note suggesting that they drafted his or her own reply based on the template I had already provided. Some took offence at this, but it had to be done. Most of the big departments devoted huge resources to letter writing. Some were more efficient than others. Letters could disappear for up to eighteen months into the notoriously inefficient Ministry of Agriculture, Fisheries and Food. My ministerial colleagues in that department were tearing their hair out in frustration. One actually went down to the MAFF mail room, stood by as the letters were opened and tracked their path through the department in an attempt to find out what the problem was. Whether he ever succeeded in finding the black hole into which they disappeared, I cannot say.

During the summer recess, ministers would take turns in signing each other's letters. This sensible arrangement broke down when one of my less collegiate colleagues declined to sign any letters but his own. I returned from holiday to find the best part of a thousand letters, each in its own orange folder, piled on the conference table in my room with more underneath in a long line of cardboard boxes. In the year 2000 I probably signed more letters than any other minister in the government.

That year I was also king of the adjournment debates. Any backbench MP who wishes to gain air time for an issue about which he or she feels strongly can apply to the Speaker for a debate on the subject which, if granted, takes place in the main chamber at the close of business. On evenings when Parliament sat late, this could be in the early hours of the morning. The subject of these debates varied widely. They could be about a constituency matter of interest only to the MP concerned and a handful of his constituents, they might concern an individual case of alleged injustice or they might be part of a wider campaign, in which case they might attract the attention of more members. Rarely, however, did they interest more than half a dozen MPs, and as often as not an adjournment debate might be held solely between the member concerned and the minister whose job it was to respond, reading speeches to each other at dead of night in an otherwise empty chamber.

The opening of an additional debating chamber in Westminster Hall greatly increased the opportunity for mini debates, some lasting as long as three hours, which meant even more work for junior ministers. Such debates worked well when the minister responding was knowledgeable on the subject under discussion. In such cases a dialogue was possible, with MPs intervening on the minister with pertinent questions to which they would receive enlightening answers. All too often, however, ministers were asked at short notice to respond on issues about which they knew little or nothing, in which case debate was less fruitful. I make no complaint. As a backbench MP, I made good use of adjournment debates, often as a way of putting ministers on the spot regarding issues they would have preferred not to talk about. Even before I was elected, half a dozen of my friends in Parliament, using notes I had provided, kept Home Office minister David Mellor up until dawn while they hammered him about the Birmingham Six case. On another glorious occasion, with the aid of several colleagues, I kept an unfortunate Foreign Office minister pinned down for four hours while he attempted to defend Britain's indefensible support for Cambodia's dreaded Khmer Rouge, a particularly disgraceful episode in which we teamed up with China, the USA and Thailand to bleed the Vietnamese who had liberated the country from one of the most murderous regimes of the twentieth century. It was a Friday and the debate should have lasted only half an hour, but the main business unexpectedly collapsed. In twenty-three years as an MP, that was the only occasion I can recall having a minister utterly at my mercy. Of course, it is not so much fun being on the receiving end. At the height of my career in the Department of Environment, Transport and the Regions, I had the dubious privilege of responding to more than forty adjournment debates in one session of Parliament. My record was four in one day.

When I wasn't busy signing letters, responding to adjournment debates and addressing conferences of experts on subjects about which I knew little or nothing, my presence was required on the Committee Corridor. Later I would work in departments that had hardly any legislation to steer through Parliament. Environment, Transport and the Regions, however, had a major legislative programme, the centrepiece of which was the Transport Bill, the first ninety clauses of which concerned the part-privatisation of the UK's National Air Traffic Services, the department in the Civil Aviation Authority responsible for providing air-traffic control at UK airports. This was controversial. Gordon Brown and the Treasury were extremely keen on it. Prescott and Brown had done a deal. In return for selling a stake in the country's air-traffic control, JP would receive the investment he needed to fund his transport plans. The Tories were content with this, but virtually no one on the Labour side was happy. Unlike many of my colleagues, however, I had no ideological objection to selling shares in NATS, providing there were no risks regarding safety (the unions were playing the safety card for all it was worth). As John Prescott once remarked, the logical extension of the argument that only state ownership could guarantee safety was that we should all travel on Aeroflot. No one who has witnessed, as I have, what happened in Vietnam when the state took control of the means of production, distribution and exchange – thereby collapsing just about all productive activity – could be too starry-eyed about public ownership. The case for selling a stake in NATS was twofold. First, that it would bring the Treasury some much-needed cash (in fact it brought in almost nothing). Second, that it would bring some badly needed private sector management to a profession that was having to grapple with significant change. Having satisfied myself that the safety regime was robust, I had no difficulty in defending the proposal, although there was no real enthusiasm for it. Even Downing Street was nervous and, had I used my various back-channels to the prime minister, I could probably have stopped it. But I wasn't about to undermine JP and so I held the line. To some effect: what had been flagged up as a considerable rebellion (at one point the whips were advising that it might not get through) soon faded.

I awaited with mounting terror the arrival of the Transport Bill. It appeared on my desk just before Christmas 1999, comprising a whopping 280 clauses and 31 schedules, together with a wodge of explanatory notes. Since I had no hope of getting my befuddled brain around the technical details, my strategy was to keep a few clauses ahead of the committee. I therefore placed the Bill in the top drawer of my desk and went home for Christmas. I returned to find that the housing minister, Nick Raynsford, had been given the job of leading for our side. Keith Hill and myself were to be his juniors. Raynsford was one of my most impressive colleagues. Despite possession of a truly Rolls-Royce mind, he was entirely lacking in the arrogance that sometimes afflicts the seriously clever. As housing minister he was completely unfamiliar with the niceties of air-traffic control. What's more, he had been ill over Christmas. Yet by the time we returned in the New Year, he had mastered the Bill. Be it ever so complex, he had only to glance at a clause to understand it. Indeed, he positively relished grappling with the intricacies. By contrast, I had yet to do any more than glance at the Bill. I came back from our first briefing with officials singing Nick Raynsford's praises to my disapproving private secretary, Jessica. She, of course, knew that my copy of the Bill had been locked in the top drawer of my desk over Christmas and replied witheringly, 'I think, Minister, he *has* read the Bill.'

The dread day came. The Tories fielded a formidable team which included Michael Portillo, who had just been re-elected at Chelsea after his surprise defeat at Enfield, and was anxious to make his mark. Bernard Jenkin led for the Opposition and he had a good understanding of what was involved. The Tories, unsurprisingly, were not ideologically opposed to selling a stake in air-traffic control, but they did have some detailed questions and one of the easiest ways to wrong-foot an inexperienced minister is to stand up and ask the meaning of Section 5, sub-clause ii(b). A phalanx of officials, the real experts, sit behind the minister furiously scribbling notes, but often the notes do not arrive in time and those that do are sometimes illegible. I have long thought that it makes no sense to pretend that the minister is all-knowing and that the solution would be to give the relevant officials a right of audience at the committee stage, but for the moment at least that is not how it works. Raynsford was completely unfazed. He volunteered to speak on all the most difficult clauses and dealt effortlessly with mischief-making from the other side. Keith Hill and I watched in awe. As long as I live I shall be grateful to Nick Raynsford.

I might have remained on the Transport Bill for many months. Those, indeed, were my instructions, even though, once the air-traffic clauses had been dealt with, I would be superfluous. However, I was needed elsewhere. A few doors further down the corridor Michael Meacher was guiding through the Countryside Bill which, among other things, implemented the right of ramblers to roam freely on mountain, moorland, heath and down. This was a commitment that had featured prominently in our election manifesto, a much more agreeable piece of legislation and one that I had no difficulty in understanding. The Tories, needless to say, representing as they did the landed interests, were implacably opposed and raised all manner of bogus objections. This was yet another piece of legislation about which Number 10 had cold feet, apparently afraid of upsetting the landowners (at this stage there seemed to be room for everyone in New Labour's big tent). Throughout its passage we were assailed by rumours that Number 10 was about to pull the plug. In the end, however, the Countryside Bill sailed through and none of the predicted disasters came to pass.

As if the Transport and Countryside Bills were not enough to be going on with, I received word that my services were urgently required on yet another committee, dealing with the Utilities Bill. We were reaching the point where I was likely to be on three Bill committees simultaneously. I could have wandered down the Committee Corridor, opened just about any door and been made welcome. The Utilities Bill was in trouble. It was badly drafted and the government's legislative programme was heavily overloaded. It was initially intended that I should move the thirty clauses relating to the water industry, but my instructions suddenly changed. It was now my job to remove them (while on no account admitting to the existence of a crisis). This I duly did with one short speech, the greatest impact I have ever had on legislation.

Overall, I was on Bill committees continuously, every Tuesday and Thursday from January to July, in addition to being minister of many other things – housing, aviation, countryside, local government, science, zoos, sustainable drainage, waste disposal, you name it ... every day was an adventure.

From the outset I had a survival strategy. On my first day the permanent secretary, Sir Richard Mottram, offered me a sound piece of advice. 'You are not going to be here long. Don't try to change the world. Just pick two or three issues where you may be able to make a difference and leave the rest.' I picked three modest aims: regulating the growth of leylandii trees, placing limits on night flights over London and making discretionary the payment of housing benefit to slum landlords. On the face of it these were all goals that ought to have been easily achievable, but in practice each proved a struggle.

Leylandii were a cause of warfare in the suburbs. They are forest trees wholly unsuited to suburban gardens. They grow at the rate of three or four feet a year and, unless maintained, can swiftly cast a shadow over a neighbour's garden. Sometimes the damage was inadvertent; sometimes they were used as a weapon. People whose lives were blighted by the remorseless growth of leylandii spent fortunes on legal actions, to no avail. Local authorities were powerless. The department received hundreds of letters each year asking for the law to be changed. It ought to have been simple enough. All that was needed was a minor amendment to the planning law, giving a local authority the power to require high hedges to be maintained at a reasonable height. Various private member's Bills, one floated by the department itself, had attempted to resolve the matter, but all came to grief. By the time I came on the scene it was clear that legislation was the only solution. If we can't sort out something as simple as this, I said to myself, we might as well all go home. Inevitably, however, it proved a great deal more complicated than I could ever have imagined. Objections flowed in from every quarter – the Home Office, the Lord Chancellor and Number 10 Downing Street. It was said that the prime minister himself had personally vetoed legislation. It was suggested that he was likely to veto even a consultation that might lead to legislation. 'What's the problem?' I asked the emissary from Downing Street. 'I bet the prime minister hasn't devoted more than thirty seconds of his time to this.' He confirmed that this was so. I pressed him and reluctantly he disgorged two names, Jonathan Powell and Anji Hunter.*

'Anji Hunter? Where does she fit in?'

'The prime minister values her political antennae.'

I later heard that she had seen Rory Bremner making jokes about the 'nanny state' (a favourite *Daily Mail* theme, although on this issue even the *Mail* was onside). Apparently, this contained a throwaway line the drift of which was, 'Do you know, the government are even proposing to regulate the size of hedges?' Result: our entire effort kiboshed.

We conducted yet another consultation. Inevitably it reached the same conclusion: only a change in the law would make any difference. Equally inevitably we were obliged to ignore the conclusion and opted instead for a 'Code of Conduct', always the last resort of governments reluctant to confront a vested interest. In co-operation with the garden centre industry (who were the cause of the problem) a leaflet

---

*Powell was Blair's chief of staff; Anji Hunter, who bore the title Director of Government Relations, was reputedly the most influential non-elected person in Downing Street.

was produced. A meeting with officials was held in Michael Meacher's office to consider a draft. It was like a scene from *Yes Minister*.

'Where,' asked Michael, 'does it actually say that it is not a good idea to plant leylandii?'

'Ah, well, Minister, it doesn't quite put it as boldly as that. We have to be careful not to upset the industry.'

In fact, as one of the officials cheerfully pointed out, the leaflet was drafted in a way that could actually be seen as encouraging the growing of leylandii – the exact opposite of what we were trying to achieve.

After several more years and much energy wasted on displacement activity, the government was finally persuaded to legislate. By this time I was long gone, though I continued to pursue the matter from the back benches. In 2003 a clause was introduced into the Antisocial Behaviour Bill giving local authorities the power to regulate high hedges. It hasn't entirely resolved the problem (some local authorities are reluctant to use the power they have been given; others resorted to charging outrageous fees), but it has made a difference.

Night flights were an even knottier problem. Between 0430 and 0600 each day sixteen long-distance flights arrive at Heathrow. The flight path runs directly across central London, disturbing the sleep of a fair swathe of the population from Greenwich to Windsor. Like leylandii, they are the subject of much complaint. Unlike leylandii, I was never in any doubt about the resistance any suggestion for change would attract.

The aviation industry is one of the mightiest vested interests in the land and has a voracious appetite. It wants more of everything: airports, runways, terminals ... and enjoys an unhealthily close relationship with government. (I was surprised to discover that a total of fourteen officials from the British Airports Authority and the airlines possessed passes to the department, enabling them to come and go as they pleased.) For their part ministers and officials alike see an expanding civil aviation industry as an essential component of economic growth and, therefore, almost always give way to the relentless demands of the industry, regardless of the impact on the environment or any other consideration. So, rearranging the night flights was always going to be an uphill battle.

Officials were against even raising the subject. I began by suggesting we invite representatives of the airlines to meet with MPs from some of the worst affected constituencies. 'I wouldn't bother, Minister. They won't turn up,' I was advised. Now why would that be, I wondered. Might it be because officials were quietly advising that this was only a junior minister on a trip of his own? I duly tapped out a note instructing officials to organise such a meeting and put it before the transport minister, Gus MacDonald. And in they came, bringing with them a long list of excuses why nothing could be done about anything, the most ludicrous of which was 'wind speeds over China'.

I could see only one way forward, and that was to make the rescheduling of the sixteen night flights conditional on something the industry badly wanted. As it happened, there was just such a weapon to hand. John Prescott was about to decide whether or not to give the go-ahead to the building of a fifth terminal at Heathrow. I, therefore, penned him a note suggesting that he make permission conditional on the rescheduling of the night flights. A meeting was arranged. Officials left me in no doubt that they were implacably opposed and, shortly before Gus MacDonald and I were due to meet with the secretary of state, they came up with legal advice that since the Secretary of State was acting in a judicial capacity it would not be right for him to discuss the subject, even with his ministers. The advice was swiftly countermanded, but by that time our meeting had been cancelled and, before it could be rearranged, I had been reshuffled. Result: Heathrow got its fifth terminal and night flights continue to disturb the sleep of half the population of central London. I note with interest the management of Heathrow are now offering to reduce night flights in return for a third runway. I'll believe it when I see it.

I had better luck with housing benefit. One day, after a decade or more in Parliament, it came to me in a blinding flash that public money was actually funding the destruction of our social fabric. In parts of Sunderland, where there were high concentrations of houses owned by private landlords – and also on some public housing estates – whole streets went into a spiral of decline. Houses became unlettable and some were firebombed by gangs of marauding youths. Anyone who was socially mobile got out, leaving behind only the desperate and the disaffected. A large part of the problem was that in many cases housing benefit travelled directly from the public purse into the bank account of the landlord without ever passing through the property for which it was being paid. As a result, landlords had little or no incentive to take an interest in either the behaviour of their tenants or the condition of their properties. Many of the properties were bought at auction by people living at the other end of the country who rarely, if ever, visited them. So blatant was this arrangement that for a period in the mid-1990s an advertisement appeared every Saturday in the property section of the *Newcastle Journal* offering houses for sale, the main selling point of which was that the tenants would all be on benefit and, therefore, required little or no management. This was especially a problem in the declining industrial towns and cities of the north. The irony was that, in the north, there was no great housing shortage. We didn't need these landlords.

The solution seemed to me obvious. There should be a presumption in favour of paying housing benefit to the tenant instead of paying it directly to the landlord. This and this alone would force landlords to take an interest in the behaviour of their tenants and it would provide tenants with leverage over landlords when it came to repairs and maintenance. When I first raised this with ministers I got nowhere. Civil servants, who tended to have a southern mindset, advised that paying housing benefit direct to tenants would lead landlords to refuse to let to tenants on housing benefit, and this would only exacerbate the general shortage of rented property in the south. I accepted this. The solution, therefore, was to grant local authorities the discretion to choose how housing benefit should be paid. Still I was getting nowhere, so I dropped a note to the prime minister. He immediately took an interest and suddenly things began to move. Eventually, from April 2008, it came to pass that housing benefit would in future, with certain exceptions, be paid directly to the tenant and not the landlord. In addition, local authorities are now allowed to designate areas with high concentrations of slum properties within which they have the power to oblige landlords to carry out repairs and maintenance. In Sunderland it had exactly the desired effect. A few weeks before I retired I received a visit from representatives of two of the city's biggest landlords who owned 400 houses apiece. One lived in Dorset, the other was local and notorious, and both complained that as a result of the new system they were finding rent hard to collect, given the type of people with whom they were filling their properties. For the first time in years they were having to spend time and money on management. 'You have to help us change the law,' they said, 'or we'll go bankrupt.' It was only with difficulty that I managed to keep a straight face.

There was one other area in which I had a modest influence, though sadly not on the Labour government. As a minister I was, of course, entitled to a car and a driver but, since ours was the department charged with encouraging people to leave their cars at home and opt for public transport, it was not good politics for ministers to be chauffeured everywhere. Every time one of our number made a speech about the need to encourage people to use bicycles or public transport, television cameras would appear at the rear of the building to film ministers climbing into their official cars. This was a regular source of embarrassment for John Prescott, whose memorable 300-yard drive from his hotel to the conference centre during the 1999 Labour Party conference was the subject of enormous ridicule.

Shaking off the Government Car Service was not easy, however. It was heavily unionised and run to a large extent for the benefit of those who provide the service rather than those in receipt of it. The drivers received a low basic wage and relied on overtime to supplement their wages. They were, therefore, keen to be kept hanging about for as long as possible. Ministers soon form a relationship with their drivers and before long found themselves inventing journeys for the sole purpose of keeping their drivers happy. I knew of ministerial colleagues who on Sunday afternoons or Monday mornings were being collected from home, hundreds of miles away, when there was a perfectly good train service, just to give the driver something to do. Others would drive the length of the country delivering and collecting ministerial red boxes, even though the Post Office operated a perfectly good special delivery service at a fraction of the price. I was determined not to go down this road and so, on day one, made clear from the outset that I did not want a car. Jessica, my private secretary, was sympathetic but pointed out that – this being the summer recess – I might find I needed one when Parliament returned in the autumn and we were a great deal busier. On this basis I agreed to retain the option of occasionally using the government car pool until the autumn. After a couple of months I discovered that the department was being charged a staggering £700 a week (at 1999 prices, remember) just to have on call a car and driver I never used. I summoned the head of the Government Car Service to invite him to justify this and, before my eyes, the price fell like a stone, bottoming at £400 a week. There we left it for the time being. Come autumn, however, Parliament returned and the numbers 3 and 159 buses continued to pass my door. I, therefore, instructed Jessica to dispense with the car. Back came the message, 'Ah, minister, that will be £4,000 depreciation for the car we had reserved for you, but which will now have to be sold.'

'Invite the head of the car service to come and discuss this with me.'

By return came the reply, 'No need, minister, your car has been reallocated.' His bluff had been called.

I recounted my struggle with the Government Car Service in the first volume of my diaries and David Cameron on reading it announced that, if he became prime minister, the service would be high on his list for reform. He was as good as his word. Most ministers no longer have dedicated drivers and are only entitled to use the car pool when they have good reason to do so. Some Cabinet ministers even ride bicycles (though, as my friend Andrew Mitchell discovered, this can get you into trouble). The number of ministerial cars and drivers now hanging about in Speaker's Court on any given day is greatly diminished (although I notice recently that it is creeping back up again). Needless to say, my name was mud within the service. For some time afterwards, when passing through Speaker's Court, I would occasionally see drivers nudging each other and whispering words to the effect, 'That's the bastard who ...'

A year passed. I counted the days to the reshuffle, and then one July morning Prescott announced that there would not be one. 'I have told Tony that I am satisfied with all my ministers and there is no need for any changes.' My heart sank. By the beginning of 2001 I was beginning to despair of rescue and then, out of the blue, came another call from the prime minister: 'Chris, I have something more up your street. How would you like to work with Clare Short at International Development?' There was nothing I would like better. And off I went with a spring in my step. The Department for International Development was a happy place full of happy people doing work they believed in. Clare, as I recounted earlier, was in most respects a brilliant secretary of state. She had transformed Britain's overseas aid programme. There was only one problem. *She didn't need a deputy.* She was, as she put it, 'policy greedy'. In five months I never saw a single piece of paper marked 'for decision'. I could have whiled away a pleasant couple of years meeting people who didn't need to be met and visiting places that didn't need to be visited, but I soon realised that I had to make up my mind whether I was a serious politician or not and, on balance, though it was a close-run thing, I decided that I was. And so, come the election, I asked to be moved up or out and was duly returned to the ranks. Where, to my pleasant surprise, I found myself re-elected to the parliamentary committee and reappointed chairman of the Home Affairs Select Committee, in both of which capacities I had far more influence than I ever had as a minister.

Two years later the call came again. By this time the New Labour project had been blown seriously off course. We were up to our necks in the wars in Afghanistan and Iraq. I was among the 139 Labour MPs who, in my case with the heaviest of hearts, had voted against the Iraq war. Seven weeks later, on the night Clare Short had belatedly resigned, I was having dinner with a friend in the atrium at Portcullis House when Jean Corston, the chair of the parliamentary Labour party, came running up. 'The prime minister is looking for you. Have you spoken to him?'

I hadn't. I went to the telephone and rang the message board in the members' lobby. Sure enough there were two urgent messages asking me to ring Number 10. I rang. 'Please hold on. He is expecting you,' said the woman on the switchboard. There followed several clicks and a long pause. 'I am sorry,' said the voice. 'He is tied up at the moment. Can you ring back in fifteen minutes?'

I went back and finished my dinner and then rang again. More clicks. More pauses and then the voice said, 'Sorry. He has gone home for the night. He will call you in the morning.' I wasn't worried. Jean Corston had told me what was afoot. Valerie Amos, who was in the Lords, had been appointed to replace Clare as secretary of state and he now needed a spokesman in the Commons. That was to be me. Later that evening, however, it occurred to me that I was due to chair the Home Affairs committee first thing next morning and I ought not to do that, if I was a minister. I went to seek the advice of Hilary Armstrong, the chief whip. 'Oh yes, I would, if I were you,' she said – a little too hastily, I thought. 'Tony hadn't realised that you had voted the wrong way on Iraq.'

'I think he had, Hilary. He and I had a fifteen-minute conversation about it on the day of the vote.'

'Well, he'd forgotten,' she said.

And in a flash all became clear. Although I had not responded instantly to the message from Number 10, Hilary had and she got straight over there to put the boot in. When I had called the first time and been advised that the prime minister was tied up, that was because Hilary was in with him trying to talk him out of appointing me.

The prime minister called first thing next morning. 'As you probably realise, there is a problem,' he said, but not to worry. He had something similar in mind for me come the reshuffle. That turned out to be the Africa job at the Foreign Office. Later that day it was announced that Hilary Benn, the prisons minister, would be the Commons minister at International Development. There was a tragic sequel. Four months later the leader of the Lords, Gareth Williams, a man universally respected, unexpectedly dropped dead. He was replaced by Valerie Amos, whereupon Hilary Benn became secretary of state. In all likelihood that would have been me. Had I responded quickly to that call from Number 10, I might have been anointed before Hilary Armstrong could have got over there. Arguably, my refusal to carry a pager cost me a seat in the Cabinet.

My two years at the Foreign Office under Jack Straw were among the happiest of my political life. Unlike Clare and JP, Jack was a secretary of state who knew how to delegate. By and large he left his ministers to get on with their jobs, expecting to be consulted only when necessary. Someone once wrote of Jack that he was the only Labour minister who appeared utterly at home in government from day one, and it was true. You had to get up very early to be ahead of Jack. A professional to his fingertips, he had always done his homework. All boxes ticked. Everything nailed down. What's more, he was widely respected because, unlike some ministers, he took Parliament seriously. He was ambitious, with an almost unerring knack of being on the winning side in any leadership struggle by the time the music stopped – witness his seamless transition from the Blair to the Brown camp in the Spring of 2007 – but somehow his ambition was never held against him. First, because of his basic decency and, second, because in any conversation with Jack, you always had a feeling that he was levelling with you.

Life at the Foreign Office was on an altogether different plane than at the other departments in which I served. I had a grand office overlooking the Durbar Court with marble fireplaces at each end and ceilings so high as to be in the clouds. Through it flowed a stream of important visitors, ambassadors, high commissioners, foreign ministers and even the occasional head of state. Official travel gave one a glimpse of life in the stratosphere. If you are the Queen or the prime minister, you dwell permanently in the stratosphere. Life in the stratosphere means that you never have to wait anywhere. Doors open without you touching them. You do not queue at airports or wait at traffic lights. I was once in a meeting with Tony Blair shortly before he was due to leave for Washington on Concorde. Alastair Campbell and members of the court were loitering in the outer office. 'Hello, Alastair,' I said. 'What time does your plane go?'

He looked at me pityingly and said, 'Ah no, Chris. It's not like that. The plane goes when we arrive. You'd love it.'

And sure enough it does. I once flew home from Nigeria with the prime minister. One minute you are dining in the High Commissioner's residence, next minute officials are bundling you into a convoy of land cruisers and, accompanied by an escort of police on motorbikes, you are racing through empty streets the thirty miles to the airport. No customs formalities or passport checks. The luggage has mysteriously found its way on board. You race up the steps of the aeroplane (the prime minister is always the last to board). The steps are removed. Doors closed. Off you go. On that occasion the prime minister had a family funeral to attend in Glasgow, but had been intending to return to Downing Street overnight and fly to Scotland next day. We were running late, however, so, when the plane reached the UK, it just carried on until we came to Glasgow, dropped off Tony and Cherie and then delivered the rest of us back to London. It sure takes the strain out of air travel.

If you are a humble minister in one of the travelling departments, you do not live in the stratosphere but you do get to visit. Every three or four weeks I would get up in my little flat in Brixton Road, tow my wheelie bag to Stockwell tube station, take the tube to Paddington and from there, the express train to Heathrow. There I would meet my private secretary. We would queue to check in. Get on a plane. Fly for perhaps nine or ten hours and come down in some interesting part of Africa. And suddenly I was de facto a head of state ...

There would be red carpets, men whispering into walkie-talkies, our ambassador or high commissioner and a foreign minister or two would be waiting to greet me. A convoy of land cruisers, sometimes with police escorts, sirens and flashing lights, would whisk us away to a grand residence. Interesting people would come to breakfast, lunch and dinner. I would be taken to see the president, prime minister, foreign minister and assorted movers and shakers. In between I would visit interesting projects, sometimes commuting between them by helicopter. At the end of three or four days my convoy would race back to the airport and, so tired that I practically kissed the steps of the plane, I would climb aboard, fly for eight or nine hours and come out the other end towing my wheelie bag as though I had been on the set of a film for the previous few days. That was my life every three or four weeks for two years.

Alas, all good things must end, and the end in British politics comes suddenly. In my case four days after the 2005 general election, just when I thought I was safe. Jack Straw was back as Foreign Secretary, most of the dismissals had already occurred and my staff were confidently expecting my return. At 3.45 p.m. on Monday, 9 May 2005, I was on the phone to my opposite number in the American State Department discussing what we were going to do about the Liberian warlord Charles Taylor.* By 4 p.m. I was no longer the minister. Dismissal was a massive blow to my fragile self-esteem, all the more so because it arrived out of the blue. Obviously The Man's opinion of me, once sufficient to defy the normal rules of political gravity, had nosedived. Later, Jack Straw, rang. 'You just fell off the end, Chris,' he said. But was that really the explanation? After two years I felt I was on top of the job. At the point where I was useful. Or so I thought. I could hover in the lobby of an African Union conference and heads of state would approach me without my having to go and seek them out. At which point The Man raised his little finger by a fraction and I was gone, and some other poor sod had to start all over again from scratch.

Personnel management was not New Labour's strong suit. Blair couldn't resist tossing all the pieces into the air and starting again. Rare was the minister who was left in place long enough to make a difference. I was the sixth Africa minister. By the time we left office there had been nine. We had thirteen Europe ministers (eleven plus Geoff Hoon, who held the job twice – once for only three months) in as many years. At the Department of Work and Pensions there were eight secretaries of state in ten years. The health and education departments were regularly turned inside out. Prisons ministers came and went almost annually. John Reid, a most capable politician, held nine ministerial posts in ten years. It was wasteful, massively destabilising and bad for morale. Several months after David Cameron had become prime minister, I ran into him. 'With all due respect,' I said, 'may I offer one piece of advice: avoid annual reshuffles.' It was a lesson he had already grasped and by and large stuck to.

Over and over I racked my brains as to why I had been sacked. At first I blamed Hilary Armstrong (who had not forgiven me for being appointed in defiance of her advice), but I don't think she was responsible for my final demise. It pains me to admit this, but I think Blair had concluded that I wasn't as capable as he had once supposed. One particular incident will have sown the seeds of doubt. It was in December 2003, a few days after our return from the Commonwealth

---

*In May 2012 Taylor was sentenced to fifty years' imprisonment by the International Criminal Court.

conference in Nigeria. At the time my star was high. I had just travelled back from Abuja with him and we had several friendly exchanges
en route. The following Monday I came down to London from Sunderland, reaching the office in the early afternoon to be told that I was
expected to go and sit next to the prime minister while he reported
back to the Commons. At this point an alarm bell ought to have rung.
I should have obtained a copy of his brief and studied it carefully. I
should have realised that Blair had taken very little interest in the
conference and probably hadn't done any more than glance at the
brief on his way over to the House. He would need help. I wandered
over, plonked myself down beside him on the front bench and sat
there soaking up atmosphere, instead of paying attention. 'What's the
answer to that?' he whispered as the Opposition spokesman sat down.
I hadn't even heard the question. I was struck dumb with terror. It
happened again. Instead of answering, I muttered something about
the Tories having awarded Robert Mugabe a knighthood (a piece of
ammunition that always came in handy in emergencies), but he just
shrugged and didn't use it. Afterwards, he left without saying a word.
I could see he was angry. In his place so would I have been too. My
star waned from then on. Even so, I survived for another eighteen
months, so I guess I must count myself lucky.

Later, long after I had left government, Douglas Hurd told me
that our high commissioner in Nigeria, Sir Richard Gozney, had taken
the unprecedented step of writing to the prime minister singing my
praises and asking that I be retained as Africa minister. Unfortunately
the letter arrived a day or two after I had been dismissed and in reply
Sir Richard received a note from the prime minister's chief of staff,
Jonathan Powell, curtly informing him that Dave Triesman was now
the Africa minister. Later, another senior Tory recounted an exchange
he had with a former permanent secretary in whose department I had
served. He had remarked that I was, 'a better minister than he
pretends'.

'A better minister than he pretends.' Not a bad epitaph to have
carved on my ministerial gravestone. I will settle for that.

Epilogue

How will it end, my life? Has anyone who has enjoyed such good fortune the right to expect a good death? Were I to go tomorrow, I would have no cause for complaint.

Over the years I have noted that there is no relationship between a virtuous life and the manner of one's death. Witness that the tyrant Stalin died peacefully in his bed while the late Pope John XXIII, a saintly man who led a life of impeccable rectitude, died in agony. But at least good Pope John, unlike many of us, had the expectation of another life to come.

We all wish for a good death and most of us know of people who have had one. The father of a friend, healthy into his mid-eighties, rose one Saturday morning, read the newspaper in his favourite armchair and then closed his eyes and fell into a sleep from which he never awoke. On the day before he died, my Vietnamese father-in-law, who during his life endured more than his share of hardship, rode around his home town on his Honda motorbike saying goodbye to close friends. He was even seen walking along the promenade by the Dakla river where, as a hungry, ragged child he had been brought up in a hut of mud and straw while his father scratched a living ferrying people back and forth in a sampan. What was he thinking on that final day? He must surely have reflected that, for all its dramatic ups and downs, his was a far better life than that of his father and that his children's lives would be better than his.

As for politicians, few led a more blessed life than the late Roy Jenkins and few enjoyed – if that is the right word – a better death.

Jenkins was arguably the most successful Home Secretary of the twentieth century, a successful Chancellor, president of the European Union (his dream job) and the author of a number of celebrated political biographies. One morning, when he was aged eighty-two and a few pages short of completing a biography of Roosevelt, his wife called upstairs to ask what he wanted for breakfast. He replied, 'Two eggs, lightly poached.' When she came back with them he had gone.

I have enjoyed more than my share of luck, having been born to a relatively prosperous family in one of the world's most prosperous countries. The absence of war meant that I missed out on both conscription and national service. After a rocky start, I have enjoyed good health, give or take the odd kidney stone. I learned to work hard, but for the most part I have had the privilege of being able to earn a living at work I enjoy, hopefully doing something useful along the way. I have two beautiful, healthy children and enjoy a comfortable retirement. No day passes without my reflecting on my good fortune. When I read about other less privileged lives I ask myself what unseen hand directed that they should live as they do and that I should live as I do.

Regrets? To be sure, I have regrets. Advice I should have listened to. People I have gratuitously upset. I wish I had passed the eleven-plus and gone to Maldon Grammar School rather than having to endure the strict regime of a Catholic boarding school, but at least it taught me the virtue of hard work. I wish I had learned a foreign language. Learned to play music. Been prime minister. But, on balance, life has worked out better than I have any right to expect.

What have I learned in my (almost) seventy years on this planet?

That life is short and one should make the most of it (although I expect most people my age have reached the same conclusion).

That it is stupid to waste time on feuds and vendettas.

That happiness comes from doing stuff, not buying stuff, and that the greatest happiness comes from helping others.

That in any walk of life it is better to go while people are asking 'Why?' rather than 'When?'

That the art of good governance (and the key to success in many other professions) is an ability to compromise, though not necessarily at the lowest common denominator.

That no religion, ideology or political party has a monopoly of wisdom.

That anyone who claims to have discovered a perfect formula for human happiness is deluded.

That although there are admirable people in all walks of life, put not thy faith in heroes; they often have feet of clay.

That one should never overlook the possibility, however remote, that one is mistaken; or that one's critics – or political opponents – are right.

That, as I have learned from the experience of my wife and her family in Vietnam, state control of the means of production, distribution and exchange does not result in greater happiness. And neither does rule by corporations. In short, big is not necessarily beautiful. Our best bet is the regulated market.

That taxation, fairly raised and efficiently used, is the subscription we pay to live in civilisation.

That an economy built on shopping does not have long to live.

That the human race must adapt to survive: if human beings continue to use the resources of the planet as if there is no tomorrow, then there will be no tomorrow.

That the great strength of capitalism is its ability to adapt to changed circumstances; its great (and potentially fatal) weakness is its voracious appetite for resources. One way or another the future is green ... or black.

I lay claim to no great insights, but it seems to me that already it is possible to identify several of the big political issues of the twenty-first century. Climate change and associated fallout is obviously one. The rise (and perhaps the implosion) of China is another. The great weakness of the Stalinist system, out of which the Chinese Communist Party grew, is that it contains no mechanism for correcting mistakes until they become catastrophes. The extraordinary current rates of growth in China cannot be sustained. The big question is what will be the impact upon surrounding countries and the world in general, if and when the Chinese economy implodes? China already has territorial disputes with just about all its eastern neighbours and is in the process of building a mighty navy. Conflict between China and Japan or Taiwan, which in turn would suck in the United States, is a long-term possibility that cannot be ruled out.

Finally, a crisis that is already upon us: the rise of the failed state. Some years ago, in Liberia, a devastated corner of West Africa, I stayed with the then US ambassador John Blaney, who argued that the rise of the failed state was likely to be one of the great challenges of the twenty-first century. He said, 'We have got to abandon our domestic hang-ups. Stop thinking twentieth-century liberal thoughts. We've got to do what helps people, what works.' Where practical, he advocated, failed states should be taken over and governed indefinitely under UN mandate. At the time he had in mind countries like Liberia, then on its third or fourth UN intervention, and Sierra Leone, where British intervention has created a fragile stability. But what of the bigger failed states such as Libya, whose inability to govern itself is already destabilising its neighbours? To be sure there is a debate to be had and some major practical difficulties to be ironed out, but we should not imagine, as we sit tight in fortress Europe, that we are immune from the consequences of their descent into chaos. On the contrary, it is rapidly becoming clear that we are not. So great is the scale of migration from Africa and the Middle East that it has the capacity to overwhelm our social systems. Already the flow of migrants from Syria, Afghanistan and elsewhere is threatening the very survival of the European Union. I have long seen this as a possibility, but it is happening much faster than I anticipated. In the longer term, climate change may create more failed states. What will happen if the great river deltas become uninhabitable? Or if the Sahara continues to spread south and west? Those who live there are not going to sit and wait to die. They are going to start moving. Some already have.

These problems are not insoluble, but they may require a mobilisation of manpower, resources and political will on a scale that we in the comfortable world have not so far been willing to contemplate. And as Ambassador Blaney suggested, they may also require some dramatic new thinking.

And what of the dear old Labour Party, of which I have been a member for about fifty years? Currently Labour is going through one of the periodic convulsions which often accompany defeat. There is nothing new in this. It happened in the 1950s and again in the late 1970s and early 80s. As we have seen before, it need not be fatal, but it would be a mistake to assume that, if we hang around long enough, the pendulum will inevitably swing back in Labour's direction. No political party (with the possible exception of the Tories) has a divine right to exist. To survive, Labour will need to convince a justifiably sceptical electorate that it has answers to the problems of the twenty-first century, and at the time of writing it is some way from doing so.

Electing Jeremy Corbyn was always going to be a high risk strategy. Much as I respect Jeremy, I did not vote for him on the grounds that in a parliamentary democracy it is folly to elect a leader who enjoys the confidence of less than 10 per cent of his parliamentary colleague. And so it has proved. It has been an interesting experiment, but always destined to end badly. To be sure, there are many mitigating factors. The election of Jeremy is yet another of the bills coming in for Iraq. As a leading opponent of the war (which I also voted against, incidentally), he was right about one of the big issues of the twenty-first century when most of the sophisticated, middle-of-the-roaders who boast of their capacity to make balanced judgements, were wrong. What a long fuse Tony Blair lit when he allied us umbilically to the worst American president of my lifetime.

The decision of the Labour national executive committee, at the urging of Ed Milliband, to allow anyone to sign up into the Labour Party in return for a payment of just £3 was another factor. Although not decisive, it brought into the party a flood of new members some of whom don't have the best interests of Labour at heart and not all of whom believe in parliamentary democracy. Witness the smattering of Socialist Worker placards at 'Save Jeremy' rallies. Jeremy was helped, too, by the fact he was up against three pleasant but lacklustre candidates, all to a greater or lesser extent tarred with the Blairite brush. Faced with a choice of four unelectable candidates, it was hardly surprising that many members decided to risk a punt on the one who was at least authentic. For what it's worth, my view was that, once elected, he should have been given two years to prove himself. There is a large grain of truth in the argument that he hasn't been given a chance. Some of those attempting to engineer his downfall were plotting and conniving within hours of his election. Unfortunately, however, Jeremy has not helped himself. His failure to throw himself wholeheartedly into the campaign to remain in the EU has played into the hands of his enemies and was arguably a decisive factor in the outcome. The clock cannot be turned back. One way or another, Jeremy needs to be replaced by someone capable of offering strong leadership in both the party and the country. Labour needs to get its act together fast. Failure to do so risks not mere defeat, but annihilation.

Whoever is in charge when the music stops has a steep hill to climb. Although the Tories have by historical standards only a small overall majority, the political realities are stark. Labour is between a rock and a hard place. Too left-wing for the southern middle classes, not left-wing enough for Scotland. Given that Scotland is not likely to return to the Labour fold any time soon, I see only one way forward – an electoral pact with the Liberal Democrats and the Greens designed to ensure that in, say, a hundred of the most marginal seats the Tories face a united opposition. Tribalists on all sides will throw their hands up in horror at the prospect, but the truth is that Labour badly needs a Liberal Democrat revival because they can win seats in places we can never hope to hold. One should never say never in politics, but the alternative is an indefinite period of Tory rule. Think about it.

In August 2010, a few months after retiring from Parliament, I finally achieved the ambition of a lifetime. After years of day-dreaming, doodling and many disappointments, I acquired a cottage with a small walled garden in a remote part of Northumberland where I intend to fade away growing vegetables and thinking great thoughts.

After forty years of inner-city living, in postal codes with some of the highest insurance costs in the country, I reckon I have served my time. In Brixton two riots passed my door. In the centre of Sunderland (where, it must be said, my family and I lived happily for twenty-five years), scarcely an hour passed without the wailing siren of a police car, fire engine or ambulance and on occasion the whirring rotors of the police helicopter hovering low overhead in pursuit of local ne'er-do-wells. Now I live in a place where the main threat to law and order comes from marauding hares – and sometimes deer – attempting to raid the communal vegetable plot. Not forgetting the fox who occasionally murders ducks on one of the three lakes. Occasionally the tranquillity of our valley is disturbed by the scream of low-flying RAF Phantoms on training flights. This is but a small price to pay for the calm that normally prevails. Almost all our thirteen windows have a view to die for.

How do we come to be here? My ambition to end my days in a walled garden dates from a stay at Chillingham in the mid-1990s. Chillingham is an enchanting medieval castle in the north of Northumberland, rescued from ruin by Sir Humphry Wakefield, a baronet descended from a long line of explorers and adventurers. On several occasions in the mid-1990s we rented an apartment there, since when Sir Humphry and I have become good friends, one of several unlikely friendships that I have struck up during the course of my life.

It was while staying at Chillingham that I noticed, a short distance from the castle, the path to it submerged in waist-high grass, an eighteenth-century walled garden that had once belonged to the castle but had long since been hived off, remaining in the ownership of the aged Countess of Tankerville, the last living inhabitant of the castle before it was abandoned in the 1930s. One evening at twilight, I waded through the grass, climbed the wall and explored. I had stumbled upon a secret world. A garden that had gone to sleep perhaps fifty years earlier. This was June and the garden was a sea of lupins. The south facing wall was lined with decaying glasshouses that once produced grapes and exotic fruit for the inhabitants of the castle. An arch in the centre led into a walled orchard, inhabited by twisted, moss-encrusted fruit trees, long past their prime.

My first thought was to see if I could buy or lease the garden with a view to setting up a charitable trust and restoring it. The aged countess lived in the adjacent Estate House with her son, the Honourable Ian. I wrote the Honourable Ian a carefully worded letter, expressing interest in his garden. Not wanting to upset him, I referred to the garden as 'unused' rather than 'abandoned'. I also expressed concern that, sooner or later, it would fall into the hands of a developer. He replied: 'Your suggestion that the garden is unused is incorrect. I use it to grow vegetables and to exercise my supposedly fierce dog.' Mention of the dog – it turned out to be a Weimaraner – caught my attention. I never trespassed again. The Honourable Ian continued,

'You are right in thinking that there is a danger of inappropriate development, but this will not happen in my lifetime and, actuarially, I can be expected to live for at least another ten years.'

He was dead by the end of the year. A couple of years later his mother, the countess, followed him to the grave. The Estate House and the attached walled garden came on the market for the first time in 200 years. It was to be sold in two lots on the understanding that whoever bought the house would have first option on the garden. Hastily I arranged for the garden to be listed. Humphry Wakefield and I then put in a joint bid for the garden only. Alas, the winning bidder wanted the garden as well as the house and with that the dream faded. The garden lies unloved and unrestored to this day.

From then on my interest was aroused. Derelict walled gardens are to be found all over the border country. Many are beyond recovery and the few that come on the market are usually part of an estate, either well beyond my means or in places so remote as to be wholly impractical. Eventually, however, after years of searching, we struck lucky. In 2005 we saw an advertisement for a cottage in a walled garden on an exquisitely beautiful estate in a valley just south of the Cheviots, eleven miles west of Alnwick, a town once designated by *Country Life* as having the highest quality of life in the country. The estate consisted of a Grade I-listed mansion incorporating an ancient Pele tower and set in a thirty-five-acre park with vast sloping lawns, three lakes, fine beech woods and a fast-flowing stream running through the grounds. The mansion had been tastefully converted into apartments and three cottages had been built in the walled garden, on the footprint of old outbuildings. One of these was for sale.

At the time we couldn't afford it, but I noted that the elderly couple living in the first cottage had the same unusual surname as a teacher at a school in my constituency. I contacted the teacher. Were the old couple any relation, I inquired. Indeed they were. 'If they ever want to sell, please let me know,' I said. Five years passed and then, just as I was about to retire from Parliament, I received a message to say they were both dead. Was I still interested? The timing was auspicious. Helped by the sale (for the second time) of television rights on *A Very British Coup*, and the proceeds of three volumes of diaries (the first of which is currently on its thirteenth reprint), what might previously have been unaffordable was suddenly within my means.

There was much to be done. The house was long, narrow and somewhat dated. Much pointing of brickwork was required to make it leak-proof. Internally we started from scratch, doubling the size of the kitchen, adding an en suite bedroom, a sun room, a porch and a wood-burning stove. Progress was hair-tearingly slow. Northumberland craftsmen are highly skilled, but they move slowly and co-ordination is not their strong point. 'He's set aside a little time for you after Easter,' my ever-optimistic architect said of the joiner he had recommended. It was November before the joiner was on site. At one point it looked as though we faced winter with a gaping hole in the side of the house where the roof of the new sun room awaited the attention of the lead-men, two elderly brothers who moved at their own pace. 'Can't you ring them?' I asked the joiner. 'No point,' he replied, 'they don't answer the telephone.'

'How do you communicate? By smoke signals?'

'Something like that.'

The garden, too, was a major operation. Although the area around the house and along one side had been cultivated, much of the rest had not. In days of yore it had been a Christmas tree plantation and the upper half was still occupied by conifers that by now had grown to heights of thirty feet and more. The first task was to remove the trees, roots and all, and that required earth-moving equipment. The removal of the trees revealed a fine stone wall that had not seen the light of day for many years. I commissioned Stephen Bean, a landscape gardener from North Yorkshire, to design a garden complete with raised vegetable beds, fruit trees, rose beds and, on either side of the lawn, wildflower areas, through which run winding paths. The soil in much of the garden, especially the forested part, was heavy, impermeable clay. Much levelling, shovelling and rotavating was required. Not to mention the importation of several tons of manure and the removal of barrowloads of stones. As with the house, there were moments of intense frustration. After heavy rain in the first year parts of the garden resembled the Somme. The water stayed for months. In the end we enlisted the aid of a man with a digger who installed field drains.

Gradually, the garden took shape. A healthy lawn emerged from the mud (it takes three hours to cut). The great advantage of a large garden is that you don't have to pile all the plants on top of each other. Spring, herbaceous and autumn flowers have their own separate beds. To one side I have created an alpine border which gives a good display in May and June. On the embankment facing the house we planted lupins, cosmos and lavender. From my garden in Sunderland I brought chunks of phlox, white and yellow marguerites and anemones. The paths are lined with catmint, Johnsons blue geraniums and old-fashioned orange calendula.

Never having grown a vegetable in my life, and being hopelessly impractical, I enlisted the aid of an experienced local gardener. In the raised beds we planted pink fir apple and charlotte potatoes, cabbages, beetroot, peas, radishes, carrots, leeks, lettuce, onions, sprouts and courgettes. The carrots proved a failure (the soil was not sandy enough) and the sprouts were attacked by a plague of caterpillars, but everything else flourished. In the first year we rather overdid the courgettes and, as a result, Ngoc spent much of the summer devising ever more ingenious recipes for consuming them. We ate them stuffed, pickled, liquidised into soup and stir-fried. No visitor was allowed to depart without an offer of a courgette or two. Outside, in a fruit cage, we harvested a modest crop of raspberries and strawberries.

Initially, at least, the fruit trees proved disappointing. The apple, pear and cherry trees espaliered along the south- and east-facing walls produced vigorous growth, but little in the way of fruit. In our first year we harvested a mere dozen plums and a similar number of apples. The second year brought a healthy crop of pears and plums, but just two apples. The third year, a plentiful crop of apples, greengages and pears, but few plums. From much older trees in the communal garden we harvested apples, damsons and blackcurrants which Ngoc turned into juice, jam and a supply of damson gin that lasted all winter.

By the south-facing wall at the far end of the garden we built a large glasshouse in the hope of growing nectarines and apricots. Both trees appear to be healthy, but so far we have not seen a single apricot. At the time of writing, however, there are signs of a promising crop of nectarines. Meanwhile the glasshouse has produced healthy crops of tomatoes, cucumbers, green peppers, aubergines and even a few galia melons.

As for the weather, we have been remarkably lucky. The first summer was like Tuscany. Not something we can count on every year, but it got us off to a good start. Around the estate there is a plentiful supply of firewood. I have acquired an axe and spend many a happy hour chopping. As Mr Gladstone discovered, there is something particularly satisfying about wood cutting.

As readers of my final volume of diaries will know, I suffered a good deal of angst about whether there would be anything useful to do after I left Parliament. I am pleased to report that, thus far at least, life has worked out much better than I could ever have hoped. A small industry developed around the diaries which I have spent a lot of time servicing. To my pleasant surprise, I discovered that the political meeting is not dead, it has simply transferred to the literary festival. In my first years after leaving Parliament I have addressed well over a hundred such events, attracting paying audiences of up to 750 (rather more than when I was an MP). I chair the Heritage Lottery Fund in the north-east and lecture part time in the politics department of Newcastle University. In 2011 I was a judge of the Man Booker Prize. True, the flow of invitations is beginning to subside and with every year that passes it seems likely that much of the rest of my life will involve cutting grass and raking leaves, but every day I count my blessings.

From the window of my study I look down through the communal gardens towards the mansion and the forested hills beyond. The light changes constantly and, come autumn, when the beech leaves change colour, the evening skyline is a blaze of yellow, brown and gold. From time to time wisps of cloud drift across the hills, as in a Chinese painting. On rainy days the hills disappear completely into the mist.

If all goes according to plan, I intend to remain in this beautiful place for the rest of my days. Ideally I shall fade away on the last sunny day of autumn after completing a final circuit of the garden propped upon my walking frame. I can already see the place where my ashes will be scattered. But not, I hope, for some time yet.

Picture Credits

The photographs have been reproduced with the kind permission of the following:

Daily Telegraph 36; News Syndication 33, 35; REX/Shutterstock 34; Stefan Cagnoni/Report Archive/reportdigital.co.uk 25, 26. All other photographs author's own.

Index